TWO VIEWS OF HELL
A Biblical & Theological Dialogue

Edward William Fudge
& Robert A. Peterson

InterVarsity Press
Downers Grove, Illinois

InterVarsity Press
P.O. Box 1400, Downers Grove, IL 60515
World Wide Web: www.ivpress.com
E-mail: mail@ivpress.com

InterVarsity Press®️ is the book-publishing division of InterVarsity Christian Fellowship/USA®️, a student movement active on campus at hundreds of universities, colleges and schools of nursing in the United States of America, and a member movement of the International Fellowship of Evangelical Students. For information about local and r egional activities, write Public Relations Dept., InterVarsity Christian Fellowship/USA, 6400 Schroeder Rd., P.O. Box 7895, Madison, WI 53707-7895.

All Scripture quotations, unless otherwise indicated, are taken from the Holy Bible, New International Version®️. NIV®️. *Copyright* ©*1973, 1978, 1984 by International Bible Society. Used by permission of Zondervan Publishing House. All rights reserved.*

Cover illustration: Scala/Art Resource, NY

ISBN 0-8308-2255-0

Printed in the United States of America ∞

Library of Congress Cataloging-in-Publication Data

Fudge, Edward.
  Two views of hell : a biblical & theological dialogue / Edward William Fudge & Robert
A. Peterson.
    p. cm.
  Includes bibliographical references.
  ISBN 0-8308-2255-0 (pbk. : alk. paper)
    1. Hell. 2. Hell—Biblical teaching. I. Peterson, Robert A., 1948- II. Title.
BT836.2 F83 2000
236'.25—dc21

00-022952

16 15 14 13 12 11 10 9 8 7 6 5 4 3 2

12 11 10 09 08 07 06 05 04 03 02 01 00

*To Robby, Matt, Curtis and David, with prayers that you would grow
to be men of God whose lives bring glory to him.*

ROBERT A. PETERSON

*Dedicated to the Christian teachers in every century
who have courageously proclaimed the biblical message
of eternal life only in Jesus Christ, despite the denunciations,
ridicule, scorn and sometimes the persecution of
the majority. This book represents
the beginning of God's public vindication of their faithful witness.*

EDWARD WILLIAM FUDGE

Contents

Acknowledgments

I want to express appreciation to the many people who had a part in my writing this book. To the administration and board of trustees of Covenant Theological Seminary for granting me a sabbatical. To colleagues who took time from busy schedules to read the manuscript and offer comments: Jimmy Agan, Hans Bayer, David Calhoun, Jack Collins, Dan Doriani, Alan Gomes, David Jones and Mike Williams. To students and other friends who improved the readability: Jonathan Barlow, Chris Crain, Bryan Cross, Deborah Kim, Floyd Simmons, Jonathan Taylor, Tara Byler Weathers and Wes Zell. To Brad Getz for sharing his linguistic expertise. To InterVarsity Press and especially Drew Blankman, who faithfully shepherded this book into the fold. To Mary Pat for her steadfast love and encouragement. To Robby, Matt, Curtis and David for not allowing our home to become boring.

Robert A. Peterson

Introduction:
What's All the Fuss About?

THAT FAMOUS THEOLOGIAN ANN LANDERS WRITES IN A JANUARY 10, 1993, column in the *St. Louis Post-Dispatch*:

> During a heated argument in the U.S. Senate back in the 1920s, one man told a colleague to go to hell. The astonished senator questioned Vice President Coolidge, who was presiding, as to the propriety of the remark. Coolidge, who had been leafing through a book, looked up and said, "I have been checking the rules manual, and you don't have to go."

Calvin Coolidge's witty remark mirrors the opinions of many today when asked about hell, "You don't have to go." Polls show that in spite of the fact that most Americans believe in the existence of hell, they do not think that they will go there. Although he was jesting, Mr. Coolidge actually had the right idea: We must consult "the rules manual." Evangelical Christians agree that the only reliable source to tell us God's truth about eternal destinies is the Bible. Consequently, they affirm the reality of hell and consider the optimism of many Americans concerning the afterlife unwarranted. Furthermore, evangelicals agree that hell is the most terrible fate that can befall a human being. But today there is no unanimity among theological conservatives concerning every aspect of the Bible's teaching on hell. Specifically, they debate the nature of hell. Does it consist of conscious punishment that lasts forever, or does it have an end? The first view is called *traditionalism* and the second *conditionalism* or *annihilationism*.[1]

At times this debate has become animated, as you will learn by hearing from two respected evangelical professors of theology, James I. Packer and John W. Wenham. Both men are British and are published by InterVarsity Press. Packer teaches at Regent College in Vancouver and is the author of the best-selling book *Knowing God*. Wenham, now deceased, was vice principal of Tyndale Hall, Bristol, and warden of Latimer House, Oxford. He is the author of the highly regarded book *The Goodness of God*. Listen, first, to Dr. Packer:

> Does it matter whether an evangelical is a conditionalist or not? I think it does: for a conditionalist's idea of God will miss out on the glory of divine justice, and his idea of worship will miss out on praise for God's judgments, and his idea of heaven will miss out on the thought that praise for God's judgments goes on (cf. Rev. 16:5-7, 19:1-5), and his idea of man will miss out on the awesome dignity of our having been made to last for eternity, and in his preaching of the gospel he will miss out on telling the unconverted that their prospects without Christ are as bad as they possibly could be—for on the conditionalist view they aren't! These, surely, are sad losses. Conditionalism, logically thought through, cannot but impoverish a Christian, and limit our usefulness to our Lord. That is why I am concerned about the current trend towards conditionalism. I hope it may soon be reversed.[2]

Strong words! And impassioned language is not confined to one side of the debate concerning the duration of hell.

> Unending torment speaks to me of sadism, not justice. It is a doctrine which I do not know how to preach without negating the loveliness and glory of God. From the days of Tertullian it has frequently been the emphasis of fanatics. It is a doctrine which makes the Inquisition look reasonable. It all seems a flight from reality and common sense. . . . I believe that endless torment is a hideous and unscriptural doctrine which has been a terrible burden on the mind of the church for many centuries and a terrible blot on her presentation of the gospel. I should indeed be happy if, before I die, I could help in sweeping it away.[3]

There you have it: Two highly regarded evangelical theologians at odds concerning how long the wicked will suffer in hell. Packer's traditional view is held by many other evangelical thinkers, including D. A. Carson and R. C. Sproul. And the conditionalist view set forth by Wenham is no mere fad—it has also been vigorously advocated by Clark H. Pinnock and is tentatively held by John R. W. Stott.

Notice that Packer's and Wenham's convictions are rooted in their hearts as well as their minds. We do not, however, mean to overplay the emotional element; both of these thinkers are committed to their respective positions for what they regard as good reasons—biblical, theological and historical.

Reflecting on why Wenham and Packer hold their views suggests a question: How does each regard the arguments advanced by those espousing the opposing view? This question is not difficult to answer. In a word, they deem the opposing arguments inadequate. Here is Packer again:

> The biblical arguments [for annihilationism] are to my mind flimsy special pleading, and the feelings that make people want conditionalism to be true seem to me to reflect, not superior spiritual sensitivity, but secular sentimentalism which assumes that in heaven our feelings about others will be as at present, and our joy in the manifesting of God's justice will be no greater than it is now. It is certainly agonizing now to live with the thought of people going to eternal hell, but it is not right to reduce the agony by evading the facts; and in heaven, we may be sure, the agony will be a thing of the past.[4]

Wenham takes strong exception to such conclusions:

> The extraordinary thing about these [traditionalist] replies [to conditional immortality] is that none of them actually addresses the arguments used by the conditionalists. . . .
>
> Packer is in some ways even more disappointing. With all his capacity for reading and digesting material and with his gift of lucid exposition, one hoped to see the conditionalist arguments carefully considered. . . . While not answering the conditionalist arguments with any seriousness, these writers do of course state their own case. They set out certain well-known texts and claim that their meaning is "obvious.". . .
>
> I would claim that the natural meaning of the vast majority of relevant texts is quite otherwise.[5]

This volume, a debate between a proponent of conditionalism and a proponent of traditionalism, addresses the bone of contention between Packer and Wenham. We will begin by introducing ourselves, explaining what the debate is not, and then set some parameters for the discussion.

Edward William Fudge is a biblical scholar and attorney who lives in Houston, Texas, and is a lifelong member of the Churches of Christ. He has written *The Fire That Consumes: The Biblical Case for Conditional Immortality.* Robert A. Peterson is Professor of Systematic Theology at Covenant Theological Seminary in St. Louis, Missouri. He has penned *Hell on Trial: The Case for Eternal Punishment.*[6]

We want to bring the debate into sharper focus by stating what is *not* the subject of this book. The debate is not over universalism, the view that all people will ultimately be saved. Although a vast number of clergy around the world hold this view, we reject it as contradicting the teaching of Scripture. Truth is not derived by taking opinion polls but by carefully studying God's Word. And the Bible will not allow universalism. Instead of portraying all of humanity as saved in the end, Jesus foretells a final separation between the righteous and the wicked. This is evident in his teaching concerning the sheep and the goats:

> When the Son of Man comes in his glory, and all the angels with him, he will sit on his throne in heavenly glory. All the nations will be gathered before him, and he will separate the people one from another as a shepherd separates the sheep from the goats. He will put the sheep on his right and the goats on his left.
>
> Then the King will say to those on his right, "Come, you who are blessed by my Father; take your inheritance, the kingdom prepared for you since the creation of the world." . . .
>
> Then he will say to those on his left, "Depart from me, you who are cursed, into the eternal fire prepared for the devil and his angels." . . .
>
> Then they will go away to eternal punishment, but the righteous to eternal life. (Mt 25:31-34, 41, 46)

There is no need to quote multiple passages; universalism is incompatible with clear biblical teaching.[7]

Another topic that is not a subject of debate in this book is that of postmortem evangelism, the idea that persons have an opportunity after death to believe the gospel of Christ. In spite of the fact that some evangelicals have adopted this position, we believe Scripture points to death as an end to the opportunity for salvation.[8] The testimony of Hebrews 9:27 seems conclusive: "Just as man is destined to die once, and after that to face judgment, so Christ was sacrificed once to take away the sins of many people."

We also agree that the Bible's general picture of the end includes the second coming of Christ, the resurrection of the dead and the Last Judgment, followed by terrible suffering for the lost. We disagree, however, as to the nature of the eternal punishment of which Scripture speaks. Based on his study of God's Word, Fudge is convinced that conditionalism is true. God will justly exterminate the wicked after they have suffered conscious punishment proportionate to their sins. The ultimate final punishment will constitute the eradication of their being, so the wicked will exist no more.

Fudge believes that this view best magnifies God's justice, fits the Bible's teaching and constitutes part of the proper motivation for evangelism.

Peterson respectfully disagrees. He is convinced for biblical and theological reasons that the suffering of the wicked in hell will never come to an end. Furthermore, it is his conviction that only this view glorifies God's righteousness, squares with biblical doctrine and provides the most important rationale for fulfilling the Great Commission.

Thoughtful readers may still ask: What is all the fuss about? Theologians like to squabble, but what difference does it really make if I adopt traditionalism or conditionalism? To completely answer these questions is the goal of the rest of this book. For now, short answers will have to do. Both writers think that our position on the subject of the debate affects our view of God, our handling of the Bible and our motivation for evangelism. In Fudge's estimation, traditionalism attributes unworthy motives to God, is based more on secular philosophy than on holy Scripture and seriously jeopardizes the church's witness. In Peterson's view, annihilationism represents wishful thinking based on a faulty portrayal of God, contradicts the clear testimony of Scripture, and if not checked, will do great harm to the task of world evangelization.

It is our goal to conduct this debate in a spirit of brotherly courtesy. We will seek to abstain from misstating one another's positions, from imputing improper motives and from using other questionable tactics that would dishonor the name of Christ.

The format is straightforward. The debaters will present the cases for their positions, Fudge affirming conditionalism and Peterson traditionalism, respectively. Then each will respond to the other's presentation.

We invite readers to join us in exploring the evangelical controversy over hell.

Part One

THE CASE FOR CONDITIONALISM

Edward William Fudge

1

AN INTRODUCTION TO CONDITIONALISM

T HE *BIBLE CLEARLY TEACHES THAT THOSE WHO PERSISTENTLY REJECT* God's mercy throughout this life will one day face him in judgment and finally be cast into hell. Hell is real. It is fearful beyond human imagination, and those who go there will never come out again. From at least the time of Augustine (A.D. 354-430), most Christians have taught that God will keep hell's inhabitants alive forever so they can suffer everlasting torment of body or soul or both, in an agony that somehow corresponds to the pain inflicted by fire.

It is not surprising that when Jonathan Edwards preached on hell, colonial Americans sometimes fainted with fright. Edwards admonished:

> To help your conception, imagine yourself to be cast into a fiery oven, all of a glowing heat, or into the midst of a blowing brick-kiln, or of a great furnace, where your pain would be as much greater than that occasioned by accidentally touching a coal of fire, as the heat is greater. Imagine also that your body were to lie there for a quarter of an hour, full of fire, as full within and without as a bright coal of fire, all the while full of quick sense; what horror would you feel at the entrance of such a furnace! And how long would that quarter of an hour seem to you! . . . And how much greater would be the effect, if you knew you must endure it for a whole year, and how vastly greater still if you

knew you must endure it for a thousand years! O then, how would your heart sink, if you thought, if you knew, that you must bear it forever and ever! . . . That after millions of ages, your torment would be no nearer to an end, than ever it was; and that you never, never should be delivered! But your torment in Hell will be immeasurably greater than this illustration represents.[1]

A century later Charles Spurgeon minced no words as he described hell's torment to his London audience:

Thine heart beating high with fever, thy pulse rattling at an enormous rate in agony, thy limbs cracking like the martyrs in the fire and yet unburnt, thyself put in a vessel of hot oil, pained yet coming out undestroyed, all thy veins becoming a road for the hot feet of pain to travel on, every nerve a string on which the devil shall ever play his diabolical tune.[2]

This style of preaching is now in rapid decline. Many advocates of the traditional view now say the fire is likely metaphorical. Hell's pains result more from deprivation than from external infliction, they explain, and are probably spiritual and emotional in nature rather than physical. The real agony will be the smitten conscience and the sense of loss, according to most of Spurgeon's and Edwards's modern descendants. Evangelist Billy Graham is among those who reject the lurid descriptions of hell once popular among advocates of everlasting torment. Says Graham in an interview:

The only thing I could say for sure is that hell means separation from God. We are separated from his light, from his fellowship. That is going to be hell. When it comes to a literal fire, I don't preach it because I'm not sure about it. When the Scripture uses fire concerning hell, that is possibly an illustration of how terrible it's going to be—not fire but something worse, a thirst for God that cannot be quenched.[3]

The fact is that the Bible does not teach the traditional view of final punishment. Scripture nowhere suggests that God is an eternal torturer. It never says the damned will writhe in ceaseless torment or that the glories of heaven will forever be blighted by the screams from hell. The idea of conscious everlasting torment was a grievous mistake, a horrible error, a gross slander against the heavenly Father, whose character we truly see in the life of Jesus of Nazareth.

Scripture teaches instead that those who go to hell will experience "everlasting destruction" in "the second death," for God is able to "destroy both body and soul in hell." The actual process of destruction may well involve conscious pain that differs in magnitude in each individual case—Scripture seems to indicate that it will. Whatever the case, God's judgment will be measured by perfect, holy, divine justice. Even hell will demonstrate the absolute righteousness of God. From Genesis to Revelation, the Bible repeatedly warns that the wicked will "die," "perish" or "be destroyed." Those who die this second death will never live again.

A growing host of respected biblical scholars now publicly question the traditional notion that God will keep the lost alive forever so he can punish them without end. These include such luminaries as F. F. Bruce, Michael Green, Philip E. Hughes, Dale Moody, Clark H. Pinnock, W. Graham Scroggie, John R. W. Stott and John W. Wenham. These men represent evangelical Christian scholarship at its best. They recognize that Scripture must judge all traditions and creeds, not the other way around. They realize that most of the church was wrong for centuries on doctrines far more fundamental than the doctrine of hell, and they understand that it would be presumptuous to suppose that the majority might not have erred on this point just as it did on others.

J. I. Packer rightly notes that "we are forbidden to become enslaved to human tradition, . . . even 'evangelical' tradition. We may never assume the complete rightness of our own established ways of thought and practice and excuse ourselves the duty of testing and reforming them by Scripture."[4] John Stott reminds us that "the hallmark of an authentic evangelicalism is not the uncritical repetition of old traditions but the willingness to submit every tradition, however ancient, to fresh biblical scrutiny and, if necessary, reform."[5] The growing evangelical rejection of the traditional doctrine of unending conscious torment is not propelled by emotionalism, sentimentality or compromise with culture but by absolute commitment to the authority of Scripture and by the conviction that a faithful church must be a church that is always reforming.

Dust Creatures in God's Image
The Bible's opening chapter tells us that there was a time when humankind did not exist, and that when God made us, he made us from dirt—from the very elements which also compose our planet. The author of Genesis allows us to watch over God's shoulder as he makes the first human (Gen 2:7). God

carefully shapes a human body from clay scooped from the earth. The Almighty stoops and breathes into its nostrils. Suddenly what began as a life-size mud doll becomes a living being! God names him *Adam*, a Hebrew word that also means "dust." Earthly elements plus the "breath of life" have become a whole man—in Hebrew "a living soul." From a rib of Adam, the story continues, God then makes Eve—also in the image of God (Gen 2:21-22).

Since humans did not exist until God formed them and gave them life, each moment of life is God's immediate gift of grace. Eventually God reclaims the breath of life and we return to the ground from which we were taken (Eccles 3:18-22). The Bible always portrays human beings within this framework of God's creation. We cannot exist for even one moment apart from God, who made us.

The gift of life. The biblical view of humans as God's dependent creatures differs sharply from the view taught by the ancient Greek philosopher Plato. According to Plato, each human being has a body that is mortal and will finally die. Plato taught that each person also has a soul that is immortal and cannot die.[6] In this way Plato continued the philosophy of his master, Socrates. As Socrates faced his own execution, he welcomed death, for to him it meant escaping the lower realm of mortal bodies and returning to the higher sphere of immortal souls. Like his student Plato, Socrates believed that the soul cannot die or cease to exist. Plato died before Jesus was born, and thus before Jesus revealed that God "can destroy both soul and body in hell" (Mt 10:28). Socrates' view also differs from the view expressed by his predecessors, the Old Testament writers, who consistently dreaded death as the end of life. Unlike those Scriptures, Socrates did not view human beings in relation to the living God.

The most notable characteristic of the dead in the Old Testament is that they are cut off from God. This is a dreadful thought because, of all the living creatures, only humans know God person-to-person. Humans alone exhibit volition and awareness of their mortality. Even though Adam lived 930 years, he too finally died (Gen 5:5). As his descendants returned his lifeless body to the soil, they must have grieved at the thought of their own mortality and the brevity of their lives. The Old Testament writers disagree with later Greek philosophers who portray humans as immortal souls entrapped for a time in mortal bodies. They picture humanity's state after death with the imagery of Sheol.[7]

Sheol—the realm of all the dead. The word *Sheol* is used in the Old Testament sixty-five times. The King James Version translators rendered it either "hell" (thirty-one times), "the grave" (thirty-one times) or "the pit" (three times). The translators of the American Standard Version simply left it "Sheol." In the New International Version the word is usually translated as "grave," though at least once it is rendered "the realm of death" (Deut 32:22). Sheol is not a physical hole in the ground, but it might well be translated "gravedom."[8] Biblical Greek writers used the word *Hades* (literally "unseen") for the Hebrew word *Sheol*, both in the Greek translation of the Old Testament and in the New Testament.

Job describes Sheol as "the place of no return, . . . the land of gloom and deep shadow, . . . the land of deepest night, of deep shadow and disorder, where even the light is like darkness" (Job 10:21-22). David calls it "the place of darkness" and "the land of oblivion" (Ps 88:12). Although individuals are sometimes pictured in the Old Testament as conversing in Sheol or engaging in other such lifelike pursuits (Is 14:9-18), the Hebrew text tells us that they are mere shades, shadows of whole persons who once lived and loved on the earth (Is 14:9).

Some writers have suggested that Sheol was a place of punishment for sin. The translators of the King James Version contributed to this misunderstanding by rendering *Sheol* as "hell." However, such faithful saints as Jacob, David and Job all expected to go to Sheol when they died (Gen 37:35; Ps 49:15; Job 14:13). Most importantly, Jesus Christ himself went to Sheol (Greek *Hades*) upon his death (Acts 2:27, 31). On the third day Jesus came back from the grave in victory, and he now holds as trophies "the keys to death and Hades" themselves (Rev 1:18). One day death and Hades also will be cast into the "lake of fire"—which is a way of saying they will cease to exist (Rev 20:13-15).

No wonder that righteous men and women throughout the Bible repeatedly express confidence that God will restore them from Sheol to enjoy life in his fellowship again (1 Sam 2:6; Ps 16:9-11). No biblical character is ever said to have placed hope in philosophical notions of natural immortality, or to have supposed that human beings have some mysterious part that cannot die. Whatever the state of mortals between earthly death and the resurrection, their only hope for survival lies in the hands of the Creator who alone is inherently immortal (1 Tim 6:16).

2

THE OLD TESTAMENT

I*F EARTHLY FAME AND FORTUNE ARE THE ONLY MEASURE, IT APPARENTLY* does not pay to serve God. We have all known godly people who have spent their entire working lives in honest labor, shared what they made with others less fortunate—then died with no fanfare, leaving little more than the clothes on their backs. Meanwhile, the well-heeled neighbor who never had time for God stashed away wealth of all kinds and exited this life with a front-page write-up. Where is God's justice in this? These questions are as old as the Bible itself. In fact, the authors of Job, Psalms and Proverbs struggle with the very same questions.

Are Good and Evil Lost on God?

Job's "friends" and the end of the wicked. Job's so-called friends argue that present calamity must be punishment for sins and that earthly prosperity is God's blessing for right living (Job 18:5-21; 20:4-29; 22:15-20; 34:10-28). Job insists that he is living proof that their perspective is mistaken, for he knows some wicked men who thrive in this life while he, with clean hands, is perishing. Although we cannot derive solid doctrine from the uninspired conclusions of Job's miserable comforters, their question will not quietly go away. Given God's moral rule over humankind, how can the wicked die rich while the righteous languish away in misery?

Psalms and Proverbs promise moral justice. The book of Psalms contains much of the same language Job's companions use. The psalmists assure us that the wicked will die, their memory will perish, and they will become as if they had never existed. These writers anticipate that the wicked will vanish like water that flows away, will melt like a slug as it moves along and will become like a stillborn child. But God will save the righteous out of death, and they will enjoy his presence forever (Ps 9; 21:4-10; 49:8-20; 58:7-8).[1] The book of Proverbs repeats these promises that the wicked will pass away, be overthrown, be cut off from the land, be no more, have their lamp put out (Prov 2:21-22; 10:25; 12:7; 24:15-20).

Psalms that anticipate final judgment. Someone might suggest that these texts all refer only to the present life, but truth requires us to acknowledge that this is not what we see on the earth. As the author of Hebrews later notes, many of the noblest promises of the psalms wait for final fulfillment in the age to come (Heb 2:5-8; 4:6-11). We now consider several other psalms whose New Testament usage projects their ultimate fulfillment into the future and that also describe the end of the wicked as total, everlasting extinction.

In Psalm 34:8-22 David praises God who delivers his people. Peter later applies this psalm's message to persecuted Christians (1 Pet 2:3; 3:10-12). Whoever fears God will discover his kindness and presence, and God will deliver them from trouble (Ps 34:8, 15-18, 22). But the wicked await a different fate. They finally will die (or "be slain" NASB) and their memory will perish from the earth (Ps 34:16, 21). The psalm reaches beyond the present life for its certain fulfillment. As surely as God is just, a day will come when the righteous will shine but the wicked will be no more (Ps 34:5, 16).

In Psalm 37:1-40 David contrasts the security of those who trust in God with the precarious position of the wicked. "A little while, and the wicked will be no more," he promises, "though you look for them, they will not be found. But the meek will inherit the land and enjoy great peace" (Ps 37:10-11). The inheritance of the righteous "will endure forever, . . . but the wicked will perish . . . [and] will vanish—vanish like smoke. . . . There is a future for the man of peace. But all sinners will be destroyed" (Ps 37:18, 20,

37-38). Again the biblical assurances do not match the world we now see. God's final justice awaits an age beyond the present. But Jesus himself assures us that this psalm speaks the truth, and he reaffirms it by quoting it to those who would follow him (Mt 5:5).

Psalm 69 sounds the desperate cry of a righteous man surrounded and out-numbered by evil enemies. New Testament writers apply its words to Jesus on the one hand (Jn 2:17; 19:28-30) and to Judas and unbelievers in Israel on the other (Acts 1:20; Rom 11:9-10). In the end the author of Psalm 69 requests that the wicked's place be deserted (Ps 69:25) and that they not be listed among the living in the book of life (Ps 69:28; see also Rev 20:15). This language is consistent with final and irreversible death, but it stands in sharp contrast to the notion that the wicked will be kept alive forever for ceaseless torment.

The Vocabulary of Divine Judgment

It is one thing to talk about divine justice and the final punishment of sin. It is quite another thing to see it happen with one's own eyes. The historical books of the Old Testament show us examples of actual judgments against the wicked in the past. More important, Jesus and the writers of the New Testament borrow the vocabulary of these events to describe God's final judgment against the lost. Unfortunately, many who have written and taught on this subject have ignored the Bible's own key to this symbolic language. If we allow the Bible to interpret itself, these Old Testament examples can teach us much about the punishment awaiting the wicked at the end of the world.

The flood and final judgment. In the structure of Genesis the saga begun with Adam and creation ends with Noah and the great flood (Gen 1—9). When they speak of the flood, both the Greek Old Testament and the Greek New Testament use the word that gives us our English word *cataclysm.* This ancient cataclysmic judgment terminated one world and ushered in another (2 Pet 3:3-6). The flood story is so important for biblical authors they use it as a metaphor both for historical judgments and for the final judgment to come. New Testament writers invoke the metaphor to explain that the final judgment will be unexpected (Mt 24:38-39; Lk 17:26-27), when they discuss its victims (2 Pet 2:5, 9) and those whom it will deliver (1 Pet 3:20-22). The flood provides examples of exemplary faith (Ezek 14:14, 20; Heb 11:7) and of divine patience (1 Pet 3:20; 2 Pet 3:5-9). Peter makes this ancient catastrophe a model of God's final wrath (2 Pet 2:5, 9; 3:3-7) as does Jesus (Lk 17:26-27).

The nature of this judgment could not be clearer. God tells Noah that he will "put an end to all people, . . . destroy both them and the earth," so "everything on earth will perish" (Gen 6:13, 17). What happened next leaves no room for doubt about the meaning of *perish* or *destroy* in this story of the end of the first world. When the flood came,

> every living thing that moved on the earth perished—birds, livestock, wild animals, all the creatures that swarm over the earth, and all mankind. Everything on dry land that had the breath of life in its nostrils died. Every living thing on the face of the earth was wiped out; men and animals and the creatures that move along the ground and the birds of the air were wiped from the earth. Only Noah was left, and those with him in the ark. (Gen 7:21-23)

Even a casual reader immediately understands the meaning of *perish, die* and *destroy* in this story. In this historical example of the end of the world, those terms mean being "wiped out," being "wiped off the face of the earth." The writers of the Bible use the same verbs to describe the eternal fate of the lost that they use to describe the judgment brought by the great flood. Just as with the flood, the ungodly will "perish," "die" and be "destroyed." These words do not require literal annihilation as a scientist might use that term. No one would protest the use of these words because the flood did not technically annihilate the physical elements of the earth or because the atoms that composed the people who perished were not literally destroyed. Yet Peter points back to what God once did in the flood as an example of what the wicked may expect at the end (2 Pet 2:5, 9; 3:3-7). There is one important difference however. Those who perished in Noah's day will live again to face God's eternal judgment (Jn 5:28-29), but those who experience the second death will be destroyed, body and soul, forever (Mt 10:28; 2 Thess 1:9).

Lessons from Sodom and Gomorrah. Genesis 19 relates the destruction of the cities of Sodom and Gomorrah. Throughout the Bible this divine judgment ranks alongside the flood as an unmistakable prototype of divine judgment.[2] After Abraham's intercessory negotiations with God to save the city, God warns Lot to gather his family and to escape with their lives (Gen 18:16-33; 19:12-17).

Then the LORD rained down burning sulfur on Sodom and Gomorrah—from
the LORD out of the heavens. Thus he overthrew those cities and the entire
plain, including all those living in the cities—and also the vegetation in the
land. But Lot's wife looked back and she became a pillar of salt.

Early the next morning Abraham got up and returned to the place where
he had stood before the LORD. He looked down toward Sodom and Gomorrah, toward all the land of the plain, and he saw dense smoke rising from the
land, like smoke from a furnace.

So when God destroyed the cities of the plain, he remembered Abraham,
and he brought Lot out of the catastrophe that overthrew the cities where Lot
had lived. (Gen 19:24-29)

This is the origin of the biblical phrase "fire and brimstone," the King
James Version's equivalent of "burning sulfur." Burning sulfur suffocates its
living victims by its fumes, and its fire devours what remains. Many of
Sodom's people undoubtedly suffered some conscious agony while they
perished, but the Bible does not call attention to that fact. Compared to
some fates, death by fire and brimstone is mercifully quick (Lam 4:6). God's
wrath descended on the sinners of Sodom and Gomorrah, "burning them to
ashes," making them "an example of what is going to happen to the
ungodly" at the end of time (2 Pet 2:6).

The writers of Scripture do emphasize the thoroughness of Sodom's
destruction. On the day after it was destroyed, Abraham went out to view
the scene. Where once a bustling city had stood he saw only "dense smoke
rising from the land, like smoke from a furnace" (Gen 19:28). God had executed his judgment, and no sound was heard in its wake. The sinners were
all gone. The silence was unbroken. Throughout Scripture from this point,
rising smoke symbolizes complete destruction (Is 34:10; Rev 14:11; 19:3).

The writers of the Bible also stress the permanence of Sodom's destruction—a one-time destruction which will last forever (Is 13:19-22; Jer 50:40).
Sodom would never rise again. In this regard Sodom illustrates the destiny
of those who Jude said would "suffer the punishment of eternal fire" (Jude
7).

Isaiah begins his prophecy with an oracle against the people of Jerusalem and Judah. They have already felt God's chastening through the Assyrians, but they did not get the message and further punishment is coming.
Some will accept correction and be blessed; others will refuse to repent and

will face even more severe punishment. Isaiah contrasts these alternate futures using vivid prophetic symbols:

> Zion will be redeemed with justice, her penitent ones with righteousness. But rebels and sinners will both be broken, and those who forsake the LORD will perish. . . . You will be like an oak with fading leaves, like a garden without water. The mighty man will become tinder and his work a spark; both will burn together, with no one to quench the fire. (Is 1:27-28, 30-31)

Here is a portrait of total destruction. Apart from God's mercy Judah's wicked would be destroyed like Sodom and Gomorrah until no one is left (Is 1:9). They would wither like an oak with fading leaves and perish like a garden with no water (Is 1:30). They would burn like tinder with no one to quench the fire (Is 1:31). If no one quenches or extinguishes a fire, it keeps consuming until there is nothing left to burn. Isaiah repeats the image of unquenchable fire at the end of his book, in a passage that Jesus quotes and applies to final judgment. Throughout Scripture unquenchable fire signifies fire that cannot be extinguished or resisted and that therefore consumes until nothing is left (Is 34:10-11; Ezek 20:47-48; Amos 5:6; Mt 3:12).[3]

Nahum prophesies God's judgment against ancient Nineveh (1:1), portraying God coming in stormy fire which no one can endure, pursuing his enemies into darkness (1:6, 8). They are consumed like dry stubble (1:10). The prophet mixes metaphors freely: God comes in fire and pursues into darkness. We need not ask how fire and darkness can coexist—each word conjures its own visual image and emotional response. Both responses are true, and they are troublesome only to the over-literalistic. Jesus also later describes final punishment in terms of both darkness and fire (Mt 8:12; 22:13; 25:30).

As we become familiar with these Old Testament symbols of judgment, we will be better able to understand the meaning of the same language in New Testament texts. And we will escape the easy temptation to explain biblical expressions in ways that have no basis in Scripture. More important, we can avoid interpreting biblical images in ways that contradict their ordinary usage throughout the Bible.

Prophetic Pictures of the End

Several Old Testament passages specifically foretell the destiny of the lost at the end of the world. According to these prophetic passages, the wicked will become like chaff or husks of wheat which the wind blows away. They will be like pottery that has been broken to pieces. The wicked will be slain and consumed and will cease to exist. They will be ashes under the soles of the feet of God's people. None of these Scripture texts even hints at anything resembling eternal conscious torment.

Psalm 1 contrasts the present and future fates of the wicked and the righteous. The godly man is like a well-nourished tree that never stops bearing fruit (1:3). We think of the Garden of Eden in Genesis or the Eternal City in Revelation. The wicked are "like chaff that the wind blows away," and their path will finally perish (1:4-6). This psalm speaks of exclusion from God's presence, a principal theme of Jesus' teaching and that of the apostles.

Psalm 2 also foretells the final fate of the lost. In Christian retrospect we see that this psalm describes Jesus Christ as the savior and judge anointed by God (Mt 3:17; Rev 2:26-27).[4] When he finally judges his enemies, he "will dash them to pieces like pottery" (2:9), which is also to "be destroyed" (2:12). When God destroys the wicked, they will resemble pottery that someone has shattered with an iron rod. Does this imagery sound like final extinction or like perpetual torment?

Psalm 110 is one of the most messianic texts in all the Old Testament and is the Old Testament chapter most often quoted in the New Testament.[5] It describes Jesus' exaltation at God's right hand (Ps 110:1), his present intercession for his people (Ps 110:4) and his final triumphant return in judgment (Ps 110:1, 5-6). Commenting on verse one of this psalm, the apostle Paul tells us that the last "enemy" to be destroyed will be death (1 Cor 15:25-26), and John describes death's annihilation by using the image of the lake of fire (Rev 20:14). Psalm 110 says that God's human enemies will be "crushed" (v. 5-6), and it pictures a time when God will be "heaping up the dead" (v. 6). These poetic statements precisely match John's explanation that the lake of fire, for human beings, means "the second death" (Rev 20:14-15; 21:8).

The eleventh chapter of Isaiah prophetically previews the person and work of Jesus Christ. New Testament writers paraphrase or echo each of its first five verses. Verses 6 through 9 picture the result of Jesus' work of redemption, and verse 10 foretells the gospel ministry among the Gentiles (Rom 15:12). Judgment will mean vindication for some and punishment for others. Jesus will "strike the earth with the rod of his mouth; with the breath of his lips he will slay the wicked" (Is 11:4). The picture is symbolic but absolutely clear: the wicked finally will be utterly destroyed.

A question concerning "everlasting burning." Defenders of the traditional view of hell as everlasting conscious torment often look for support to Isaiah's question "Who of us can dwell with everlasting burning?" (Is 33:14), as if it supports the notion that God will keep the wicked alive forever to burn them everlastingly. When we read this passage carefully, we see that it teaches the exact opposite.

Foreign armies afflicted Israel in Isaiah's day, but in Isaiah 33:10-24 the prophet foretells a day when the wicked will be burned up. That day will come at the end of the world. Then God's people will "see the king in his beauty and view a land that stretches afar" (Is 33:17). They will look on the eternal Jerusalem (Is 33:20). They will never be ill again, and all their sins will have been forgiven (Is 33:24). God will "arise," and the wicked will be unable to protect themselves. They will ignite themselves by their own sins, producing a fire that "consumes" them (Is 33:10-11). They will blaze as easily as "cut thornbushes" and burn as thoroughly "as if to lime" (Is 33:12). No metaphor could describe a destruction more complete.

How strange, then, that some attempt to find everlasting conscious torment in verse 14 of this passage, which says:

> The sinners in Zion are terrified;
>   trembling grips the godless:
> "Who of us can dwell with the consuming fire?
>   Who of us can dwell with everlasting burning?"

Admittedly, this verse may be somewhat confusing at first glance. How can a "consuming" fire involve "everlasting" burning? However, this verse does not envision the wicked *living* forever in fiery torment. Instead, it portrays a fire with which no wicked person can *possibly* "dwell." Verse 15 answers the question verse 14 asks. Only the person who "walks righteously and speaks what is right," who rejects extortion and bribes, who avoids evil in every form—only this one can coexist with the God whose holiness is a consuming fire that burns up all sin and whoever will not repent of it.

Food for fire and maggots. The last verse in the book of Isaiah says of the righteous at the end of time, "And they will go out and look upon the dead bodies of those who rebelled against me; their worm will not die, nor will their fire be quenched, and they will be loathsome to all mankind" (Is 66:24).

For nearly three millennia, this verse has been among the most often-quoted Scripture passages concerning final punishment. Yet it might also be the most misunderstood, misused and misapplied passage in the Bible on that subject. We must read the context, which foretells a time when God will execute judgment "with fire and with his sword," when many will be "slain" and will "meet their end together" (66:16-17). Then the righteous and their descendants will endure forever, and "all mankind" will worship God, for the wicked will no longer be alive (66:22-23).

This symbolic picture of the future reflects an actual incident that Isaiah describes in chapter 37 of his book. The savage Assyrians had surrounded Jerusalem and good King Hezekiah prayed to God. That night "the angel of the LORD went out and put to death a hundred and eighty-five thousand men in the Assyrian camp. When the people got up the next morning—there were all the dead bodies!" (Is 37:36).

In chapter 66 Isaiah anticipates the same scene on a massive scale at the end of time. In this prophetic picture, as in the historical event of Isaiah's day, the righteous view "the dead bodies" of the wicked. They see *corpses*, not living people. They view *destruction*, not conscious misery. Discarded corpses are fit only for worms (maggots) and fire—both insatiable agents of disintegration and decomposition.

To the Hebrew mind, both worms and fire signify disgrace and shame (Jer 25:33; Amos 2:1). Worms and fire also indicate complete destruction, for the maggot in this picture does not die but continues to feed so long as there is anything to eat. The fire, which is not "quenched" or extinguished, burns until nothing is left of what it is burning. According to God's prophet Isaiah, this is a "loathsome" scene, which evokes disgust rather than pity (Is 66:24; see the same word in Dan 12:2). This scene portrays shame and not pain. This passage of Scripture says nothing about conscious suffering and certainly nothing about suffering forever.

It is inexcusable to interpret language from this text, whether quoted directly or indirectly from the mouth of Jesus (Mk 9:48), to give a meaning diametrically the opposite of Isaiah's clear picture. Yet that is exactly what traditionalist interpreters have done without exception, down to the present day.[6]

Two kinds of resurrection. Daniel 12:1-2 provides one of the few explicit Old Testament references to the resurrection of both the good and the evil. This prophecy clearly says that "multitudes" will awake from the dust of the earth, but that they will be raised in two forms: "some to everlasting life" and "others to shame and everlasting contempt" (Dan 12:2). The Hebrew word translated "contempt" here is the same word translated "loathsome" in Isaiah 66:24 where it describes unburied corpses. The shame and contempt here are "everlasting" because the loathsome disintegration of the wicked will never be reversed.

Daniel predicts a future time when those who are "wise" will understand his end-time prophecy. All who know the gospel are privileged to be included in that category, for the New Testament reveals clearly what Daniel only hinted at. According to the New Testament, all those who have died will be raised again when Jesus comes (Jn 5:28). The saved will be raised immortal and incorruptible (1 Cor 15:52-54; Rom 2:6-7; 2 Cor 5:4). Those who are raised to shame and everlasting contempt will not be raised immortal but rather for condemnation (Jn 5:29). They will be judged, expelled from God's presence and finally die again forever in the lake of fire—in what Revelation calls the second death (Rom 6:23; 2 Thess 1:9; Rev 21:8). Evangelical commentator Robert H. Mounce well describes the second death as "the destiny of those whose temporary resurrection results only in a return to death and its punishment."[7]

The closing chapter of the Old Testament contrasts the final destinies of the saved and the lost. God's "great and dreadful day" will come when those who revere him will leap for joy in the healing rays of the sun of righteousness (Mal 4:2, 5). Arrogant evildoers will then become like "stubble" and "that day . . . will set them on fire" (Mal 4:1). This all-consuming fire will leave them without "a root or a branch," an expression which removes any hope of a remnant or a survivor (Mal 4:1; contrast this with 2 Kings 19:30; Is 11:1; 53:2). It will be too late for repentance. There will be no restoration or escape. Those lost will be "ashes" under the soles of the feet of the saved (Mal 4:3).

Because these expressions are similes and metaphors, we ought not to take them literally. At the same time, these figures of speech accurately portray the reality they describe. The righteous will rejoice in God's salvation and the wicked will be gone forever. This is the Old Testament's final word on the topic. God's next prophet, John the Baptizer, will march out of the desert, demanding repentance in view of the approaching judgment fire. He also will warn of a time when the wicked will be judged and finally burned up (Mt 3:12).

Between the Testaments

During the tumultuous period between Malachi and Matthew, pious Jews wrote the books contained in the Apocrypha and the pseudepigrapha, as well as the Dead Sea Scrolls. The Apocrypha are books found in the Greek translation of the Old Testament and, later, in the Roman Catholic Bible. The pseudepigrapha ("false writings") have never been included in the canonical Scriptures, although, as the name indicates, they purport to have been written by ancient biblical characters.

The Dead Sea Scrolls reflect the ideas held by an ascetic community of Jews who lived at Qumran, near the Dead Sea, during the first and second centuries before Christ. The Apocrypha and pseudepigrapha were not easily available in English until early in the 1900s; the Dead Sea Scrolls were first translated in the mid-twentieth century. Before these documents came to light, advocates of the traditional position commonly argued that first-century Jews taught everlasting conscious torment and that since Jesus did not explicitly dispute the point, he must have held the same view himself. For such a supposedly uniform Jewish view they relied on Edersheim or Josephus or even Philo of Alexandria.[8]

This resulted in a twofold error. First, traditionalists ignored the rich Old Testament background of the teaching of Jesus and failed to take his teaching on its own terms. Second, they mistakenly assumed from secondary and dubious sources that Jewish intertestamental thought was united on this subject. The simple fact is that these intertestamental Jews were living, breathing, thinking folks who sometimes disagreed on theological subjects.[9] Informed scholars today acknowledge this fact and reject the older notion that Jesus' contemporaries all held one opinion about the destiny of the lost.[10]

The Apocrypha generally repeats Old Testament language concerning the final destiny of the lost. It warns the wicked that they will not escape God's judgment but will surely die. Worms will be their end. They will pass away like smoke or chaff. They will burn up like straw. The righteous may hope for a resurrection and blessed life with God, the Apocrypha says, but the wicked have no such hope.

The single exception in the Apocrypha to this Old Testament view occurs in the book of Judith (150-125 B.C.), the account of a Jewish heroine who saves her people from an evil king. In the end, Judith leads Israel in a great victory song that concludes with the words:

> Woe to the nations that rise up against my race;
> The Lord Almighty will take vengeance of them in the day
>   of judgment,
> To put fire and worms in their flesh;
> And they shall weep and feel their pain for ever. (Judith 16:17)

Judith's fire and worms come straight from Isaiah 66:24, but she gives them a meaning entirely different from the prophet's. Isaiah envisioned the unburied corpses of God's enemies, exposed to shameful destruction by fire and worms. Judith introduces the novel idea of everlasting conscious pain—an idea borrowed, no doubt, from the pagan Greek notion that souls are immortal and cannot die. Judith's fire and worms do not destroy. They torment. They do not consume their victims from outside. They create horrible agonies inside the bodies of the wicked. Instead of being destroyed by the fire and worms, the damned in Judith's story "feel their pain forever." This is the first time this concept appears in Hebrew literature. It is certainly not found in the Old Testament Scriptures, the authors of which consistently expect the wicked to die, to perish and be no more. Our choice of authorities is clear: the prophet Isaiah or the uninspired author of the book of Judith.

The pseudepigrapha also shows a variety of Jewish ideas regarding the final fate of the lost. Some passages in the pseudepigrapha, like Judith in the Apocrypha, seem to express the expectation that the lost will suffer unending conscious torment.[11] Most often, however, the books known as the pseudepigrapha simply reflect the Old Testament writers' view of the sinner's ultimate total extinction. These texts say repeatedly that God will destroy the lost by fire. The overwhelming testimony of these books is that sinners finally will perish from the earth, never to be seen again.

Of the Dead Sea Scrolls translated so far, all agree that the lost will be totally destroyed, body and soul, forever. Their unknown authors evidently agreed with the consistent teaching of the Old Testament on the subject. They also agreed, as we have seen, with most of the pseudepigrapha and with all of the Apocrypha, with the exception of the one passage in the book of Judith.

Because the vast writings of the Apocrypha, pseudepigrapha and many of the Dead Sea Scrolls are now available in English, even nonscholars today can know that not all first-century Jews believed in everlasting torment. There is no longer any reason for anyone to conclude that Jesus endorsed the notion of everlasting torment because it was "the Jewish view." Instead of being misled by a minority view expressed in intertestamental literature, we must examine New Testament teaching in its context and take it at face value unless there is good reason to do otherwise. As we attempt to understand the New Testament, our most valuable tool will be the inspired revelation contained in the Old Testament. On this subject, as on all others, the Bible is its own best interpreter.

3

THE TEACHINGS
OF JESUS

IF WE ACCEPT JESUS' AUTHORITY, WE MUST BELIEVE THAT HELL IS REAL AND that it will be the ultimate fate of the lost. Indeed, Jesus tells us more about the final end of sinners than any other speaker or writer in the New Testament. But is it possible that we have read into Jesus' words meanings that we merely assumed to be correct about the nature of that fate?

Teaching Using the Imagery of Fire
Certainly, much of Jesus' teaching about the final fate of the lost involves the imagery of fire. But because we are so accustomed to that imagery, we might find it surprising to discover the many other illustrations that our Lord uses to describe the fate of the wicked. In this section we will look carefully at what Jesus says concerning final punishment using the imagery of fire. In the next section we will examine what Jesus says about the end of sinners using images other than fire. But before we look at Jesus' own teaching, we must quickly hear a word from his forerunner, John the Baptizer.

Burned up like chaff. The Old Testament closes with a promise that "Elijah" will come to prepare Israel for the day of the Lord (Mal 4:5-6). The New Testament opens with John the Baptizer, who is Malachi's "Elijah" and Isa-

iah's "voice of one calling in the desert" (Mk 1:2-4). As Matthew tells the
story (3:1-12), the Pharisees come out to investigate John, who admonishes
them to flee God's wrath like desert reptiles fleeing before a wilderness
blaze.

"The ax is already at the root of the trees," John announces, "and every
tree that does not produce good fruit will be cut down and thrown into the
fire" (Mt 3:10). Every orchard owner recognizes the image, which is plain
on its face. Trees with bad fruit are burned, as are unfruitful vines and useless weeds. For Jesus and for John these images represent sinners, whether
false prophets, hypocritical hearers or fruitless disciples (Mt 7:19; 13:40; Jn
15:6). In each case their fate is that they will be burned up.

John tells his morally mixed audience that Jesus will "baptize you with
the Holy Spirit and with fire" (Mt 3:11). This promise includes believers,
whom Jesus baptizes in the Holy Spirit (1 Cor 12:13), and unbelievers,
whom he will plunge into the fire of future judgment (2 Thess 1:7-10). Jesus
is both Savior and Judge, at his first and second advents respectively, and
John the Baptizer mentions both of these roles using the language of the
reaper. "His winnowing fork is in his hand, and he will clear his threshing
floor, gathering his wheat into the barn and burning up the chaff with
unquenchable fire" (Mt 3:12). Because God's fire is irresistible and cannot be
quenched, it keeps burning and consuming until nothing is left. Anything
that is put into unquenchable fire is finally burned up. We have seen the
image of unquenchable fire throughout the Old Testament prophets, always
describing fire that cannot be resisted or put out. Not surprisingly, such a
fire consumes, reduces to nothing and burns up whatever is put in it (Ezek
20:47-48; Amos 5:6; Mt 3:12).

Burned like useless trees. In Matthew 7:15-23 Jesus warns against false
prophets. He foretells the end of such religious frauds in these words:
"Every tree that does not bear good fruit is cut down and thrown into the
fire." But what will happen to the evildoers in this fire? Jesus contrasts the
few who find life with the many whose end is destruction (Mt 7:13-14). The
choices in this context are to live or to be destroyed. There is no mention
here of eternal life in torment or of anyone suffering agony forever.

Burned like weeds. Jesus also predicts the destiny of the lost in his parable
of the weeds, recorded in Matthew 13:30-43. In this story the owner of a

field allows wheat and weeds to grow together until the harvest. "At that time," the owner says, "I will tell the harvesters: First collect the weeds and tie them in bundles to be burned; then gather the wheat and bring it into my barn" (Mt 13:30). Jesus interprets the image:

> As the weeds are pulled up and burned in the fire, so it will be at the end of the age. The Son of Man will send out his angels, and they will weed out of his kingdom everything that causes sin and all who do evil. They will throw them into the fiery furnace, where there will be weeping and gnashing of teeth. Then the righteous will shine like the sun in the kingdom of their Father. (Mt 13:40-43)

Jesus says that this word picture accurately depicts what the angels will do to sinners at the end of the world. The lost finally will be burned up like weeds. The promise that "the righteous will shine like the sun" reminds us of Daniel 12:3 or Malachi 4:1-3, in which the righteous enjoy the healing rays of the "sun of righteousness" but the wicked turn to ashes under their feet.

"Weeping" and *"gnashing of teeth."* When Jesus says that there will be weeping and gnashing of teeth in the fiery furnace at the end of the world, what does he mean? Should we imagine the damned enduring horrible pain forever—yet unable to die because God has made them immortal for this very purpose? Or is there a better, biblical explanation?

Weeping is a common biblical symbol for fear, misery or extreme grief—often because of God's judgment on sinners. The Jews wept when Jerusalem was destroyed and when they were exiled from their homeland (Is 22:12; Lam 1—5). People sometimes weep over the death or destruction of others (Is 16:9; Jer 9:1; Rev 18:9). James warns the rich to weep for fear of God's coming judgment (Jas 5:1). Those finally lost will have reason and occasion enough to weep, but eventually that weeping will stop.

The image of people gnashing (or *grinding,* to use a more modern term) their teeth appears throughout the Old and New Testaments, and it always describes the fury of people who are so enraged at others that like wild beasts they could literally devour their victims (Job 15:9; Ps 37:12; Lam 2:16). A familiar example occurs in the story of the death of Stephen, whose enemies rushed at him to kill him, gnashing their teeth in uncontrollable rage (Acts 7:54).

Psalm 112:1-10 offers a most interesting preview of the wicked gnashing their teeth at the end of the world. The psalm primarily describes the happy destiny of the righteous (Ps 112:1-9), but it ends with the fate of the wicked. "The wicked man will see and be vexed, he will gnash his teeth and waste away; the longings of the wicked will come to nothing" (Ps 112:10). This psalm depicts the ungodly as they see the saved of the earth going to their reward and are so infuriated that they gnash their teeth in rage. Meanwhile, like the horrible witch in *The Wizard of Oz*, the wicked disintegrate and waste away until nothing of them is left. The widespread assumption that weeping and gnashing of teeth describe the ceaseless agony of souls in unending conscious torment originated long after the Bible was written and has no basis in the Word of God.

Discarded into the fiery furnace. In Matthew 13:48-50 Jesus also tells a parable about a great fishnet which caught all kinds of fish. When the fishermen emptied their catch on the shore, they "collected the good fish in baskets, but threw the bad away" (Mt 13:48). Hear Jesus' explanation: "This is how it will be at the end of the age. The angels will come and separate the wicked from the righteous and throw them into the fiery furnace, where there will be weeping and gnashing of teeth" (Mt 13:49-50).

Again Jesus emphasizes exclusion—this time in a "fiery furnace." We know what a fiery furnace is intended to do from the story of Daniel's three friends. Nebuchadnezzar's fiery furnace did not destroy Shadrach, Meshach and Abednego because God miraculously intervened to save their lives. However, no one will be delivered out of God's fiery furnace at the end of the world. God's furnace will destroy both body and soul (Mt 10:28). From the "second death" there will never be restoration, resurrection or recovery. Hell's destruction will never end. No wonder Paul refers to it as "everlasting destruction" (2 Thess 1:9).

A proof text that doesn't prove. People frequently refer to Jesus' story of the rich man and Lazarus (Lk 16:19-31) as if it supports the notion of unending conscious torment. Popular author Larry Dixon devotes half of his discussion of Jesus' teaching to this one parable.[1] Even taken literally, however, the story concerns only the intermediate state of two Jewish men who died while Jesus was still teaching on the earth.[2] Furthermore, the context shows no connection with the topic of final punishment, and Jesus' "punch line" in this story is on another subject altogether.

The parable relates to its context from first to last. For example, the story comes immediately after Jesus' teaching on covetousness and stewardship (Lk 16:1-13). The rich man's only known sin is his selfish neglect of Lazarus. The Pharisees sneer at Jesus' teaching, and he warns them against self-justification, reminding them that God knows their hearts and that he often detests what people value highly (Lk 16:14-15). Then Jesus illustrates this truth with the parable of the rich man and Lazarus, two men about whom people have one opinion but God has a very different opinion. The Pharisees live in the most critical of times when God's kingdom is being preached, yet they waste every opportunity to hear and obey God (Lk 16:16-17). Jesus warns them about that very thing, then tells this story about another man who makes the same mistake while he is alive and whose brothers continue it after he is gone.

Few serious interpreters attempt to take the details of the story literally. To do so would require us to imagine the saved and the lost conversing with each other after death, in full view of each other and at close range. We also would have to think of literal tongues that burn with literal fire and literal water that does not cool them,[3] not to mention physical bodies that can be tortured by fire but which somehow do not burn up.

Even if this story were historical narrative rather than a parable, and even if Jesus had told it in answer to a question about the afterlife (which, of course, he did not), and even if we ought to understand all of its details literally (which no one says we should), the parable of the rich man and Lazarus still would tell us absolutely nothing about the *final* destiny of the damned. We should not misuse this parable by trying to make it teach the traditional doctrine of unending conscious torment. That notion is simply not there.

Jesus' teachings that mention Gehenna. Jesus tells us more about hell than does anyone else. But we must ask whether the picture that he intended to portray is the same picture that we have learned to imagine when we hear the word.

On one occasion Jesus pricks the rationalistic pride of the scribes by condemning hateful thoughts and contemptuous words as well as murderous acts. Jesus warns: "Anyone who is angry with his brother will be subject to judgment. . . . Anyone who says to his brother, 'Raca,' is answerable to the Sanhedrin. But anyone who says, 'You fool!' will be in danger of the fire of hell" (Mt 5:22).

This is the Savior's first specific reference to Gehenna, which the English Bible traditionally translates as "hell." The word meant nothing to Gentiles unfamiliar with the geography of Jerusalem, and it appears outside the Gospels only once in the New Testament, in a passage which does not concern the final end of the lost (Jas 3:6). Later we will see how New Testament books written for Gentiles or for Jews living outside Palestine describe the fate of the lost. But to Jesus' Jewish hearers in their homeland, Gehenna had a long and gruesome history.

The Greek word *Gehenna* is the translation of a Hebrew expression meaning the "Valley of Hinnom." This was an actual site, located southwest of the old city of Jerusalem. A deep, waterless gorge, the valley had this name early in Hebrew history (Josh 15:8; 18:16). Later it became the abominable site of child sacrifices to the pagan god Moloch in the days of Ahaz and Manasseh (see 2 Kings 16:3; 21:6), earning it the additional name *Topheth*, which means a place to be spit on or abhorred (Is 30:33).

The same valley may have been the place used to burn corpses in the days of Hezekiah, after God slew the 185,000 Assyrian soldiers in one night (Is 37:36). Jeremiah predicted that this horrible valley would some day be filled with Israelite corpses as well (Jer 7:31-33; 19:2-13). The first-century Jewish historian Josephus says that this valley was heaped with the dead bodies of Jews following the Roman siege of Jerusalem in A.D. 69-70. It is commonly said that Gehenna served as Jerusalem's garbage site in Jesus' day. If that is so, his hearers would have known Gehenna as an abhorrent place where maggot and fire raced to consume the garbage, refuse and offal dumped there each day.

During the time between the Testaments, the word *Gehenna* became a familiar Jewish term for the fiery pit in which the godless will meet their final doom. It is called "the station of vengeance" and "future torment" (2 Baruch 59:10-11), the "pit of destruction" (*Pirke Aboth* 5:19) and the "pit of torment" (4 Esdras 7:36). From about the time of the apostle Paul the rabbis spoke of Gehenna as the intermediate state of the dead and, later, as a place of purgatory.[4] Given its horrible history, *Gehenna* was a well-known local term for the fiery place of judgment to come. But given its rich diversity of meaning, this place-name alone cannot tell us all that we need to know about the nature of the punishment awaiting those who go there. However, Jesus himself supplies additional details concerning punishment in Gehenna, or hell.

Jesus says that hell is so terrible that one should avoid it even at the cost of a cherished body part. The loss of one limb in the present is more desirable than the loss of the total self in the hereafter.

> If your right eye causes you to sin, gouge it out and throw it away. It is better for you to lose one part of your body than for your whole body to be thrown into hell. And if your right hand causes you to sin, cut it off and throw it away. It is better for you to lose one part of your body than for your whole body to go into hell. (Mt 5:29-30)

Jesus' verbs emphasize the ideas of rejection, banishment and expulsion. "Throw" away eye or hand, he says, rather than having your whole body "thrown" away on the day of judgment. The picture is one of total loss—like the loss inflicted by fire.

On another occasion Jesus warns: "Do not be afraid of those who kill the body but cannot kill the soul. Rather, be afraid of the One who can destroy both soul and body in hell" (Mt 10:28). Man's killing power stops with the body and ends with the present age. And the only death any human can inflict is temporary, because God will raise the dead and give the righteous eternal life. But God's ability to destroy has no limits. It reaches deeper than the physical and further than the present. God can kill both body *and* soul, forever. Far from lessening the anxiety of sinners, this understanding of Jesus' words ought to intensify their dread. The words *kill* and *destroy* are parallel and interchangeable in this passage.

Luke records the same teaching in these words: "Do not be afraid of those who kill the body and after that can do no more. But . . . fear him who, after the killing of the body, has power to throw you into hell. Yes, I tell you, fear him" (Lk 12:4-5).

Luke's sequence of events matches that described in Isaiah 66. In both Luke and Isaiah, God first slays his enemies, then throws their dead bodies into the consuming fire (Is 66:16, 24). The pagan philosopher Plato taught that souls are immortal and cannot be destroyed. Many Christians have rea-

soned about hell from that same point of error.[5] But Jesus, the Son of God,
stresses the exact opposite: God can kill the soul as easily as he can kill the
body. And God can destroy both body and soul in hell.

The greatest person in the kingdom of heaven is the one most like a little
child, Jesus instructs the ambitious disciples (Mt 18:1-4), and woe will come
to whoever hinders one of God's little ones in the path of faith (Mt 18:6-7). It
is better to forfeit a member of the body if necessary, Jesus continues, in
order to escape total destruction that will be forever.

> If your hand or your foot causes you to sin, cut it off and throw it away. It is
> better for you to enter life maimed or crippled than to have two hands or two
> feet and be thrown into eternal fire. And if your eye causes you to sin, gouge
> it out and throw it away. It is better for you to enter life with one eye than to
> have two eyes and be thrown into the fire of hell. (Mt 18:8-9)

Gehenna is the "eternal" fire for two reasons. First, it is not part of the
present age but of the age to come. It does not belong to time but to eternity.
Second, those who go into it suffer everlasting destruction. When the
unquenchable fire finally destroys the lost, they will be gone forever. The
Bible calls the fire that fell from heaven and destroyed Sodom "eternal fire"
for that very reason (Jude 7). Once destroyed, Sodom was never seen again.

Mark recounts Jesus speaking of sinners being thrown into or going into
hell (Mk 9:43-48). Mark also quotes Isaiah's description of hell as a place
"where their worm does not die, and the fire is not quenched" (Mk 9:48).
But what kind of worm is this? Is it a "worm" of conscience, of remorse, of
physical or spiritual pain? If we allow the Bible to interpret itself, we do not
have to guess. As we have already discovered, Jesus is quoting from Isaiah
66:24. And the "worm" in Isaiah is a maggot, a devouring worm. What it
eats is already dead. The devouring worm is aided by unquenchable fire
that cannot be put out and that therefore continues to destroy until nothing
remains. And when that destruction is completed, it will last for all eternity.

Punishment will be eternal, but of what will it consist? Perhaps the most
famous of all of Jesus' words concerning final punishment comes at the end
of the parable of the sheep and the goats (Mt 25:31-46). Shepherds in Judea
often care for mixed flocks including both sheep and goats. At night the
shepherds separate the sheep from the goats, because the goats require protection from the cold, while the sheep prefer open air. This practice pro-

vided the setting for Jesus' parable. In this story of final judgment Jesus tells those on the right hand to "take your inheritance, the kingdom prepared for you since the creation of the world" (Mt 25:34). Jesus' first sermon in Matthew names this reward (Mt 5:3) and so also does this, his last sermon in Matthew's Gospel. To those on the left hand the Son of Man says: "Depart from me, you who are cursed, into the eternal fire prepared for the devil and his angels" (Mt 25:41).

Both destinies have been "prepared" and are described as "eternal," but the Lord emphasizes the contrast between these two destinies: life or fiery punishment (Mt 25:46).

The word *punishment* tells us that the destiny of the lost issues from a judicial sentence. They are sent away to this fate. The word *punishment* does not tell us the nature of the penalty, however, or of what it actually consists. In our own criminal justice system *punishment* has a wide variety of meanings. It might mean a monetary fine or perhaps a brief time in jail or even a life sentence to prison. The worst punishment of all, however, is capital punishment—although the actual act of execution lasts only a few minutes at most. We do not measure capital punishment by the time required to carry it out but in terms of its lasting consequences. We consider it the greatest punishment of all because it forever deprives its victims of the remainder of their anticipated lives.

Saint Augustine, whose endorsement of the traditional view of conscious, unending torment practically guaranteed its status as orthodox doctrine, had to admit that this is true of capital punishment. "Where a very serious crime is punished by death and the execution of the sentence takes only a minute, no laws consider that minute as the measure of the punishment but rather the fact that the criminal is forever removed from the community of the living."[6] In this light it will not surprise us to learn that the word translated "punishment" in Matthew 25 originally meant "to cut short." By the time of Jesus it also meant "to prune" or "to cut down." The Old Testament uses this word at times to describe punishment by death (1 Sam 25:31; Ezek 21:15).

This punishment is called "eternal" for two reasons. First, it is the punishment of the age to come, not a punishment meted out by either man or God in this present life. Second and more importantly, it is called "eternal" because it will last forever, as the apostle Paul later specifically details. When Jesus comes at the end of the world, Paul explains, he will punish the wicked with "everlasting destruction" (2 Thess 1:9). Once destroyed, they will be gone *forever*. Jesus mentions in Matthew 25 the fate of the wicked in the most general of terms (eternal punishment), but Paul tells us its specific nature (everlasting destruction). Even Jonathan Edwards, whose name is best known today for his vivid preaching about the torments of hell, concedes that irreversible extinction would properly be called "eternal punishment."[7]

Teachings Without Mentioning Fire

We have considered Jesus' teachings about final punishment that use language involving fire. However, our Lord also taught much on this subject without referring to fire or to Gehenna as such.

Teachings from the Sermon on the Mount. Jesus' familiar Sermon on the Mount recorded in Matthew 5—7 contains no fewer than five separate messages about final punishment.

Jesus warns his disciples early in the Sermon on the Mount, "I tell you that unless your righteousness surpasses that of the Pharisees and the teachers of the law, you will certainly not enter the kingdom of heaven" (Mt 5:20). The Pharisees and scribes were old hands at seeking right standing with God, but they went at it the wrong way. Jesus makes it very clear that whoever enters the kingdom of heaven will do so totally apart from any claims of personal merit—whether by rationalistic arguments like the scribes or by pseudopiety like the Pharisees. One must receive God's righteousness as an undeserved gift. Those who lack this true righteousness will be denied admission into the kingdom of heaven—which is itself a terrible punishment, no matter what else is involved. And according to Jesus, as we have seen and will see again, far more is involved than that.

Jesus also stresses that men and women must get right with God now if they hope to avoid the wrath to come at the end of the world. In this passage the Lord uses the figure of a prisoner who never gets out of jail.

> Settle matters quickly with your adversary who is taking you to court. Do it while you are still with him on the way, or he may hand you over to the judge, and the judge may hand you over to the officer, and you may be

thrown into prison. I tell you the truth, you will not get out until you have paid the last penny. (Mt 5:25-26)

The assumption seems to be that the man in this story cannot possibly discharge his debt and that he will never get out of prison. Since God will destroy both body and soul in hell, no one will exit who enters there. We do not need to invent a doctrine of everlasting torment to understand or explain these words of our Lord.

The gate through which people enter on the way to "life" is narrow and small, Jesus warns in Matthew 7:13-14. There is another gate, a wide one through which many now press, but it leads to "destruction." Jesus admonishes the disciples: "Enter through the narrow gate. For wide is the gate and broad is the road that leads to destruction, and many enter through it. But small is the gate and narrow the road that leads to life, and only a few find it." Here Jesus shows us a picture of the kingdom of God in the form of a walled city with gates that are opened each morning but closed every night and when danger threatens. When the gates are closed, people can enter only by the "narrow gate"—a small gate built into the main gate—and then only those whose names are officially recorded on the city's role of living inhabitants (its "book of life," if you please). In this passage the final alternatives are "life" or "destruction."

Jesus warns that hypocrites will also seek admission into the kingdom in the last day but will be turned away (Mt 7:21-23). Although they will claim to have prophesied, exorcised demons and performed miracles in Jesus' name, he will nevertheless disown them and banish them from his presence. "Then I will tell them plainly, 'I never knew you. Away from me, you evildoers!'" (Mt 7:23). Jesus borrows the last statement from Psalm 6:8, where David rebukes hypocrites among God's people in Israel. A chief element of final punishment is banishment from God's life-giving presence.

Jesus concludes the Sermon on the Mount with the parable of the wise and foolish builders, recorded in Matthew 7:24-27. The foolish man omits the foundation when he builds, and his house crumbles before the storm. "The rain came down, the streams rose, and the winds blew and beat against that house, and it fell with a great crash" (Mt 7:27). Matthew says the house had a great "fall," but Luke literally says it had a great "ruin" (Lk 6:49 NASB). Throughout the Greek Old Testament the word here translated "ruin" stands for a divine judgment of destruction.[8] The New Testament uses the verb form of the same word to describe nets ripping, wine bottles bursting and the state of a body that is torn to pieces by wild hogs—three forms of destruction for the objects involved (Lk 5:6, 37; Mt 7:6).

Luke adds that the destruction came immediately—"the moment the torrent struck"—and that it was "complete" (Lk 6:49). Anyone who has helplessly witnessed a hurricane flattening a house, or has watched in horror as a tornado swept through a nearby dwelling, or has seen a flood demolish and wash away a building knows just how sudden and severe such destruction can be. The symbol is powerful and easy to understand. Jesus' parable also reflects imagery used by the prophet Ezekiel to portray God's storm of judgment that totally destroys the wicked.

> Therefore this is what the Sovereign LORD says: In my wrath I will unleash a violent wind, and in my anger hailstones and torrents of rain will fall with destructive fury. I will tear down the wall you have covered with whitewash and will level it to the ground so that its foundation will be laid bare. When it falls, you will be destroyed in it; and you will know that I am the LORD. (Ezek 13:13-14)

Weeping and gnashing (grinding) of teeth. Earlier we encountered Jesus' imagery of "weeping" and "gnashing of teeth" in Gehenna, or hell. But Jesus also uses those expressions in word pictures that include no specific mention of fire.

On one occasion Jesus warns presumptuous Israelites that their place in God's kingdom is not guaranteed. "I say to you that many will come from the east and the west, and will take their places at the feast with Abraham, Isaac and Jacob in the kingdom of heaven. But the subjects of the kingdom will be thrown outside, into the darkness, where there will be weeping and gnashing of teeth" (Mt 8:11-12).

Those who come "from the east and the west" are most certainly Gentiles (Is 59:19; Mal 1:11). The "subjects of the kingdom" in Matthew's Gospel are undoubtedly faithless Jews to whom (in Luke's account) Jesus directly addresses this harsh warning (Lk 13:28). Those rejected will be "thrown outside, into the darkness."

The King James Version uses the phrase "outer darkness," which has become a familiar part of our language about hell. We picture a lighted house full of merriment, the area outside the door dimly lit by the lamps inside and the region beyond the perimeter of the lamplight where darkness rules. Those expelled from the festivities inside the house are thrown out into that "outer darkness."

Both Matthew and Luke literally say that *there*, in the outer darkness, will be weeping and gnashing of teeth. As we have already found, we do not need to imagine that God keeps people alive forever, torturing them without end, in order to understand that there will be "weeping and gnashing of teeth." In this passage these activities are not even mentioned in the context of fire. Scripture's imagery concerning final punishment is more diverse than we have sometimes acknowledged.[9]

In Matthew 22:1-14 Jesus tells the parable of the wedding banquet, which ends tragically when the king discovers an improperly clad guest. The man is speechless and without excuse. "Then the king told the attendants, 'Tie him hand and foot, and throw him outside, into the darkness, where there will be weeping and gnashing of teeth.' For many are invited, but few are chosen" (Mt 22:13-14). We have previously seen this picture of expulsion into darkness, where there is weeping and gnashing of teeth.

In Matthew 24:45-51 the Lord tells the story of a reckless and profligate servant who is left in charge of his master's household, only to be caught by surprise when his master suddenly returns. The story ends with a warning concerning watchfulness: "The master of that servant will come on a day when he does not expect him and at an hour he is not aware of. He will cut him to pieces and assign him a place with the hypocrites, where there will be weeping and grinding of teeth" (Mt 24:50-51).

Luke, whose version of the story does not mention "weeping and gnashing of teeth" and uses the word *unbelievers* rather than *hypocrites* (12:46), continues where Matthew stops, adding a new element to the picture:

> That servant who knows his master's will and does not get ready or does not do what his master wants will be beaten with many blows. But the one who does not know and does things deserving punishment will be beaten with few blows. From everyone who has been given much, much will be demanded; and from the one who has been entrusted with much, much more will be asked. (Lk 12:47-48)

Again Jesus foretells degrees of punishment based on light spurned and opportunity neglected. But no one in this story is tormented alive forever. The worst fellow is cut in pieces and thrown out. The example of such terrible punishment is indeed sufficient to smite the conscience of any sensitive soul.

People today sometimes pity the "one-talent man," but Jesus portrays him in the parable of the talents as "lazy" and "worthless" (Mt 25:26, 30). In the end he loses what he originally had and is thrown "outside, into the darkness, where there will be weeping and gnashing of teeth" (Mt 25:30). Only Matthew describes the master's return, but Luke adds a subplot and some additional characters—a group of citizens who refuse to acknowledge the master's authority (Lk 19:11-27). In the end they are arrested and executed. This detail teaches us about final punishment, but it says nothing about everlasting torment.

Additional teachings on final punishment. Jesus reminds his hearers that people cannot ultimately destroy life but that God can kill with such finality that nothing survives. He says, "Whoever finds his life will lose it, and whoever loses his life for my sake will find it" (Mt 10:39). Jesus presents the same two options in Matthew 16:25-26, where he adds a rhetorical question. Of what advantage is it to people, Jesus asks, if they gain the whole world but lose their own lives? In the larger context Jesus is explaining his own approaching death and resurrection to life, and we ought to read his words *life* and *death* at face value. Jesus warns against attempting to save one's own life, and he promises that all who lose their lives for the Lord will find them in the end. No person in this world willingly exchanges life for any amount of riches. Jesus could not say it more plainly. Some will *lose life* when Jesus comes to judge, but others will *find life*.

At the Last Supper Jesus tells the Twelve that one of them will betray him. "The Son of Man will go just as it is written about him. But woe to that man who betrays the Son of Man! It would be better for him if he had not been born" (Mt 26:24; see also Mk 14:21).

Some people argue that only unending conscious torment could be worse than never having been born. However, the same language appears in one of the intertestamental books attributed to Enoch. The people in question perish and their lives come to an end (*1 Enoch* 38:2, 5-6). Jesus says that Judas's fate is worse than nonbirth, not that nonbirth is a fate worse than death.

John 3:16, perhaps the most-memorized verse among evangelicals, contrasts the final alternatives beyond this present life. Some people will enjoy "eternal life" but others will "perish." We ought to take these words at face value. There is no scriptural reason to explain them any other way.

We learn from Matthew 11:22-24 that it will be "more bearable" for Tyre and Sidon on the day of judgment than for Korazin and Bethsaida, and "more bearable" for Sodom than for Capernaum. Jesus' imagery that Capernaum will "go down to the depths [or Hades]" comes from Old Testament warnings against Babylon and Tyre (Is 14:13, 15; Ezek 26:19-21). If these sayings refer to God's judgment of individual people rather than to cities as such, then they only confirm what we have found before. Whatever conscious suffering hell's victims do endure will be based on perfect, divine justice in each individual case.

Present Choices and Eternal Consequences

Woven throughout Jesus' teachings about final punishment is his insistence that now is the time to make ultimate decisions. Present choices will have eternal consequences.

Some Pharisees once saw Jesus heal a demon-possessed man and attributed his astounding power to the prince of demons. Jesus warned them: "The blasphemy against the Spirit will not be forgiven. Anyone who speaks . . . against the Holy Spirit will not be forgiven, either in this age or in the age to come" (Mt 12:31-32).

In Mark's account Jesus expresses the same idea using the adjective *eternal:* "Whoever blasphemes against the Holy Spirit will never be forgiven; he is guilty of an eternal sin" (Mk 3:29). Luke 12:10 states simply that "he will not be forgiven." The "eternal sin" is not a sin committed forever. It is the specific sin of blasphemy against the Holy Spirit. Because this sin will never be forgiven, its *consequences* last forever. It is "eternal" in its results. The New Testament speaks in the same way of eternal salvation (Heb 5:9), eternal judgment (Heb 6:2), eternal redemption (Heb 9:12), eternal punishment (Mt 25:46) and eternal destruction (2 Thess 1:9). In each case, the outcome is everlasting, not the process. God will not be forever saving or judging or redeeming or punishing or destroying. He accomplishes each activity, then stops. But the results of each activity last forever.

In John 3:36, John the Baptizer explains that believers in Christ will have "eternal life;" rejecters of Christ experience the alternative: "God's wrath remains" on them. John's Gospel emphasizes the present aspect of both states. Already the believer enjoys eternal life. Already God's wrath rests on the person who rejects the life that Jesus offers. The statement reminds us of Moses' warning to Israel that if one of them breaks God's covenant, God's curses not only will come ("fall" NIV) on him but will "rest" (NASB) on him as well (Deut 29:20). The Hebrew text literally says the curses "lie down" on the covenant breaker, evoking the image of a beast of prey. In the same way, warns Jesus, God's wrath "remains" on the one who rejects him, for he alone can turn it away.

Jesus says that "a time is coming when all who are in their graves will hear his voice and come out—those who have done good will rise to live, and those who have done evil will rise to be condemned" (Jn 5:28-29). Although the Sadducees denied that there would be a resurrection of the body, the Pharisees and many others in Israel waited with strong hope for that event (Acts 23:60). Jesus' words here remind us of Daniel's ancient resurrection prophecy (Dan 12:2). The word *condemned* clearly indicates a judicial verdict, but that word alone does not reveal the actual sentence. Jesus' emphasis here is that people's present response to him determines their postresurrection fate.

4

THE WRITINGS
OF PAUL

I*T SHOULD NOT SURPRISE US THAT A MAJOR PORTION OF NEW TESTAMENT* revelation concerning final punishment comes from the pen of the apostle Paul or that what he says is straightforward and easy to understand. What is not easily understood is why Paul's teaching has so often been ignored. Perhaps it is because that teaching so obviously contradicts the popular notion that God intends to immortalize the wicked in order to torment them forever. As we will see, the apostle's actual teaching is exactly opposite of that widely accepted tradition.

God will avenge evil. The first point Paul makes is that God sees evil and that eventually he will call sinners to give account for their actions. Paul urges his converts to live holy lives and to abstain from moral uncleanness, warning that "the Lord will punish men for all such sins" (1 Thess 4:6). Paul literally says that the "Lord is Avenger," a phrase which also appears in the Greek text of Psalm 94:1. This passage does not tell us how God will "avenge" or what his punishment will involve, but Paul also makes that plain as we will shortly see.

Exclusion from the kingdom. We already have seen Jesus' frequent warnings that the wicked will not be admitted into the kingdom of heaven. Paul

makes the same point in Galatians 5:16-21, noting that the Spirit who frees
believers from legalism also forbids fleshly license. Those who "live like
this will not inherit the kingdom of God" (Gal 5:21). Although this passage
focuses on exclusion from eternal bliss rather than infliction of pain, it only
begins to paint Paul's full picture of the final wages of sin. The ungodly will
not simply slip away from God's judgment, silent and unobserved. Instead
they will come face to face with the wrath of their holy Creator, the
almighty God of the universe.

God's wrath awaits the lost. According to Paul the final punishment of the
wicked will demonstrate God's righteous wrath against sin. Throughout
the Old Testament God's wrath against sin results in the total destruction of
the sinner. The prophets paint an awesome mosaic of divine wrath and
destruction—a mosaic which includes raging floods, destroying storms,
slaying swords, flowing blood, consuming moths, devouring worms, consuming fire and ascending smoke. The Old Testament also shows us historical examples of God's wrath poured out in the past—such as the flood of
Noah's day and the everlasting obliteration of Sodom and Gomorrah.

Romans 2:6-11 and 2 Thessalonians 1:6-10 contain Paul's most detailed
discussion of final punishment. Both passages concern the justice of God's
judgment—regarding suffering Christians and their persecutors (in Thessalonians) and regarding the faithful and the impenitent (in Romans). God's
justice comforts and inspires the faithful (Thessalonians), even as it warns
the careless and the indifferent (Romans). God

> "will give to each person according to what he has done." To those who by
> persistence in doing good seek glory, honor and immortality, he will give
> eternal life. But for those who are self-seeking and who reject the truth and
> follow evil, there will be wrath and anger. There will be trouble and distress
> for every human being who does evil: first for the Jew, then for the Gentile;
> but glory, honor and peace for everyone who does good: first for the Jew, then
> for the Gentile. For God does not show favoritism. (Rom 2:6-11)

God will judge all people fairly and individually. To those who persistently do good God will give eternal life, which Paul says will also include
"glory, honor and immortality." His mention of "immortality" reminds us
again of the ancient Greek philosophers, but the contrast between biblical
authors and pagan Greeks in the use of this term is striking. Whenever the

Bible attributes immortality to human beings, it always describes the *bodies* (never disembodied souls or spirits) of the *saved* (never of the lost) after the *resurrection* (never in the context of this created world as we know it).[1]

Paul informs us that not everyone will experience immortality or eternal life. Those who prefer evil over truth and pleasing themselves over pleasing God will receive "wrath and anger . . . trouble and distress." Wrath and anger describe the scene from God's standpoint. Trouble and distress portray it from the perspective of the lost. *Wrath* appears often in passages concerning final judgment, and the synonym *anger* intensifies the meaning.

The original readers of Romans (who knew the Greek Old Testament) would have been likely to likely remember Zephaniah 1:14-18 as they read Paul's words here. Zephaniah speaks of "the day of the LORD's wrath," and also of "wrath" and "distress" (the same word Paul uses for "trouble"). Zephaniah mixes metaphors freely. Sinners' "blood will be poured out like dust and their entrails like filth" (Zeph 1:17). God will "consume" the whole world in "the fire of his jealousy" (Zeph 1:18). The two scenes share a single meaning: God "will make a sudden end of all who live in the earth" (Zeph 1:18). The notion of everlasting torment is nowhere in Paul's detailed picture—or in Zephaniah's before it.

In Romans 1:18 Paul announces: "The wrath of God is being revealed from heaven against all the godlessness and wickedness of men who suppress the truth by their wickedness." In the previous verse Paul says that the gospel "reveals" God's righteousness. Our English word *apocalypse* (revelation) comes from the noun form of Paul's verb *revealed* in both passages, as does our adjective *apocalyptic*. These words relate to the end of the world, when all that is now hidden will be uncovered. Then Jesus also will be revealed as he is (2 Thess 1:7; 1 John 3:2). However, we do not have to wait until the end to see what God's wrath means, for God has revealed it in the death of Jesus. The cross of Christ portrays the divine wrath against sin more vividly than any apocalyptic description of the end ever could, no matter how imaginative or vivid its terms. What the cross shows us is a picture of total destruction and death from which God alone can deliver.[2]

The epistle we call 1 Thessalonians was probably Paul's earliest letter, written in A.D. 50-51 from Corinth. Its recipients were themselves new believers who had only recently "turned to God from idols to serve the living and true God, and to wait for his Son from heaven, whom he raised from the dead—Jesus, who rescues us from the coming wrath" (1 Thess 1:9-10). Paul tells these believers that they need not fear, "for God did not appoint us to suffer wrath but to receive salvation through our Lord Jesus Christ" (1 Thess 5:9). Paul reassures them that the righteous will "live together with him," an outcome exactly opposite the destruction awaiting the lost (1 Thess 5:10). This epistle closes in the same way that it opens, with the final alternatives of "wrath" or "salvation."

The wicked will finally be destroyed. Throughout his epistles the apostle Paul tells us plainly that the punishment awaiting the wicked is destruction. This finally is the meaning of God's wrath against sin.

God will avenge in wrath on the day he has appointed, which Paul (like the Hebrew prophets before him) calls "the day of the Lord" (1 Cor 5:5; see Acts 17:30-31). The expression stands in contrast with "human day," the literal term translated "man's judgment" in 1 Corinthians 4:3 (KJV). Today people have their say, but tomorrow God will have his. Throughout Scripture the "day of God's wrath" is also "the day of redemption." The New Testament also calls it "the day of Christ" or "the day of our Lord Jesus Christ" (Phil 2:16; 1 Cor 1:8). This "day" will be unexpected, sudden and inescapable. Paul insists that "destruction will come on the [the lost] suddenly, . . . and they will not escape" (1 Thess 5:2-3). Paul also says that this "destruction" is "everlasting" (2 Thess 1:9).

The word translated here as "destruction" occurs in the New Testament only in Paul's writings. The incestuous Corinthian is to be delivered over to Satan "so that the sinful nature may be destroyed" (1 Cor 5:5). Paul uses a form of this same word when referring to the "destroying angel" who wiped out a generation of Israelites in the wilderness (1 Cor 10:10). The author of the epistle to the Hebrews (whether Paul or someone else) uses a variant form of this Greek word to identify the "destroyer" who slaughtered the firstborn throughout Egypt (Heb 11:28). In these last two passages the word clearly involves execution, extermination and death. Contrary to the assumptions of many traditionalists, scientific notions of physical annihilation are entirely beside the point.

"If anyone destroys God's temple," warns the apostle in 1 Corinthians 3:17, "God will destroy him." Dissension and factions are among acts of the sinful nature which lead to "destruction" or "corruption." *Destroy* in this verse is the translation of the verb form of the Greek noun meaning "corruption" or "destruction" (Gal 5:20; 6:8).

Paul encourages embattled believers at Philippi with the prospect that their very persecution is a sign of God's coming judgment, when the alternative fates will be salvation or destruction. Do not be "frightened in any way by those who oppose you," he encourages. "This is a sign to them that they will be destroyed, but that you will be saved—and that by God" (Phil 1:28). *Destroyed* here translates a noun form of the verb Paul used when he wrote that "all who sin apart from the law will also perish apart from the law" (Rom 2:12).

Today crosses crown our church steeples and adorn our sanctuaries. It might be hard for us to remember that there are people who "live as enemies of the cross of Christ." Of such individuals Paul says: "Their destiny is destruction, their god is their stomach, and their glory is in their shame. Their mind is on earthly things" (Phil 3:18-19).

The destiny of sinners is "destruction." Two verses later the apostle contrasts "destruction" with being immortalized in glory. Jesus will transform believers' bodies to be like his glorious body. Let there be no mistake about it: God will raise the wicked to face judgment. But their certain destiny is destruction. Because they have served their carnal appetites as their god, they will not enjoy immortality but will perish.

Although the final destruction of the lost may involve conscious suffering, its primary horror is that those who are destroyed will not enjoy eternal life. Paul presents the final alternatives like this: "The one who sows to please his sinful nature, from that nature will reap destruction; the one who sows to please the Spirit, from the Spirit will reap eternal life" (Gal 6:8).

The New International Version has *destruction* instead of *corruption*, which is what Paul literally wrote. Paul elsewhere uses the same word to describe perishable food and the decaying world order (Rom 8:21; Col 2:22). Peter uses it to refer to animals destined for slaughter (2 Pet 2:12); Christian literature of the second century uses the same word for an abortion or a miscarriage, a gruesome but vivid example of "destruction."

Four times in his writings Paul speaks of "mortal" things that eventually are corrupted and decay, each time choosing a Greek adjective from the same family as the word translated "destruction." Mortal creatures are contrasted with the immortal God (Rom 1:23), and the crown that "will not last" stands opposite one that lasts forever (1 Cor 9:25). Twice Paul contrasts our present body, which is "perishable," with the glorified resurrection body, which will never perish (1 Cor 15:53-54). Paul's statement in Galatians 6:8 also contrasts the product of the flesh on the one hand and the harvest of the Spirit on the other. The first brings forth corruption (think of a miscarriage). The second produces eternal life. The natural opposite of life is death, not eternal life in misery.

Sometimes this word has a figurative or metaphorical sense. Paul uses its verb form to refer to destroying a house, a girl's virginity, a man's financial standing or someone's morals. Even in those figurative uses of the word, however, the building *as building* no longer exists, the maiden's *virginity* is forever gone, the man's *financial security* is annihilated, and the individual's *good character* that once existed is no longer to be found. The very fact that a word can have a figurative sense presupposes an ordinary and literal sense that gives meaning to the extended usage. There is no good reason to look for some special, figurative meaning of *destruction* when the Bible uses it to portray the final end of sinners. Its primary meaning is the most natural reading.

On an upbeat note, even present persecution and trials inspire hope and joy in view of God's coming judgment. Suffering believers may know that "God is just" and that he will even the score. That is Paul's theme in 2 Thessalonians 1:5-10. The King James Version says Jesus will "be revealed from heaven with his mighty angels, in flaming fire taking vengeance." The New International Version and Revised Standard Version turn the phrase around, saying that Jesus "is revealed from heaven in blazing fire with his powerful angels" (NIV) or "is revealed from heaven with his mighty angels in flaming fire" (RSV).

This entire passage parallels Isaiah 66 in several interesting respects.

1. The Thessalonians, like the faithful Israelites whom Isaiah comforted, were being excluded by their fellow citizens (1 Thess 2:14-16; Is 66:5).

2. In each case the faithful anticipate God's reversal of circumstances (2 Thess 1:5-7; Is 66:6, 14).

3. Both Paul and Isaiah speak of "inflicting" or "repaying" vengeance.

(The KJV and the RSV correctly translate the phrase in 2 Thessalonians 1:8 as inflicting or taking vengeance.)

4. Both passages picture the Lord coming in "fire" (2 Thess 1:7; Is 66:15).

If we read Paul against the background of Isaiah 66:15-24, the fire in this passage appears to be a means of God's vengeance. In Isaiah, God comes "with fire," brings down "his rebuke with flames of fire" and "with fire" executes judgment. The rebuke and judgment of fire result in "many . . . slain by the LORD" (Is 66:15-16). The chapter ends with the "dead bodies" of the slain being given over to fire and worm so that they become "loathsome to all mankind" (Is 66:24). Throughout the Bible the fire that symbolizes God's holiness also destroys those who do not reverence him. The same heavenly fire which lit the altar also destroyed Aaron's irreverent sons (Lev 9:24—10:3). The God who is called "a consuming fire" is jealous for his glory (Deut 4:24; Heb 12:29). Those who reject the sin offering he has provided are not only left without a sacrifice for sin, they also must wait in "fearful expectation of judgment and of raging fire that will consume the enemies of God" (Heb 10:26-27).

This background prepares us to read Paul's statement that the wicked will finally be "punished with everlasting destruction" (2 Thess 1:9). That this destruction is a "penalty" emphasizes that it is the result of a lawful process in accordance with what is right. The word *penalty* comes from the same root word as does the word *just* in verse six and the word *vengeance* (*punish* NIV) in verse eight. This punishment of destruction is also "eternal"—in two senses. It is eternal in a qualitative sense, because it belongs to the age to come and not to the present order of created space and time. But the future destruction of the lost will also be eternal in a quantitative sense if we imagine quantities of time, because it will never end. Once destroyed, the wicked will never be seen again. The *result* is everlasting, not the *process*.

What does it mean that the wicked "will be punished with everlasting destruction . . . from the presence of the Lord and from the majesty of his power" (2 Thess 1:9)? The original language also appears in the Greek text of Isaiah 2:10, 19, 21, and it may be interpreted two ways. Either the everlasting destruction proceeds from God's presence, or it involves exclusion from the divine presence. The King James Version allows the first; the Revised Standard Version, New American Standard Bible and New International Version all translate to mean the second. Both are likely true.

When God comes to punish sinners, the whole earth shares in the consequences. Isaiah saw a vision in which the earth finally "falls—never to rise
again;" its inhabitants "are burned up, and very few are left" (Is 24:6, 20).
Jeremiah also had a vision which was a reversal of the creation story, as if
one watched a video of Genesis 1 run from back to front (Jer 4:23-26). The
prophet watches as people disappear from the land and birds from the air.
The fruitful ground becomes a barren desert. Mountains tremble and shake.
The lights go out of the heavens. Finally, the earth is "formless and empty,"
just as it began.

Now we have come full circle. Paul tells the Thessalonians that God will
punish the wicked—with everlasting destruction which proceeds from his
presence and removes the wicked from his presence forever. Jesus Christ
will be glorified and marveled at among the believers, and God's faithful
people will enjoy his presence without end. This too was part of Isaiah's
vision of God's great day.

> They raise their voices, they shout for joy;
>> from the west they acclaim the LORD's majesty.
> Therefore in the east give glory to the LORD;
>> exalt the name of the LORD, the God of Israel,
>> in the islands of the sea.
> From the ends of the earth we hear singing:
>> "Glory to the Righteous One." (Is 24:14-16)

Nothing in Paul's language in 2 Thessalonians requires or even hints at
immortalized sinners or everlasting conscious torment. Instead, Paul's
words agree consistently with the former Scriptures, where time and again
the end of sinners is made plain. They will perish, be destroyed, be burned
up and be gone forever. The new element in Paul's picture is the role of
Jesus Christ.

Anathema *means "devoted to destruction."* In case the ordinary vocabulary of death and destruction is not absolutely clear, several times in his
writings Paul uses a special word that leaves no room for confusion or
mistake. That word is *anathema*, a transliterated Greek word. Paul warns
that the gospel of Jesus Christ is so important that anyone who diverges
from it risks eternal consequences. "But even if we or an angel from

heaven should preach a gospel other than the one we preached to you, let him be eternally condemned! As we have already said, so now I say again: If anybody is preaching to you a gospel other than what you accepted, let him be eternally condemned!" (Gal 1:8-9; see also 1 Cor 16:22).

The New International Version says "eternally condemned" and the Revised Standard Version and King James Version say "accursed," but Paul actually wrote "anathema." The word literally refers to something set aside to be kept, as an offering that might be hung on a temple wall after being devoted to a god. Because offerings devoted to the true God were commonly burned or otherwise destroyed, this word also refers to anything "accursed" or dedicated to destruction. Paul tells the Romans that he would sacrifice himself as one marked for destruction (anathema) to save his Israelite brethren (Rom 9:3). Of course, Paul was himself a sinner in need of salvation, and he could not carry out the task of becoming accursed for others. What happened on Golgotha was the proper fate of one made "anathema," although the innocent Jesus was there in the place of us sinners (1 Cor 12:3; 1 Pet 2:24).

The word *anathema* is used in the Greek Old Testament to refer to the Canaanites whom Israel "totally destroyed" (Num 21:2-3). *Anathema* describes the spoils of war set apart for destruction, including the city of Jericho and its spoils, which Achan took (Deut 7:26; Josh 6:17-18; 7:12). Achan himself paid the very penalty that the word implies. He was utterly destroyed—stoned to death, burned with fire and covered with rocks (Josh 7:25-26). When Paul used the word *anathema*, it already had deep roots in biblical literature, with a very specific meaning. We do not need to give it an entirely different meaning when used of final punishment, nor is anyone justified in doing so. If even an angel from heaven preaches a different gospel, Paul says that that one is "anathema"—devoted to utter destruction.

The wages of sin is death. Several times Paul comes right out and says that the end of the lost will be to die, a term to which humans everywhere instantly relate. For Paul *destruction* and *death* are interchangeable. We should not look for hidden meanings in these words, different from their common, ordinary usage.

It is "God's righteous decree," for example, that those who renounce known truth and give themselves over to depravity "deserve death" (Rom

1:21-32). That was God's first word on the subject to Adam and Eve in the Garden (Gen 2:17). Plato would later teach the Greeks that death was a friend that separated the immortal soul from the imprisoning mortal body, a notion that appears nowhere in the Word of God. Scripture always portrays human life as God's gift and death as the inevitable punishment for sin. Paul speaks for all Scripture authors when he warns that "the wages of sin is death" (Rom 6:23). Throughout the Bible this "death" stands in stark contrast to eternal "life."

The death which is appointed to all human beings to experience is the end of this animated earthly person (Gen 2:7; Eccles 12:7). But temporal death is not the end of the story—for either the saved or the lost. Both groups will be raised, although the nature of their resurrection bodies will differ greatly. In the resurrection God will transform the saved from mortal into immortal and they will never die again. The wicked, on the other hand, will not be given immortality, and they finally will perish in the second death—which is the everlasting and total destruction of both body and soul in hell.

Twice Paul says that sin results in "death," the alternative to "eternal life." In Romans 6:21 he asks: "What benefit did you reap at that time from the things you are now ashamed of? Those things result in death!" Two verses later he concludes: "For the wages of sin is death, but the gift of God is eternal life in Christ Jesus our Lord." Eternal life stands opposite eternal death, which for Paul means "perishing," "destruction" and "corruption."

Sinners will finally perish. No wonder Paul says that sinners will finally perish—whether they are Jewish sinners or Gentile sinners (Rom 2:12). God will judge righteously in every case and each person will be judged according to the light he or she rejected. This "perishing" is the alternative fate to "immortality," and it will happen to those whom God will raise from the dead in a mortal, corruptible and destructible state.

Of course, the word translated "perish" is sometimes used figuratively—for example, of ruined wineskins or spoiled food (Mt 9:17; Jn 6:12). But that fact is misleading if taken alone. The word translated "perish" appears ninety-two times in the New Testament, thirteen times in Paul's letters. Most often it refers to actual death. Sometimes it is contrasted with enduring, eternal life. This same Greek word is the regular term for the "lost" or for those who are "perishing." Peter uses the same Greek word to describe the fate of the world that was destroyed by the flood (2 Pet 3:6). Both Paul and Jude use it to describe Israel's destruction in the wilderness (1 Cor 10:9-10; Jude 5). To "perish" would be the fate of dead Christians if Christ had not been raised (1 Cor 15:18). This is the word used so often to describe the final punishment of the wicked at the end of the world. We should allow the Bible to explain itself and give this word rendered "perish" its natural and obvious meaning.

Paul's language in its philosophical context. In Paul's day philosophers and common folk alike discussed the subject of human immortality. Some argued that every soul is immortal by nature and denied that any soul can ever pass out of existence. They mistakenly used the terms Paul uses to describe the destiny of the saved, as if those words apply to both the saved and the wicked. Others in Paul's day taught that when people die they perish completely and forever, both body and soul, and that there is no future life of any kind for any person. They mistakenly used the very words Paul uses to describe the destiny of the lost, as if they applied to both the saved and the wicked.

In that context Paul uses all these words very carefully. Some terms—such as *immortality, glory* and *indestructible*—he applies only to the saved. Others—such as *die, perish, destroy* and *corrupt*—he applies only to the lost. This common usage of the Greek language in Paul's day led the New Testament translator R. F. Weymouth to exclaim, as he listened to popular preaching on final punishment:

> My mind fails to conceive a grosser misinterpretation of language than when the five or six strongest words which the Greek tongue possesses, signifying "destroy," or "destruction," are explained to mean maintaining an everlasting but wretched existence. To translate black as white is nothing to this.[3]

5

THE REST OF
THE NEW TESTAMENT

W E HAVE EXAMINED JESUS' TEACHINGS CONCERNING FINAL PUNISH-
ment and all the passages on this subject from the writings of Paul. We look
now at the teachings of other New Testament writers concerning the ultimate doom of the lost.

What Acts Says
It is informative to discover what the earliest gospel evangelists said concerning the final fate of those who reject God's mercy, and to note the contrast between their descriptions of that destiny and the pictures we have
seen presented, for example, by Jonathan Edwards and Charles Spurgeon.

While in Athens during his second missionary trip, the apostle Paul
addressed a company of pagan philosophers who regularly gathered for
discussion at the Acropolis. Luke records the substance of Paul's remarks in
Acts 17:19-33, which concluded with this startling announcement: "[God]
has set a day when he will judge the world with justice by the man he has
appointed. He has given proof of this to all men by raising him from the
dead" (Acts 17:31).

Although Paul declared that judgment is certain and that it will be just, he did not specify here the outcome of that judgment for the lost. However, in another passage also found in Acts, Peter did say what the fate of the wicked will be, and we turn to that passage next.

In Acts 3:23 Peter paraphrases Moses' warning to Israel found in Deuteronomy 18:15, 19. Peter warns that Jesus is the prophet of all prophets, and whoever rejects him "will be completely cut off from among his people." Peter chooses a verb, used only this one time in the entire New Testament, that means "to destroy utterly" or "to root out."[1] The same verb is common in the Greek Old Testament, however, where it translates the regular Hebrew verb for capital punishment or total extermination. The same word describes God's destruction of the world by the flood (Gen 9:11) and the fate of evildoers in general. Daniel also applies this word to the coming Messiah who would suffer the fate due to sinners (Dan 9:26).

What Hebrews Says

The epistle to the Hebrews highlights Christ's perfect, saving sacrifice by which God forgives and forever sets right all who truly put their trust in him. But the author of this book also speaks concerning the consequences of willfully rejecting the mercy of God in Christ.

The author of Hebrews reminds his readers that God used angels to deliver the law to Moses and that violation of the law carried a death penalty. But Jesus is far greater than angels, he explains, both in his person and in his position. The unknown author of Hebrews then asks, "How shall we escape if we ignore such a great salvation . . . announced by the Lord?" (Heb 2:3-4). The answer is obvious: there will be no escape. The epistle closes with the same question with which it opened: "If they did not escape . . . how much less will we, if we turn away from him who warns us from heaven?" (Heb 12:25). The plain answer is that there is no escape.

God expects those who taste new life in Christ to go on to maturity, according to Hebrews 6:1-10. God blesses fruitful farmland, and he will also bless productive believers. This passage warns professing believers who do not demonstrate the fruit of salvation that "land that produces thorns and thistles is worthless and is in danger of being cursed. In the end it will be burned" (Heb 6:7-8). Literal thorns and thistles are part of the curse brought on by human sin (Gen 3:17-18). The land here represents "worthless" disci-

ples who claim to know Christ but who bear no fruit. Such people will
finally be "burned." One does not burn a field of briars to cause them pain
but to destroy what is useless. Surely this figure does not illustrate something directly opposite to what it pictures.

Christ's atoning sacrifice was offered once for all time, and it was perfect
in design, sufficient for its purpose and everlasting in its results. Whoever
relies on that sacrifice can approach God boldly, confidently and continu-
ally, according to Hebrews 10:12-27. But the same truth also implies a serious warning. For if someone rejects this offering, there is not another
offering anywhere in the universe that God will accept in its place. Those
who "deliberately keep on sinning" therefore thrust away the only hope of
salvation. They can anticipate "only a fearful expectation of judgment and
of raging fire that will consume the enemies of God" (Heb 10:26-27). We
have encountered this consuming fire many times throughout the Old and
New Testaments.

This consuming fire is nothing other than God's holiness, viewed from
the standpoint of one who despises it, "for our 'God is a consuming fire.' "
This statement found in Hebrews 12:29 is a direct quotation from Moses'
warning to Israel (Deut 4:24). "This fire of God is not a passing thing; it is of
his very essence."[2] Indeed, "it is a dreadful thing to fall into the hands of the
living God" (Heb 10:31).

Rebels who rejected the law of Moses "died without mercy" (Heb 10:28).
We remember the earthquake that devoured rebellious Korah, Dathan and
Abiram, with their possessions and their entire families. We recall covetous
Achan and his household, whom Israel stoned to death, then burned with
fire and buried with rocks. We remember irreverent Nadab and Abihu,
whom God struck down with heavenly fire, or presumptuous Uzzah,
whom God executed on the spot when he reached out and touched the ark
of the covenant. The author of Hebrews warns that our greater salvation in
Christ also carries greater responsibility. Anyone who consciously and consistently rejects this salvation will be punished even "more severely" (Heb
10:29) than those wrongdoers who perished in Old Testament times. In
addition to whatever conscious torment it might involve, the "second
death" is worse than the first death because it lasts forever and because it
means missing out on eternal life.

However, the author of Hebrews does not expect his readers to be among the lost. "We are not of those who shrink back and are destroyed," the author continues, "but of those who believe and are saved" (Heb 10:39). Throughout the New Testament, "destruction" is the opposite of being "saved." There is no reason to think of unending conscious torment.

What James Says

The short epistle of James offers a fascinating glimpse into the faith and experience of Jewish believers in Jesus—faithful Hebrew men and women who probably were never called "Christians" (although they accepted Jesus of Nazareth as the promised Messiah), who met in synagogues (rather than churches) for worship and fellowship and who stressed the practical aspects of serving God more than they did theoretical doctrinal questions.

Our responsibility is to obey God's law, not to sit in judgment on others. James tells us two reasons why this is true. "There is only one Lawgiver and Judge, the one who is able to save and destroy. But you—who are you to judge your neighbor?" (Jas 4:12). Since God gave the law, only he has the right to call people to account regarding it. Besides, only God can execute any judgment sentence—for good or for ill. The final alternatives are salvation or destruction.

"Misery" awaits the wicked rich, according to James 5:1-6. To his listeners who "have lived on earth in luxury and self-indulgence," James warns of a time when hoarded gold and silver will "eat your flesh like fire." They thought they were acquiring security, but they had really "fattened" themselves for "the day of slaughter." The well-spread banquet table somehow looks different if it is the last meal before execution.

The culprit behind human sin is evil desire. In time, wicked desire "gives birth to sin; and sin, when it is full-grown, gives birth to death" (Jas 1:15). The image reminds us of Paul's warning that whoever lives to please the sinful nature will reap "corruption" (Gal 6:8), the same word used in the postapostolic church for a miscarriage or abortion. James's statement here is in contrast to his statement three verses later that God gave believers birth so that they could be "a kind of firstfruits" of his new creation. The *new creation* stands over against *death*. Those are the two alternatives when the present age has passed away.

James closes his epistle as he opened it—by warning of the death at the end of sin's road. He urges his readers to guard and protect each other: "Whoever turns a sinner from the error of his way will save him from death and cover over a multitude of sins" (Jas 5:19-20). James literally says "save a soul from death," but the New International Version accurately conveys the meaning by using the personal pronoun. The salvation of which James speaks is salvation from the second death.

Four times in his short letter James refers to the end of sinners. One time he says it is misery followed by "slaughter." Once he says it is "destruction." And twice he says it is "death." Everlasting torment is nowhere in the picture.

What Peter Says

First Peter was probably written as a manual for new Christians, to be studied in connection with baptism. Second Peter is a follow-up letter, written as Peter faced his own approaching death, intended to prepare its first readers to go on without the apostle's personal guidance. The believers to whom Peter wrote both these letters were a minority in an unbelieving culture in which being a Christian more often meant persecution than popularity.

If you suffer for the sake of Christ, Peter urges, do not be ashamed but rather praise God for the privilege. "For it is time for judgment to begin with the [house] of God; and if it begins with us, what will the outcome be for those who do not obey the gospel of God?" (1 Pet 4:17).

Peter's reference to judgment beginning with the house of God draws from one of Ezekiel's visions. In the vision God showed Ezekiel the idolatry that caused Judah to be taken into Babylonian captivity (Ezek 8). Those who had been faithful to God received a protective mark on their foreheads; the rest were to be slaughtered without mercy (Ezek 9:4-5). God ordered the destroyers to "begin at my sanctuary" (Ezek 9:6). Peter says that the time has come again for God's judgment, again commencing at God's house—this time his spiritual house, the church.

In his second epistle Peter warns of scoffers who will conclude that "everything goes on as it has" and will therefore mock God's warning of coming judgment (2 Pet 3:4-9). The generation which perished in the flood had the same opinion, yet their world "was deluged" by the flood and was "destroyed" at God's command (2 Pet 3:6). By the same word from God "the present heavens and earth are reserved for fire, being kept for the day of judgment and destruction of ungodly men" (2 Pet 3:7). Peter's statement here suggests that the fire that will melt the elements will also accomplish the destruction of ungodly men. He uses the same verb *(perish)* and noun *(destruction)* to describe both the sudden end of the old world in Noah's day and the future end of ungodly men.

In 2 Peter 1:1-3 the apostle warns of false teachers who bring seductive heresies but who finally will be condemned and swiftly destroyed. Both terms are familiar New Testament words for the end of the lost. Neither word carries any inherent meaning of everlasting conscious torment. *Condemnation* refers to God's judicial sentence. *Destruction* is the everlasting outcome of the judgment of condemnation. As we have seen time and again, Jesus warns that God can destroy both body and soul in hell (Mt 10:28), and Paul says that God will punish the lost with everlasting destruction (2 Thess 1:9).

Peter illustrates his own warning with specific examples of God's past judgments. We have already examined two of those illustrations in detail. They are the flood that destroyed the old world and the destruction of Sodom and Gomorrah by fire from heaven. Both prototypes involved a total destruction that exterminated sinners and annihilated their sinful way of life forever. The destruction of Sodom and Gomorrah illustrates especially well the final end of the wicked. God condemned these cities, Peter says, "by burning them to ashes, and made them an example of what is going to happen to the ungodly" (2 Pet 2:6). The Revised Standard Version says that "by turning [them] to ashes he condemned them to extinction."

Peter employs a rarely used verb that literally means "to cover with ashes" or "to reduce to ashes." Nonbiblical Greek writers describe the eruption of Mount Vesuvius by using this verb. The same image of fiery desolation appears throughout Scripture. It is a picture of total destruction by fire from God, a destruction that Scripture paints even more vividly by adding the adjectives *unquenchable* (the destructive force of this fire cannot be stopped) and *eternal* (this fire's destruction will never be reversed).

Peter also illustrates God's ability to detain the ungodly for judgment by using the example of fallen angels now held in "gloomy dungeons" in "hell" awaiting judgment (2 Pet 2:4). "Hell" here is not *Gehenna* but literally *Tartarus*, a word that is borrowed from classical Greek literature and appears in Scripture only here. In the *Odyssey* Tartarus is the place where the Titans were chained for endless punishment. Homer and Plato also call the place *Hades*, which the Greek Old Testament uses to translate the Hebrew word *Sheol*. Whatever one makes of this passage and the angels in Tartarus, it adds nothing to our understanding of the final doom of human sinners, because it concerns angels, not people, and because it speaks of detention before the judgment rather than punishment following the judgment.

Peter next describes the false teachers' crimes and then returns to their punishment. He confidently predicts that these men, like brute beasts "born only to be caught and destroyed," also "will perish" (2 Pet 2:12). Both *destroy* and *perish* represent the same Greek word, which in Galatians 6:8 is translated "destruction" (NIV) or "corruption" (KJV). Brute beasts and wicked people come to the same final end, though the people must first face God's judgment, sentence and consuming fire.

"Blackest darkness is reserved for them" (2 Pet 2:17). Jude completes this thought by forming a simile in verse 13 of his letter, comparing the spurious teachers to "wandering stars, for whom blackest darkness has been reserved forever." If there is continuing fire we would also expect continuing light, but Peter and Jude write of darkness instead. Like the comparisons with the destruction of Sodom and with the death of brute beasts, this image also suggests total extinction.

What Jude Says

Seeing the influence of some "godless men, who change the grace of our God into a license for immorality and deny Jesus Christ our only Sovereign and Lord," Jude urges his readers to "contend for the faith that [God has] once for all entrusted to the saints" (Jude 3-4). God will punish evildoers and he will protect all who continue in his love.

Like Peter, Jude recounts past examples of God's righteous judgment. Unfaithful Israel was "destroyed" in the wilderness. Sodom and Gomorrah "serve as an example of those who suffer the punishment of eternal fire" (Jude 7). The word translated "example" here was used by secular Greek writers in commercial contexts to refer to samples of corn and produce. Wicked people can observe the destruction of Sodom and Gomorrah and know what they can expect when God judges them.

The Bible nowhere even hints that Sodom and Gomorrah's inhabitants are presently enduring conscious torment. Jude means just what he says. The sinners of Sodom are "set forth for an example, suffering the vengeance of eternal fire" (KJV). This passage defines "eternal fire." It is a fire that destroys sinners totally and forever. Peter also notes that God condemned these cities "by burning them to ashes, and made them an example of what is going to happen to the ungodly" (2 Pet 2:6).

Because God is fully able to keep his people from falling, Jude urges his readers to keep themselves in God's love (Jude 21, 24). They are also to care for one another: be tender with some; "snatch others from the fire and save them; to others show mercy, mixed with fear—hating even the clothing stained by corrupted flesh" (Jude 22-23).

The image of being snatched from the fire comes from Amos 4:11, in which the prophet reminds a remnant: "You were like a burning stick snatched from the fire" when God overthrew some as he once had Sodom and Gomorrah. When death and destruction came on some among Israel, Amos reminds the survivors, you were snatched from the fire in the nick of time—like a stick already beginning to burn. The same language recurs in Zechariah when God says to Satan: "The LORD rebuke you. . . . Is not [Joshua the high priest] a burning stick snatched from the fire?" (Zech 3:2). Here the "fire" is the Babylonian exile, from which many who entered never returned. Joshua had been spared, and Satan now seeks to destroy him.

Jude's statement concerning "the clothing stained by corrupted flesh" probably is a reflection of the same passage in Zechariah. In the next verses Joshua stands dressed in filthy clothes before the angel. The filthy clothes are removed and replaced by rich garments and a clean turban. The angel tells Joshua: "See, I have taken away your sin, and I will put rich garments on you" (Zech 3:4). The drama is fulfilled in the New Testament when believers are "clothed" with Christ and dressed in perfect righteousness to stand before God.

For Jude those snatched from the fire are given "eternal life." However, "eternal fire" (the opposite of "eternal life") is the punishment awaiting the

wicked—the same punishment of which Sodom and Gomorrah are examples. Their fate is everlasting destruction, blackest darkness forever. Just as
the indescribable light of God's presence identifies eternal life for the
immortal saved, so absolute, unending darkness portrays the everlasting
destruction of those who perish in the second death.

What 1 John Says
The apostle John closes his first epistle with the admonition: "There is a sin
that leads to death, . . . and there is sin that does not lead to death" (1 Jn
5:16-17). The definition of these two types of sin is uncertain, but their alternate results are clear.

The final choices are "death" and "not death." A person is either dead or
alive. There is probably not a clearer, more expressive word in English or a
word grasped any more easily by common people of all times and places
than *death*. We have no need to explain it away—nor any right to explain it
away. This word *death* means just what it says.

The Last Word from the Last Book
John did not invent the symbols he uses in Revelation, and they do not origi-
nate with this book. Most of the images that jump off the book's pages appeared
hundreds of years before in the prophetic books of the Old Testament. Many of
these symbols also appear in a body of apocalyptic (from the Greek word translated "uncovering" or "revelation") literature written between the time of the
Old Testament and that of New Testament. The book of Revelation is also
known as the Apocalypse. It is written by John and comes from the same Spirit
of prophecy who spoke through the Old Testament writers. Those Old Testament writings, more than any other literature of any description, are still our
best guide to understanding the sometimes bizarre characters and often puz-
zling events revealed in this final book of Scripture.

We may compare the code language of apocalyptic imagery to the ste-
reotypes of modern cartoons. When we see a man with a light bulb in a bal-
loon over his head, we know he has an idea. A string of Zs tells us the
person is snoring. Political cartoons also use symbolic language to communicate. Everyone recognizes Uncle Sam, standing there in his stars and
stripes. No one has to explain what the elephants and donkeys mean dur-

ing an election year in the United States. These all are examples of symbols that have taken on a life of their own.

But suppose a farmer in Tibet happened to find a magazine containing these same cartoons. The very symbols that communicate so clearly to us would only bewilder our imaginary friend in Tibet. Having never seen a real light bulb, the farmer wouldn't know how to start thinking about drawing one. If the farmer did know what a light bulb is, the cartoon might be even more confusing, especially if the farmer tried to understand the cartoon in a literal way. The same symbols that speak so clearly to an audience that is familiar with their meaning, actually confound or even mislead another audience that does not know what the symbols signify. Revelation's symbols do not mean whatever a commentator wishes to invent. Their meaning in almost every instance clearly comes from the prophetic writings of the Old Testament Scriptures.[3]

Finally, we should remember that the focus of Revelation is not on the visions themselves but on Jesus Christ, the risen and coming Savior of the world and the Lord of history. The first words of the last book of the Bible tell us its main purpose and its full name. Its name is not "Revelations" or even "Revelation," but "The Revelation *of Jesus Christ.*" If we are wise, we will also keep in mind the universally accepted rule of interpretation that requires us to interpret obscure passages in the light of passages that are clear, not the other way around.

Suffering that ends in death. After an introductory scene in which Jesus appears to John, who is in exile on Patmos, the book of Revelation continues with seven letters, dictated by Jesus himself, addressed to church congregations in the Roman political province known as Asia Minor. One of these letters is directed to the church at Pergamum.

Jesus warns the church at Pergamum that some of their own number have followed the errors of Balaam, an Old Testament character who put money ahead of proclaiming God's truth. Some have accepted other erroneous ideas advocated in their town. They must all repent, Jesus warns, or "I will soon come . . . and will fight against them with the sword of my mouth" (Rev 2:14-16). In neighboring Thyatira a false prophetess called Jezebel has led some professing believers into idolatry and sexual immorality. Seeing no repentance, Jesus warns that he will "cast her on a bed of suffering," will "make those who commit adultery with her suffer intensely" and will "strike her children dead" (Rev 2:20-23). All these statements may refer to temporal judgments, perhaps of a lingering or even terminal disease. Insofar as they describe final punishment, however, they picture a suffering that ends in *death*.

Destruction. Another section of the book of Revelation pictures a huge angel blowing seven loud trumpet blasts, with a climactic world event following each blast. When the seventh trumpet sounds, John hears loud voices in heaven. They announce good news: God has triumphed gloriously over his enemies. The kingdom is the Lord's. Then John sees twenty-four heavenly elders, who respond: "The time has come for judging the dead . . . and for destroying those who destroy the earth" (Rev 11:18). Both times the verb *destroy* is used in this verse, it translates a strong Greek word that John uses only one other time (Rev 8:8-9). There, a burning mountain is thrown into the sea, turning waters into blood, killing living creatures and destroying a third of the ships. Outside Revelation, the same word describes what moths do to clothes (Lk 12:33) and what the natural process of aging does to the physical body (2 Cor 4:16).

The third angel's judgment message. It is not at all clear that Revelation 14:9-11 is even speaking about final punishment, yet advocates of everlasting conscious torment sometimes speak as if this were the Bible's principal passage on the subject. If this text does concern the ultimate end of sinners, it still does not require us to conclude that God will keep them alive forever to inflict everlasting pain. But let us scrutinize the passage carefully, phrase by phrase. This is not to play games with the text but rather to prove ourselves worthy evangelicals who "deal thoroughly and honestly" with any Scripture in order "to carefully and painstakingly ascertain the meaning of the passage in its original setting."[4]

In Revelation 14:1-5 John recounts his vision of a beautiful mountain named Zion, which stands for the reward awaiting God's people who serve him faithfully. There stands Jesus, pictured as a Lamb, and he is accompanied by 144,000 of his people, a number symbolizing the firstfruits of God's redeemed servants. Three angels appear and announce God's judgment in language that becomes progressively stronger. The third angel cries out with a loud voice:

If anyone worships the beast and his image and receives his mark on the fore-
head or on the hand, he, too, will drink of the wine of God's fury, which has
been poured full strength into the cup of his wrath. He will be tormented
with burning sulfur in the presence of the holy angels and of the Lamb. And
the smoke of their torment rises for ever and ever. There is no rest day or
night. (Rev 14:9-11)

This third angel's announcement includes four elements, all familiar
images in the biblical vocabulary of divine judgment:
☐ drinking the wine of God's fury poured out full strength into the cup of
his wrath
☐ being tormented with burning sulfur in the sight of the angels and of the
Lamb
☐ the smoke of their torment rising for ever and ever
☐ having no rest day or night
Some people have interpreted these expressions as if they require us to
imagine the lost suffering endlessly in conscious agony. That is a possible
interpretation—if we ignore how the Bible itself uses the same language elsewhere. In other words, this passage about the third angel's judgment message
provides us with an outstanding opportunity to let the Bible interpret itself
rather than importing meaning into its symbolic language based on a presup-
position about final punishment, even once that has been held a long time.

The cup of God's wrath is a frequently used Old Testament symbol of
divine judgment.[5] Biblical authors picture God mixing the cup in varying
strengths, signifying degrees of punishment (Ps 75:8; Jer 25:15-38). This cup
sends God's people reeling, but it does not destroy them and they later
recover (Ps 60:4; Is 51:22). Other recipients are not so blessed. The prophets
use language like this: The Edomites will "drink and drink and be as if they
had never been" (Obad 16). God commands his enemies to "drink, get
drunk and vomit, and fall to rise no more" (Jer 25:27). Jesus drank this
"cup"—and it referred to his death—but God removed the cup from his
hand by raising Jesus from the dead (Mt 26:39). Elsewhere in Revelation the
image of God's cup of wrath includes "torture and grief," but it ends in
"death, mourning and famine," and in consumption by fire (Rev 16:19;
18:7-9; 19:15). The image of the "cup" is entirely consistent with everlasting
destruction in the second death.

As we have already seen, throughout the Old Testament, from the destruction of Sodom onward, burning sulfur symbolizes absolute and total destruction.[6] We have also seen the origin of the image of rising smoke in the aftermath of Sodom's fiery destruction. When Abraham went out the next morning to look on the scene, all he saw was "dense smoke rising from the land, like smoke from a furnace" (Gen 19:27-28). Nothing else remained. All was silent. But the rising smoke testified more eloquently than words that a city with all its inhabitants and vegetation had been wiped off the face of the earth. Isaiah uses the same picture of ascending smoke to describe Edom's total destruction. Again there is "burning sulfur" and a fire which "will not be quenched night and day" (Is 34:9-10). Because this fire is irresistible, it consumes whatever comes into its path. Then "its smoke will rise," for the fire has completed its appointed destruction—and it rises "forever," meaning that the destruction will never be reversed (Is 34:10-15).

John's vision of the fall of Babylon, recorded in Revelation 18, also clarifies the meaning of this image. A heavenly voice calls out for divine vengeance against the wicked city (Rev 18:6). God answers the cry with plagues of death, mourning and famine, then destroys the city with a consuming fire (Rev 18:8). Merchants and kings bewail the "torment" they see, but all they behold is the rising smoke of a destruction now completed (Rev 18:9-10, 15). Rising smoke signifies destruction completed, not people suffering conscious agony.

The Greek language can describe an action or event in several ways with reference to time, depending on the grammatical form that is used of a word.[7] John here uses the genitive case-form with *day* and *night* to describe a kind of time. The people in John's vision have no guarantee of rest during the day, and there is no hope that relief will come at night. They suffer during the daytime and also at nighttime. This statement does not require us to understand that the suffering lasts all day and all night (although that may be true) or that it lasts for an infinite number of days and nights. It requires that we understand only that the sufferers are not immune to their torment at any time of the day or night so long as that torment may last.

John uses the same form of the expression "day and night" to describe the living creatures praising God, the martyrs serving God, and Satan accusing God's people (Rev 4:8; 7:15; 12:10). In each case the thought is the same: the action described does not occur exclusively during the daytime or at nighttime. But this does not mean it goes on forever, or even nonstop. For example, Paul says that he worked and that he prays "night and day" (1 Thess 2:9; 3:10). The apostle did not work or pray nonstop. Sometimes he prayed at night, sometimes during the day, and he worked the same way. Isaiah 34:10 also illustrates this sense of "night and day." The prophet begins the sentence by saying that Edom's fire "will not be quenched night and day," and he ends the same sentence by saying that "its smoke will rise forever." Edom's fire would not be limited to a day shift or a night shift; it burned in the daytime and in the nighttime. But when it had consumed all that was there, it would go out, although its rising smoke would remain as a memorial to God's thorough destruction.

The fall of Babylon. Although the Old Testament prophets sometimes use *Babylon* to mean the literal city, they also use the name at times as a symbol of opposition to God's kingdom. John uses *Babylon* the same way. To his original readers the term would probably indicate Rome. Revelation 18 describes the fall of Rome (Babylon)—and of every ungodly world power, in every age and under any name, which sets itself in opposition to God. When John paints Babylon's fall, he does so with pictures borrowed from Old Testament portrayals of divine judgment against ungodly cities, including literal Babylon, Nineveh and especially Tyre (Is 21:1-10; Ezek 27; Nahum 1—3).

This judgment against spiritual Babylon includes plagues and torture, grief and death, mourning and famine, but it finally ends in consumption by fire (Rev 18:4, 7-8). When the ruin is complete, the smoke of the city ascends for all to see (Rev 18:9, 18). Smoke that goes up forever describes eternal destruction but not everlasting conscious torment, as we have seen earlier (Rev 19:3; see also Is 34:10).

The lake of fire and brimstone. As the book of Revelation closes, John provides the Bible's last description of final punishment. It is the fiery lake of burning sulfur, or in the King James Version, the lake of fire and brimstone (Rev 19:20; 20:10, 15; 18:8). This symbol is found nowhere else in the Bible, although the Old Testament provides a similar vision of a fiery river which flows out from God's flaming throne (Dan 7:9-10). There, a character pictured as a terrifying fourth beast is "slain and its body destroyed and thrown into the blazing fire" (Dan 7:11). Insofar as Daniel's vision sheds light on our topic, it suggests that the lake of fire thoroughly consumes whatever goes in it.[8]

In John's visions in Revelation, two characters called the beast and the false prophet are thrown into the lake of fire (Rev 19:20; 20:10). According to many Bible scholars these are not actual people but represent governments which persecute believers and false religions which support those governments. Neither institution will be perpetuated forever, nor could either suffer conscious, sensible pain. Other Bible students think the beast and false prophet are actual persons, but even then they are different from ordinary human sinners. Whether we understand them to be specific persons or impersonal forces, the fate of the beast and false prophet does not define the final destiny of wicked human beings. If they stand for wicked governments and perverse religions, clearly the lake of fire represents their annihilation. Whatever the case, sound biblical interpretation requires us to explain the mysterious sayings of Scripture in light of its many plain statements, and not the other way around.

Revelation 20:7-10 seems to be the strongest biblical picture supporting the traditional view of unending conscious torment. It symbolically portrays evil's last great assault against good, resulting in evil's final defeat and everlasting destruction. The vision builds on the imagery of Ezekiel 38 and 39, down to the very code names "Gog" and "Magog." Satan's hordes surround the camp of God's people, but as in the days of Elijah, fire comes down from heaven and devours them (Rev 20:9; 2 Kings 1). The army is toasted in its tracks, but Satan himself is "thrown into the lake of burning sulfur, where the beast and the false prophet had been thrown" (Rev 20:10).

As John watches his vision, he then sees the beast, the false prophet and the devil "tormented day and night for ever and ever" (Rev 20:11). If the beast and false prophet symbolize wicked governments and false religion, they will be totally wiped out. That is clearly what the lake of fire means in the case of death and Hades. If the beast and false prophet stand for some kind of personal beings, their fate is different from that of lost men and women as consistently described throughout the rest of the Bible. John does say that certain humans will end up in the fiery lake, but each time he mentions humans, he is careful to explain that the lake of fire means the "second death" (Rev 20:14-15; 21:8). The contrast to this unending death is everlasting life (Rev 20:15; 21:4, 6; 22:1-2).

As John watches, he sees the earth and sky disappear. He sees all the people who have ever died assembling to be judged before God's great white throne. "Then death and Hades were thrown into the lake of fire" (Rev 20:14). This clearly pictures the final annihilation of death and dying. The time finally will come when death itself will pass away. More than seven centuries before John, Isaiah had looked to a time when God will "destroy the shroud that enfolds all peoples, the sheet that covers all nations," when "he will swallow up death forever" (Is 25:7-8). The apostle Paul also predicts, "The last enemy to be destroyed is death" (1 Cor 15:26), and John says that destruction occurs in the lake of fire. Paul's statement is a comment on Psalm 110, which also portrays the destruction of God's human enemies as the heaping up of dead bodies (Ps 110:6). That imagery matches John's twice-made statement: The "lake of fire" or the "fiery lake of burning sulfur . . . is the second death" (Rev 20:14; 21:8).

The first time human beings are mentioned as being in the lake of fire is in Revelation 20:15, which says: "If anyone's name was not found written in the book of life, he was thrown into the lake of fire." John later contrasts the destiny of "he who overcomes," who inherits the new heavens and new earth, with that of the lost, who "will be in the fiery lake of burning sulfur" (Rev 21:7-8). It is here that John says for the second time: "This is the second death" (Rev 21:8). Twice John tells us that the wicked end up in the lake of fire. But both times he carefully identifies the lake of fire as "the second death."

Because John's explanation that the lake of fire is the second death is so clear, those who hold to the idea of everlasting conscious torment seem to go out of their way to contradict what it says. One theologian approvingly quotes Philo the Jew, a contemporary of the apostle Paul, who speaks of a "kind of death remaining deathless and dying."[9] Such statements are at obvious odds with the universally understood usage of the word *death*. Rather than the wicked experiencing a "deathless death," John tells us that there will be a second death—and that that death itself will die and be no more.

6

A FINAL WORD

FOR CENTURIES THE MAJORITY OF CHRISTIANS HAVE BELIEVED THAT GOD will somehow make the lost indestructible so that they will suffer horrible, conscious agony and pain forever. According to this tradition, the wages of sin is not really *death* but *eternal life in torment*. Although this tradition is very old and highly popular, it cannot be justified by a careful reading of the Word of God. Quite the contrary, the notion that the wicked will live forever in inescapable pain contradicts the clear, consistent teaching of Scripture from Genesis to Revelation.

Jesus Christ warns his hearers of the terrible consequences of rejecting God's gift of eternal life. The alternative, he says, is to be condemned and destroyed, to lose one's life and to perish. People should fear God's wrath, Jesus warns, because God is able to destroy both body and soul in hell. Jesus compares such a fate to that of dead trees or weeds that are burned up, to that of a house destroyed by a hurricane, to that of someone crushed by a huge, falling boulder.

According to Jesus the lost have plenty to fear. They might die now in great earthly honor and wealth. But God sees what humans do not see; God looks on the heart. One day God will raise the wicked to face him in judgment. At the conclusion of his judgment he will banish them from his presence forever, to a place Jesus compares both to fire and to deepest darkness. The lost will see the saved going with God to eternal reward. They will weep and grind their teeth in anger, but God's sentence will be carried out. They will be destroyed, both body and soul, forever. That punishment will never be reversed, and it will be as everlasting as will be the life of the saved with God.

Paul's epistles present the final choices of salvation and wrath, life and death. Paul says that the lost will "die," "perish" and be "destroyed." Paul explains the "eternal punishment" of which Jesus warned and specifies that it will be "eternal destruction." Once destroyed, the lost will never be seen again.

The rest of the New Testament describes the final destiny of the wicked in many ways, without ever using the word *Gehenna* (hell). Yet the alternatives are stark: either to be saved or to be destroyed. For the person who refuses God's salvation there will be no escape. In the end the lost will perish as in Noah's flood. They will be destroyed like Sodom and Gomorrah. They will perish like brute beasts that are slaughtered. Their end will be eternal darkness. They will meet their doom in the second death.

The Bible has much to say about the end of the wicked—far more, in fact, than has commonly been supposed. We must be very careful lest we communicate something the Bible does not say. What we believe about the final punishment of the lost affects our understanding of the nature of human beings. Do we really understand what the Bible makes so plain—that only God has immortality and that every moment of our existence (now or in the age to come) is his wonderful, gracious gift?

What we say concerning final punishment also reflects on God's character. He is absolutely holy and perfectly just. On that, Scripture is too plain to be misunderstood. But are we to believe that God, who "so loved" the world that he gave his only Son to die for our sins (Jn 3:16), will also keep millions of sinners alive forever so he can torment them endlessly throughout all eternity? Is that the God we see revealed in the personal ministry of Jesus of Nazareth, who told his disciples that whoever has seen him has seen the Father?

No, no—a thousand times no. God is indeed a "consuming fire," as both the Old and New Testaments tell us. He will punish those who refuse his salvation, and not one of them will escape. There will be degrees of punishment, and the destructive process will allow plenty of opportunity for that. But whatever conscious suffering may be involved, the unrighteous will all finally die. It will be just as God warned Adam in the Garden, as he told Ezekiel centuries later, as he said through Paul still later and as he twice said through John in the closing pages of Scripture: the wages of sin is *death*. The soul that sins shall *die*. The final end of the lost is the lake of fire, which is the second death. Life or death—these are the final two alternatives. Both that life and that death will last forever.

The good news of the gospel shines even more brightly in view of the two contrasting fates. These biblical truths free us from pagan notions of indestructible souls which even God cannot destroy, of vindictive deities who delight in tormenting their victims, of men and women doomed to writhe in agonizing pain forever and ever without end. When we are freed of those unbiblical traditions, the wonderful Gospel text found in John 3:16 becomes even more precious and meaningful to us: "God so loved the world that he gave his one and only Son, that whoever believes in him shall not *perish* but have eternal *life*." If you forget everything else in this book, remember that verse. If we let it mean what it says, it is enough.

Response

A Traditionalist Response to Conditionalism

Robert A. Peterson

In THE SPRING OF 1992 I TAUGHT FOR THE FIRST TIME WHAT HAS become a favorite elective: Systematic Theology 658, Eternal Destinies. I will never forget the effect that reading the first edition of Edward Fudge's *The Fire That Consumes* had on my small group of students. They took Fudge's challenge to their traditional view of hell very seriously. As they began to read his book and consider his case for annihilationism, they came to class complaining of physical symptoms including headaches and churning stomachs. I gave them credit for not being dismissive but earnestly considering Fudge's arguments.

When they were about halfway through Fudge's book, however, a great change came over them. Fear gave way to confidence, and even anger. The more closely they looked at Fudge's case for conditionalism, the less they were impressed. What had once seemed like a powerful case crumbled in their hands as they took apart one argument after another.

So it is with Fudge's contribution to this debate. If readers are unfamiliar with the issues involved, Fudge's presentation, considered as a whole, may seem persuasive. But upon closer inspection, the case for conditionalism is not nearly as convincing as it initially seems. In fact, when the sum is evaluated on the basis of its parts, the case is weak.

Techniques That Do Not Advance the Debate

Edward Fudge uses many arguments to present his case for the ultimate annihilation of the lost. I will evaluate his arguments in the next section. At present I undertake a preparatory task.

Fudge uses techniques that do not advance the debate. I will refrain from passing judgment on his motives; I do not know why he uses these techniques. He does use them, however, and I want to highlight them to help us focus on more substantial matters. I count four such techniques: straw-man arguments, the argument from silence, ostentatious use of Greek, and emotionally charged language.

1. Straw-man arguments. Fudge and I have each authored a book of over two hundred pages on the doctrine of hell. So we can each learn what arguments our partner in debate used previously by consulting his book. Fudge appears not to have done this. At least nine times Fudge mentions and then refutes specific traditionalist positions.[1] But I have never used any of the bad arguments Fudge refutes, so when Fudge refutes them, he is not refuting my case for traditionalism. Fudge is using straw-man arguments: setting up weak positions that are easy to "burn." What is he accomplishing? He gives readers the impression that he is scoring points because nine times he says what traditionalism stands for and nine times he shows traditionalism to be in error.

I could set up straw-man positions for annihilationism that Fudge doesn't hold and refute them one by one. But since Fudge doesn't use those positions, I won't refute them. Instead, I will try to refute the positions he does hold.

2. The argument from silence. More than ten times Fudge employs the argument from silence against traditionalism.[2] For example, he writes, "None of these Scripture texts even hints at anything resembling eternal conscious torment," and "Neither word carries any inherent meaning of everlasting conscious torment" (pp. 30, 69). But this type of argument carries very little weight. It is an argument from silence, from what the

Bible does not say rather than an argument based on what the Bible does say.

A traditionalist could say at numerous points, "This passage on hell says nothing about the lost being exterminated and existing no more." Readers should not allow the argument from silence to sway them, because it appeals to emotion, not reason. When one reads ten times that this or that passage doesn't hint at X, it is easy to conclude that the Bible says nothing about X. But basing such a conclusion on the argument from silence is a mistake.

3. *Ostentatious use of Greek.* Fudge appeals to the Greek words of the New Testament more times than I have attempted to count. A few times this appeal constitutes a part of Fudge's argument, and this is appropriate. I do not always find his use of Greek in argumentation convincing, but he has the right to use it. Usually, however, Fudge's appeal to Greek words does not serve to advance his argument. But it does give readers the impression of scholarship, of authority. I know because I have taught Greek profession-ally for twelve years and adult Sunday school for twice that long. I try not to begin many sentences in Sunday school with "The Greek says . . ." Why? Because I know that to do so overwhelms people in the class. Their faces say, "He knows Greek, so who can argue with him?"

In a debate book aimed at a popular audience, the debaters need to be careful how they display their scholarly tools. It is easy to give an appear-ance of correctness by frequently referring to Greek. But the mere mention of Greek words does not prove a case. Rather, the proof is in the debater's ability to explain the teaching of Holy Scripture.

4. *Emotionally charged language.* Fudge wants to base his case for condi-tionalism on biblical exposition; and indeed he argues extensively from Scripture. Unfortunately, however, he frames his biblical case with inflam-matory language. He begins with "lurid" (Fudge's adjective) quotations from Edwards and Spurgeon, cites Billy Graham, and then *wham!*

> The fact is that the Bible does not teach the traditional view of final punish-ment. Scripture nowhere suggests that God is an eternal torturer. It never says . . . that the glories of heaven will forever be blighted by the screams from hell. The idea of conscious everlasting torment was a grievous mistake, a horrible error, a gross slander against the heavenly Father whose character

we truly see in the life of Jesus of Nazareth. (p. 20)

This approach is not worthy of a Christian gentleman like Edward Fudge. I hold to the traditional view of hell. But I most certainly do not think that "God is an eternal torturer" or that "the glories of heaven will forever be blighted by the screams from hell." And although I think Fudge's annihilationism is a serious error, I do not accuse him of "gross slander against the heavenly Father."

Fudge concludes his piece in much the same tenor:

These biblical truths free us from pagan notions of indestructible souls which even God cannot destroy, of vindictive deities who delight in tormenting their victims, of men and women doomed to writhe in agonizing pain forever and ever without end. (p. 82)

Here Fudge uses emotionally charged language to misrepresent my view. My commitment to traditionalism does not stem from "pagan notions" but from my understanding (be it correct or incorrect) of the Holy Scriptures. I do not believe that God cannot destroy persons in hell—or any other persons. Rather, I believe that God teaches in his Word that he won't destroy them. Regardless of our view of the duration of hell, it is unwise, uncharitable and unfair for us to compare our opponent's view of God to a belief in "vindictive deities who delight in tormenting their victims."

There is a place for emotion in Christian theology. If we do not have convictions about what we believe, then we should not teach or write. But holding deeply felt convictions is one thing and using inflammatory language to ridicule an opponent's position is another. And that is what Fudge has done to introduce and conclude his piece.

I urge readers to look past the four techniques that I have criticized. Do not base your verdict as to who wins the debate on these techniques. Instead, read our presentations of the two views with open minds and hearts, test everything by the Word of God and reach your own conclusions.

In the interest of fair play I add one more thing. Obviously I am not impressed by Fudge's employment of these techniques. I will leave it to readers to judge whether Fudge has played the game according to the ground rules that we laid down on page 15. But in fairness to him I want to state that although these techniques do not advance the debate between us, neither do they prove Fudge wrong. Even as readers should not embrace Fudge's position because of the techniques, neither should they reject his view simply because he employs these methods.

Putting those techniques to the side, we see that Fudge presents a case for conditionalism based on five types of arguments: those from history, hermeneutics, linguistics, theology and Scripture.

Arguments from History

Fudge appeals to history to make his case for conditionalism. I will consider two of his arguments: that traditionalism is pagan in origin and that Jonathan Edwards taught that annihilation could properly be called eternal punishment.

Pagan origins. According to Fudge, traditionalism has its origins in paganism. He claims that because it is pagan in origin the church's traditional view of hell is mistaken. The church fathers who believed in eternal conscious punishment were misled by Platonic philosophy into believing in the immortality of the soul. Their belief in eternal conscious punishment is a result of their belief in immortality. Because souls live forever, their punishment in hell must last forever too. Fudge's clearest statement is on pages 43-44: "The pagan philosopher Plato taught that souls are immortal and cannot be destroyed. Many Christians have reasoned about hell from that same point of error."[3]

In contrast, Fudge believes that when human beings die, no immaterial part (soul or spirit) survives. Instead, the whole person expires and ceases to exist until the resurrection. I refute this unbiblical notion on pages 171-74, where I pointed to six passages that teach that death is the separation of our material and immaterial parts and that our soul or spirit departs from the body at death.

How are we to evaluate Fudge's argument that traditionalism is pagan in origin and hence false? First, it is important to note that Fudge does not argue for his viewpoint. Instead, his footnote 5 notwithstanding, he merely states his case seven times. Here Fudge confuses assertion with argument. A simple *assertion*, a statement of belief, does not constitute proof. By contrast, an *argument* gives reasons for believing something is true. Fudge gives no evidence but simply states that traditionalists borrowed their notion of the immortality of the soul from Greek philosophy. He therefore does not prove his claim.

Fudge here commits the logical fallacy of begging the question. He merely assumes that his view is correct and traditionalism wrong. Because the consensus of the historic church is overwhelmingly against annihilationism, Fudge is faced with a problem. How can he account for the fact that the worthies of church history believed in traditionalism not annihilationism? The best Fudge can do is to argue that they taught eternal punishment because they believed in the immortality of the soul, an idea they borrowed from Plato. But mere statement does not constitute proof.

Furthermore, Fudge's claim is not substantiated by a study of church history. As I demonstrate in my chapter entitled "The Road to Traditionalism," it is erroneous to argue that Tertullian, Augustine, Thomas Aquinas, Martin Luther and John Calvin, to name my first five figures, believed in eternal conscious torment because they were influenced by Greek philosophy. Instead, each of the five based his arguments for eternal punishment on scriptural exposition rather than on philosophy.

Additionally, Fudge mistakenly equates traditionalists' belief in immortality with that of Plato: "No biblical character is ever said to have placed his hope in philosophical notions of *natural* immortality, or to have supposed that human beings have some mysterious part that cannot die" (p. 23, italics mine). Plato held to the soul's natural or inherent immortality. By contrast, evangelical Christians hold that God alone is inherently immortal (1 Tim 6:16) and that he confers immortality to all human beings.

Fudge commits another logical fallacy, that of imputing guilt by association. Even if he could prove that the fathers borrowed their idea of immortality from Plato, that wouldn't prove them wrong. Plato's ideas are a mixture of error and truth. He believed in the existence of God, for example. So to simply trace an idea to Plato does not prove it to be false.

Finally, Fudge also errs when he asserts that belief in the immortality of the soul drives the traditional view of hell. Actually, he has it backward. I do not accept traditionalism because I believe in the immortality of the soul. Rather, I believe in the immortality of human beings (united in body and soul after the resurrection of the dead) because the Bible teaches that there will be "eternal punishment" for the lost and "eternal life" for the saved (Mt 25:46).

Jonathan Edwards on annihilation and eternal punishment. Fudge claims that Jonathan Edwards called annihilation eternal punishment. He writes, "Even Jonathan Edwards, whose name is best known today for his vivid preaching about the torments of hell, concedes that irreversible extinction would properly be called 'eternal punishment' " (p. 46).

Anyone familiar with Jonathan Edwards's views on hell knows that Fudge has made a mistake. I say this for two reasons. First, in his writings Edwards repeatedly affirms traditionalism and condemns annihilationism. Although I demonstrate this on pages 123-24, here I offer further evidence. John H. Gerstner, who devoted considerable time to studying the writings of Edwards, penned *Jonathan Edwards on Heaven and Hell,* in which he lists ten of Edwards's arguments against annihilationism. I will cite only the first four of those arguments.

> Furthermore, Edwards annihilates annihilationism. The wicked in the world to come will beg for annihilation, but Edwards will not allow this hope. He destroys it with a battery of arguments. First, the Bible teaches eternal punishment. It is eternal, for the very word used for eternal life is used for eternal death. And this punishment implies pain, which annihilation is not. Annihilation is the relief which the wicked, begging for, will never receive. As the sermon on Revelation 6:15-16 poignantly describes, "Wicked men will hereafter earnestly wish to be turned to nothing and forever cease to be that they may escape the wrath of God." Second, it is also clear that the wicked "shall be sensible of the punishment they are under." Third, degrees of punishment preclude annihilation. Fourth, "the Scripture is very express and abundant in this matter that the eternal punishment is in sensible misery and torment and not annihilation."[4]

Plainly Edwards opposes annihilationism.

This brings me to the second reason that Fudge errs in claiming that Edwards is willing to call annihilation "eternal punishment." Edwards's words in the very passage that Fudge cites reveal Fudge's mistake. After refuting the view that the wicked will suffer for a time in hell and then enjoy eternal blessedness, Edwards discusses annihilationism. This view differs from the preceding one because its proponents hold that after the wicked "shall suffer misery to such a degree, and for so long a time, as their obstinate wickedness in this world *deserves* . . . then they shall be annihilated."[5]

Edwards gives an immediate evaluation, "On this I would observe, that there is nothing got by such a scheme; no relief from the arguments taken from Scripture, for the proper eternity of future punishment." Let me paraphrase Edwards's archaic English. He means that nothing is achieved by this scheme of combining temporary suffering with eventual annihilation. This view does not adequately explain the biblical arguments for the future everlasting punishment of the lost.

The key here is the adjective *proper* in the expression "the proper eternity of future punishment." Edwards understands "the proper eternity of future punishment" to consist in everlasting punishment, which he then demonstrates. He goes to some lengths to show that annihilationism is in error, concluding with the words "So this scheme overthrows itself."[6] I do not accuse Fudge of impure motives here. He errs because of his zeal for annihilationism and his consequent tendency to read that doctrine into the words of historical (as well as biblical!) writers when it isn't there.

Arguments from Hermeneutics (the Study of Biblical Interpretation)

Throughout his essay Fudge insists that conditionalism is the crystal-clear teaching of both the Old and New Testaments. If people "allow the Bible to interpret itself" (pp. 26, 44, 75), read the Scriptures "at face value" (pp. 50, 51), give words their "common, ordinary usage" (pp. 29, 61), their "natural and obvious meaning" (p. 63), then they will find that the Bible is "easy to understand" (pp. 48, 53) and "means what it says" (pp. 71, 72, 82) when it repeatedly teaches annihilationism.

Annihilation in the Old Testament. In Fudge's estimation the Old Testament transparently teaches annihilationism. Let's subject this claim to scrutiny. Commenting on Paul, Fudge summarizes what he regards as the teaching of "the former Scriptures." In the Old Testament "time and again the end of sinners is made plain. They will perish, be destroyed, be burned up and be gone forever" (p. 60). Indeed, on pages 24-34 Fudge marshals many Old Testament passages that use what is commonly called "the vocabulary of destruction." That the language of destruction is used in the Old Testament with great variety of vocabulary is not debatable. This does not mean, however, that these Old Testament passages teach annihilationism.

It is crucial to the debate to consider what aspect of God's punishment is in view. The great majority of the Old Testament passages that Fudge cites in support of conditionalism do not speak of the final fate of the wicked at all. Instead, they speak of God visiting the wicked with premature death. At first glance Fudge's list of "destruction" passages from the Old Testament seems impressive. On closer inspection, however, few of the passages he cites are relevant to the debate.

I will cite a few examples. Psalm 34 says, "Evil will slay the wicked; the foes of the righteous will be condemned" (v. 21). Does the psalmist speak of God punishing the wicked in this life or at the Last Judgment? The question is clearly answered in verse 16: "The face of the LORD is against those who do evil, to cut off the memory of them *from the earth*" (italics added). The psalmist is not writing about the final fate of the lost, but of God shortening their earthly lives.

It is the same for the numerous references to the plight of the ungodly in Psalm 37. Because of God's anger they will "perish . . . vanish like smoke" (v. 20), be "cut off" (vv. 22, 28, 34, 38) and "be destroyed" (v. 38). Are these statements about annihilation or about God removing the ungodly from the earth? Plainly the latter, as the psalm makes clear. "Do not fret because of evil men . . . for like the grass they will soon wither, like green plants they will soon *die away*" (vv. 1-2, italics added).

These verses do not teach that God will exterminate sinners after the Last Judgment; rather they speak of the Lord visiting them with untimely physical death now. This conclusion is confirmed by the contrast between the fate of the lost and the blessing of the righteous in the land: "Evil men will be cut off, but those who hope in the LORD will inherit *the land*. A little while, and the wicked will be no more; though you look for them, they will not be found. But the meek will inherit *the land* and enjoy great peace" (vv. 9-11, italics added). Psalm 37 does not speak of the final fate of the unsaved consisting of exclusion from the new earth; rather it tells of God's judgments against them on the present earth. As a result of these judgments, "the offspring of the wicked will be cut off" (v. 28), that is, experience premature death. By contrast, "the righteous will inherit the land and dwell in it forever" (v. 29).

Fudge objects that the statements about the destruction of the wicked in

Psalms 34 and 37 "do not match the world we now see. God's final justice awaits an age beyond the present" (p. 26). Of course God's final justice awaits the last day. But these psalms do not predict that day. Fudge's objection that the words of woe against the ungodly "do not match the world we now see" is shortsighted. Indeed, the Old Testament is replete with examples of God bringing temporal destruction on those who rebel against him: the Noahic flood, the judgment on Sodom and Gomorrah, the plagues on Egypt, the eradication of the Canaanites, God's slaying of 185,000 Assyrians in a single night (2 Kings 19:35) and so on.

Fudge cites Old Testament cases of God executing earthly judgments against sinners as if they pertained to the Last Judgment. But before claiming that a passage supports annihilationism or traditionalism, one must determine that the passage speaks of the final destiny of the lost.

This is why I include a time frame for each of the ten passages that I adduce as evidence for the traditional view of hell (see p. 130). I establish the fact that all ten passages speak of the final destiny of the unsaved before I explain the passages. I do so because of annihilationists' tendency to appeal to texts that do not pertain to the topic of hell. Fudge exhibits this very tendency. As a result, his claim that the natural and obvious meaning of the Old Testament supports annihilationism is false. In fact, as in the case of his historical argument, Fudge here commits the logical fallacy of begging the question. He does not prove that the Old Testament passages he cites speak of annihilationism; he merely assumes it when he confuses temporal judgments with the Last Judgment.

At least two Old Testament passages do speak of the final end of the wicked: Isaiah 66:24 and Daniel 12:2. I point readers to my exposition of these passages on pages 130-36. Here I will refer to Fudge's treatment of these texts to illustrate that his hermeneutic is not as plain and simple as he claims.

In Isaiah 66:24 Fudge takes the expression "the dead bodies" literally and then blunts the sense of the imagery of the fire and worm. Isaiah says, "their worm will not die, nor will their fire be quenched." Fudge says that "the maggot . . . does not die but continues to feed so long as there is anything to eat. The fire . . . burns until nothing is left of what it is burning" (p. 32). Is this letting the Bible interpret itself? To the contrary, Fudge has altered the prophet's meaning to fit annihilationism. Because Isaiah speaks of undying worm and unquenchable fire, he intends for readers to understand "the dead bodies" as referring to resurrected human beings who suffer the second death, that is, experience everlasting disgrace in hell. Jesus' interpretation of Isaiah 66:24 in Mark 9:43-48 confirms the traditionalist interpretation. Jesus warns his hearers of being thrown into hell where "their worm does not die, and the fire is not quenched."

Daniel speaks of the resurrection of human beings to one of two fates: "some to everlasting life, others to shame and everlasting contempt" (Dan 12:2). This parallelism is straightforward. If we interpret Daniel's words at face value, we will find them easy to understand. The fates of the righteous and the wicked are both eternal. The saved enjoy everlasting life; the lost consciously endure everlasting contempt.

Unfortunately, Fudge doesn't regard this interpretation as obvious. Instead, after correctly stating that the word translated "contempt" here is rendered "loathsome" in Isaiah 66:24, he incorrectly concludes that Daniel 12:2 teaches annihilationism. The fact that both passages use the word *loathsome* does not mean that Fudge is justified in jumping from Daniel 12 to Isaiah 66, failing to deal with Daniel 12:2 on its own terms. Fudge states that "the shame and . . . contempt" of Daniel 12:2 "are 'everlasting' because the loathsome disintegration of the wicked will never be reversed" (p. 33). He begs the question. Daniel says nothing about disintegration; rather, he contrasts the fates of the righteous and unrighteous and modifies both fates with the adjective *everlasting*. To interpret the text according to common usage is to conclude that even as the godly will experience "everlasting life" so the ungodly will experience "shame and everlasting contempt."

Annihilation in the New Testament. Fudge claims that the New Testament also makes frequent and clear affirmations of conditionalism. In fact, he explains repeated New Testament references to judgment as death, destruction and perishing in this way. Unlike most of the Old Testament passages he cites, most of these passages do deal with final destinies. Nevertheless, there are at least two problems with Fudge's claim that these passages teach annihilationism.

First, Fudge is again guilty of assuming his conclusions because he fails to offer his reasons for reaching them. Instead, he substitutes frequent statement of his view for evidence for it.

I agree that New Testament writers commonly use the vocabulary of destruction to refer to the final fate of the wicked. But I do not agree with Fudge that these passages teach annihilationism. In fact, whether the Bible teaches traditionalism or annihilationism is the subject of the debate between us. Neither of us has the right to assume that simply quoting New Testament texts proves his position. But that is exactly what Fudge does repeatedly. It is not necessary, however, to interpret the New Testament vocabulary of destruction literally as teaching annihilationism. Rather, it is possible to understand it figuratively as teaching traditionalism.

As annihilationist Harold Guillebaud admitted, "It is not denied that *if* it were clear beyond question from Bible teaching elsewhere that the doom of the lost will be everlasting torment, it would be quite possible to understand 'death,' 'destruction' and the like as meaning a wretched and ruined existence."[7] Guillebaud is correct. Much of the New Testament vocabulary of destruction could be understood as teaching either traditionalism or annihilationism. For that reason Fudge must make a case that the New Testament vocabulary of destruction signifies annihilationism. And that he fails to do.

Second, at least some of the New Testament vocabulary of destruction is incompatible with annihilationism. Consider 2 Thessalonians 1:9. Paul says the wicked "will be punished with everlasting destruction and shut out from the presence of the Lord and from the majesty of his power." Fudge says that "everlasting destruction" means that the punishment of the lost will occur in the future and that "it will never end." With those conclusions I heartily agree. Then he adds, "Once destroyed, the wicked will never be seen again." So, according to Fudge, "everlasting destruction" means annihilation without re-creation. But this conclusion clashes with the rest of the apostle's sentence. "They will be punished with everlasting destruction and shut out from the presence of the Lord and from the majesty of his power" when he comes again (2 Thess 1:9).

Doesn't unbelievers' being shut out from the presence of the Lord imply their existence? Not according to Fudge, who writes, "God will punish the wicked—with everlasting destruction that proceeds from his presence and removes the wicked from his presence forever" (p. 60). Fudge explains this in more detail in *The Fire That Consumes*. He says that God will remove the wicked from his presence by permanently annihilating them. They are removed from his presence because he is everywhere, and after annihilation they are nowhere.[8] This is not interpreting judgment passages according to their "natural and obvious meaning" (p. 63) but twisting that meaning to fit annihilationism. The natural and obvious meaning of an "everlasting destruction" that involves being "shut out from the presence of the Lord and from the majesty of his power" is that the wicked exist forever in a state of absolute ruin away from the blessed presence of Christ the King. They are separated from the presence of his joy, not from his omnipresence because they have been exterminated.

The New Testament vocabulary of destruction does not teach annihilationism. As further evidence of that fact, I point out that the word *destruction* cannot bear Fudge's meaning in Revelation 17:8, 11. There "destruction" is prophesied for "the beast." We read two chapters later that the beast and false prophet are "thrown alive into the fiery lake of burning sulfur" (Rev 19:20). Although in an earlier book Fudge states, "In the case of the beast and false prophet, therefore, the lake of fire stands for utter, absolute, irreversible annihilation,"[9] they are still there "one thousand years" later (Rev 20:7, 10). Furthermore, John teaches that the beast, the false prophet and Satan "will be tormented day and night for ever and ever" (Rev 20:10). The beast's "destruction," therefore, is not annihilation but eternal punishment!

Fudge errs, then, when he claims that the words *destruction* and *perish* and their synonyms signify the final extinction of the wicked. This claim cannot be established from a study of all of the judgment passages that use these words. In fact, the only passages that can be made to conform to annihilationism are those in which the words are used as shorthand without further explanation. I conclude, therefore, that Fudge's argument from hermeneutics is largely a smoke screen. The Bible is not crystal clear in teaching annihilationism. In fact, it does not teach annihilationism at all. It does use the vocabulary of destruction, and it would be *possible* to read annihilationism into many passages that simply mention "death," "being destroyed" and the like. Nonetheless, we ought not do so, because other passages—even other passages using the vocabulary of destruction—are incompatible with annihilationism.

Arguments from Linguistics

Fudge also offers arguments from linguistics. As I mentioned in the introduction to this rebuttal, his ostentatious use of Greek gives the appearance of scholarship. The important thing, however, is not how many Greek words are mentioned but the correctness of the arguments when set against the plumb line of Holy Scripture. Now it is time to put two of his linguistic arguments to the test: the argument about the word *eternal* when it is used with nouns of action and the argument about word studies.

The word eternal *with nouns of action.* Fudge puts forth an argument concerning the word *eternal* when it is used with nouns of action. He selects six occurrences of nouns used with the adjective *eternal:* "eternal sin" (Mk 3:29), "eternal salvation" (Heb 5:9), "eternal judgment" (Heb 6:2), "eternal redemption" (Heb 9:12), "eternal punishment" (Mt 25:46), and "eternal destruction" (2 Thess 1:9 NASB). Fudge argues, "In each case, the *outcome* is everlasting, not the *process.* God will not be forever saving or judging or redeeming or punishing or destroying. He accomplishes each activity, then stops. But the results of each activity last forever" (p. 51, emphasis added).

Why does Fudge use this argument? He does so in order to prove that the church is mistaken in its traditional understanding of two passages: Matthew 25:46, which speaks of "eternal punishment," and 2 Thessalonians 1:9 (NASB), which speaks of "eternal destruction." According to Fudge, these verses do not teach everlasting conscious punishment. Rather, the "punishment" and "destruction" of the unsaved is a once-for-all act that has "eternal" consequences. When Scripture speaks of "eternal punishment" and "eternal destruction," it means that once the wicked are annihilated, they never will be re-created.

I will offer four responses to Fudge's argument. First, it is important to note that Fudge is not the first annihilationist to put forth the argument based on the word *eternal* with nouns of action. Others have used the argument before him.[10] It is curious, however, that none of these writers cites a single authority on linguistics. It appears that Fudge follows earlier conditionalists in using a contrived argument to buttress his position.

Second, this argument cannot pass muster in the field of linguistics. It is an example of the logical fallacy that D. A. Carson calls "selective and prejudicial use of evidence."[11] Why does Fudge find only six nouns of action among the seventy nouns used with *eternal?* Specifically, why omit "eternal *life*" (Mt 25:46; Lk 18:30), especially when Jesus pairs it with "eternal punishment" in Matthew 25:46? Is "life" excluded because it is a person or thing and not an act or process? Or is "life" excluded because "eternal life" does not conform to the pattern in which *eternal* supposedly refers to the results of the action and not to the action itself? It looks like Fudge has selected examples that fit his theory and ignored others that don't. This is the selective use of evidence.

Fudge errs when he asserts that *eternal* used with the six nouns refers to the result of the action, not to the action itself. Consider his treatment of "eternal salvation" in Hebrews 5:9: "Jesus is not forever saving his people: he did that once for all. . . . This salvation is eternal because it is the everlasting result which issues from the once-for-all process or act of saving."[12] Whereas it is true that according to the writer of Hebrews Jesus saves once for all, it is also true that he forever saves his people. This idea is taught in Hebrews 7:24-25: "Because Jesus lives forever, he has a permanent priesthood. Therefore he is able to save completely those who come to God through him, because he always lives to intercede for them." So Fudge's "rule" that *eternal* with nouns of action refers to results and not process does not hold. In Hebrews 5:9 it refers to both.

Third, I will evaluate Fudge's linguistic argument by doing what he does not do—appeal to linguistic authority. Linguists acknowledge the ability of language to communicate the result of action. The basic distinction is between expressions that are *telic*, that "have natural culminations," and those that are *atelic*, that "do not have to wait for a goal for their realization."[13] The linguistics books I consulted, however, do not speak of telic and atelic nouns but rather of telic and atelic verbs and especially of telic and atelic sentences. For example, Carlota S. Smith illustrates the difference between telic and atelic sentences thus: "Mary walked in the park (atelic); Mary walked to school (telic)." The second sentence has a well-defined end point, but the first does not.[14]

Moreover, linguists insist that for sentences to qualify as telic "there should be both a process leading up to the terminal point as well as the terminal point."[15]

Evaluated in terms of the science of linguistics, the conditionalists' argument based on the use of *eternal* with nouns of action leaves much to be desired. Conditionalists apparently have made up a set of categories: telic and atelic nouns. Can they cite legitimate linguistic authority for this? It appears to be a set of categories contrived to get around the Bible's teaching of everlasting punishment in Matthew 25:46 and everlasting destruction in 2 Thessalonians 1:9.

Furthermore, how can an adjective *(eternal)* used with a noun convey the process and end point needed to constitute a telic expression? This seems impossible. The burden of proof lies with conditionalists to demonstrate that this argument is linguistically sound and cogent.

Fourth, Fudge compounds his error when he applies his conclusion concerning *eternal* with nouns of action to "eternal punishment" in Matthew 25:46. He adds faulty logic to faulty linguistics when he draws a parallel from the criminal justice system to eternal destinies. He correctly points out that capital punishment is a worse punishment than life in prison. But he errs when he infers that because capital punishment is worse than life imprisonment so also annihilation is a worse punishment than eternal conscious torment (p. 45). This is absurd. I would rather spend life in prison than be executed. But who would choose everlasting torment over extinction of being? Annihilation means the end of suffering, not the worst possible punishment as Fudge insists.

Therefore, Fudge's argument based on uses of *eternal* with nouns of action is contrived and false. Instead of appealing to such arguments, interpreters ought to give heed to the way words are used in their biblical contexts. When Jesus contrasts "eternal punishment" with "eternal life" in Matthew 25:46, the meaning of the two expressions is not difficult to understand. The suffering of the ungodly in hell will last as long as the bliss of the godly in heaven—forever. Likewise, if we allow the expression "eternal destruction" mentioned in 2 Thessalonians 1:9 to be defined by the words that follow it, the expression means that the unsaved will experience forever the loss of all that is worthwhile in human life by being separated from the blessed presence of King Jesus.

The study of words. The argument about the use of the adjective *eternal* with nouns of action is only one of Fudge's ways to move the discussion from the immediate context of the verse in question to other matters.

Another such strategy is to appeal to word studies in order to try to blunt the Scripture's teaching of eternal punishment.

In his treatment of Matthew 25:46, where Jesus contrasts "eternal punishment" with "eternal life," Fudge not only gives attention to the word *eternal*, he also investigates the word *punishment*. He writes, "It will not surprise us to learn that the word translated 'punishment' in Matthew 25 originally meant 'to cut short.' By the time of Jesus it also meant 'to prune' or 'to cut down.' The Old Testament uses this word at times to describe punishment by death (1 Sam 25:31; Ezek 21:15)" (p. 45). The implications of Fudge's argument are obvious. Because *punishment* originally meant "to cut short," "eternal punishment" in Matthew 25:46 means an eternal cutting short, that is, annihilation. Because the same word is used in the Old Testament to describe punishment by death, "eternal punishment" in Matthew 25:46 means an eternal death, that is, annihilation.

Even though some of these facts are accurate, Fudge's presentation is misleading because of what he fails to mention. The word translated "punishment" *(kolasis)* in Matthew 25:46 did originally mean "checking the growth of trees." But the same Greek-English lexicon that records that fact says that the word also means "chastisement, correction." Specifically, it lists one place in the Bible where the word means "checking the growth of trees," four where it means "chastisement, correction," and three, including Matthew 25:46, where it speaks of divine "retribution."[16] It is misleading to mention only references that can be construed as supporting one's position while not mentioning those that can't. This is to commit the logical fallacy of "a selective and prejudicial use of evidence."[17]

Fudge claims that "by the time of Jesus" *kolasis* meant also "to prune" or "to cut down." This claim is misleading. The standard dictionary of New Testament Greek defines the word *kolasis* as "punishment" and offers two categories of usage. The first, labeled literal, includes these definitions, "to undergo punishment" and "long-continued torture." The second category, "of divine retribution," includes "of eternal damnation," "of hell." Under this heading the dictionary translates *kolasis* used with *eternal* as "eternal punishment" and cites Matthew 25:46 along with seven other references in early Christian literature. The only biblical reference besides Matthew 25:46 is 1 John 4:18, for which the dictionary translates *kolasis* as "fear has to do with punishment."[18]

Although Fudge does not supply it, I have located the source for his claim that in Jesus' time *kolasis* meant "to prune" or "to cut down."[19] According to my examination of this source, Fudge's presentation is misleading. It is inaccurate for Fudge to claim that this dictionary defines the noun *kolasis* as "to prune" or "to cut down." It does not. Instead, it lists those meanings for a related verb form *kolazo*. It also lists "to punish" as a meaning of this verb and cites seven examples.

Moreover, this dictionary's presentation of *kolasis* contradicts Fudge's argument. It gives "punishment" and "deprivation" as meanings, and with reference to Matthew 25:46 it translates a fragment outside of the Bible thus: "For the evil-doers among men receive their reward not among the living only, but also await *punishment* and much torment."[20] Here again, therefore, Fudge is guilty of the prejudicial and selective use of evidence.

There are greater problems with Fudge's assertions about the meaning of the word translated "punishment" *(kolasis)* in the Old Testament. Fudge cites 1 Samuel 25:31 and Ezekiel 21:15 as occurrences of the word that "describe punishment by death" (p. 45). In fact, the word does not occur in the Greek Old Testament in those places. Neither does any cognate (word of related origin). Fudge is in error when he claims that *kolasis* occurs in 1 Samuel 25:31 and Ezekiel 21:15. Furthermore, the standard lexicon of the Greek Old Testament lists the following meanings for the word *kolasis:* "chastisement, punishment, vengeance, that which brings about punishment, stumbling block, trap."[21] Fudge simply has not done his linguistic homework. The occurrences of *kolasis* in the Old Testament do not support taking it to mean punishment resulting in irreversible annihilation in Matthew 25:46; rather they support the rendering of "eternal punishment" that we find in commonly used English Bible translations such as the NIV, NRSV and NASB.

I conclude, then, that Fudge fails miserably in his attempt to open the door for an annihilationist understanding of Matthew 25:46 by appealing to the study of the Greek word rendered "punishment" in the expression "eternal punishment." The standard dictionaries (in chronological order) of classical Greek, the Greek Old Testament, the Greek New Testament, the papyri and the church fathers do not support his claim. Rather, a study of them discloses that he has engaged in a selective presentation of evidence and in the dispensing of information that is at times correct, at times only partially correct and at times even incorrect. The five dictionaries support the traditional understanding of "eternal punishment" in Matthew 25:46. Although there is some value in considering the original meaning of a word, of much greater importance is the way the word is used in context. In this case the meaning of "eternal punishment" is determined by Jesus' contrasting it with "eternal life." The fates of the righteous and the wicked are alike in that both involve conscious everlasting experience. The righteous shall forever enjoy eternal life in the presence of their Lord and Savior; the unrighteous will forever suffer eternal punishment away from that joyous presence.

Arguments from Theology

Fudge also bases his argument for annihilationism on the doctrines of humanity and the atonement. Specifically, he finds evidence for annihilationism in conditional immortality and in the fact that Christ suffered the pains of hell in his death.

An argument from conditional immortality (conditionalism). Fudge argues for annihilationism on the basis of conditional immortality, commonly referred to as conditionalism. Some definitions are in order. Annihilationism is the view that the wicked will ultimately be exterminated and exist no more. Fudge does not like to be called an annihilationist because he thinks that this term conjures up ideas of the Jehovah's Witnesses in people's minds. The Jehovah's Witnesses, unlike Fudge, hold that when lost persons die, they forever cease to exist and that only faithful Witnesses will be raised from the dead. Fudge holds a different view: all persons will be resurrected, the righteous to eternal life and the wicked to terrible punishment, then the wicked will experience the final blow, destruction without recreation. This is Fudge's understanding of eternal punishment—irreversible annihilation.

Fudge dislikes the term *annihilationist* and prefers to be called a conditionalist, an advocate of conditionalism. This is the view that God created human beings mortal, not immortal. He gives the gift of immortality only to the saved, who consequently live forever. The unsaved, however, do not receive the gift of immortality and, according to Fudge, are consequently annihilated after their resurrection.

I do not like the terms *traditionalism* and *traditionalist*. *Traditionalism* has come to be used to designate the traditional view of hell, eternal conscious punishment. A traditionalist is an advocate of that view. I do not like these terms because they suggest that people hold to the view simply because of tradition. I hold to traditionalism because I am persuaded that at least ten biblical passages teach it, as I argue later. But whether I like those terms or not, I am stuck with them. I am a traditionalist who holds to traditionalism.

Similarly, although Fudge does not like the terms, he is an annihilationist who holds to annihilationism. In fact, he is both a conditionalist and an annihilationist. He is a conditionalist because he holds to conditional immortality. He does not hold that human beings are created immortal by God. Instead he believes that only regenerate persons receive the gift of immortality. Fudge combines his belief in conditional immortality with the view that God will raise the dead. Because Fudge holds that the ultimate judgment of God upon the lost will be their extinction of being, he is an annihilationist. Although the terms *conditionalism* and *annihilationism* technically are not synonyms, I have used them as synonyms throughout this book because that is how they are used in theological writing.

It is time to point out some of the problems with Fudge's conditionalism/annihilationism. His clearest statement occurs in the context of Paul's mention of immortality in Rom 2:6-11:

> Whenever the Bible attributes immortality to human beings, it always describes the *bodies* (never disembodied souls or spirits) of the *saved* (never of the lost) after the *resurrection* (never in the context of this created world as we know it). (pp. 54-55; italics in original)

Fudge rejects the idea "that human beings have some mysterious part that cannot die" (p. 23). He contends that no human beings are created immortal by God and that there is no immaterial part of human beings that survives in an intermediate state between death and resurrection.

How do these ideas stand up to biblical scrutiny? Not very well. Although Fudge is technically correct about the Bible's use of the words *immortal* and *immortality,* he reaches an erroneous conclusion. He confuses word and concept. The Bible does not have to use a particular word or words in order to communicate a concept. For example, a writer can teach about the church without using the word *church*. He could speak of the people of God, the body of Christ or the temple of the Holy Spirit to refer to the concept of the church.

So it is in this case. It is true that the words *immortal* and *immortality* are used in the Bible to refer only to God and to resurrected saved persons. It is wrong, however, to conclude from that fact that the immortality of unsaved persons is denied in the Bible. Matthew 25:41 records Jesus' teaching that the wicked will experience "the eternal fire prepared for the devil and his angels." The description of that fire in Revelation 20:10 reveals that it involves being "tormented day and night for ever and ever." If humans suffer the same fate as the devil, who will experience eternal conscious torment, then humans too will suffer eternal conscious torment. It isn't important whether one calls this fate "immortality" or not. It is important, however, to affirm what the Bible affirms concerning the unsaved—they will suffer forever in hell along with the devil.

Five verses later in Matthew 25 we read Jesus' classic statement concerning the destinies of human beings, unsaved and saved, respectively: "Then they will go away to eternal punishment, but the righteous to eternal life." We learn from these words that the destinies of all human beings are everlasting. Some will forever enjoy eternal fellowship with God; others will forever suffer eternal misery in hell.

In summary, although Matthew 25:41 and 46 do not use the words *immortal* and *immortality*, there Jesus teaches that all human beings will exist forever in either heaven or hell. Fudge errs when he rejects the immortality of the lost.

Similarly, Fudge's rejection of the survival of human beings in the intermediate state contradicts the clear teaching of Scripture. Luke 23:43 records Jesus' promise to the forgiven thief, "Today you will be with me in paradise." Jesus thus assured the man that after death they would be together in heaven on that very day. Because their bodies were left on the crosses and taken down, Jesus was not speaking of going to paradise in the body. Instead, he was speaking of their spirits going there. This is what Jesus meant three verses later when he said from the cross, "Father, into your hands I commit my spirit" (Lk 23:46). Jesus' body remained on the cross after his death. But his human spirit, inseparably united to his divine nature, went immediately to be with the Father in heaven.

Other Scriptures teach the same truth. In Philippians 1, Paul expresses his difficulty choosing between life and death. He wants to live and serve the Philippians, but he longs to "depart and be with Christ, which is better by far" (Phil 1:23). Paul doesn't speak of "soul" or "spirit," but, as is his custom when speaking of the intermediate state, he simply uses a personal pronoun—"*I* desire to depart and be with Christ." Because he contrasts departing this life to be with Christ with "living in the body" (v. 22) and remaining "in the body" (v. 24), his meaning is plain. Paul looks forward to death in Christ because it will mean immediate blessing in his presence in heaven. Of course, this involves existing outside of his body. Amazingly, although such an existence is temporary and even abnormal, Paul calls it "better by far." It is far better because at death Paul will forever be done with sin and will experience the nearness of Christ in a way impossible in this life.

Fudge believes that human beings cease to exist at death and are nonexistent until the resurrection. This view encounters difficulty in maintaining continuity of personhood, as I will point out (pp. 171-74). If we completely cease to exist when we die, with no immaterial part surviving death, how is it that we are the same persons who are raised? It is better to call this resurrection a re-creation. The human beings who once existed no longer exist. The new human beings whom God will re-create are not the same persons who died. They cannot be the same persons, because those persons ceased to exist at death.

Above I cited Fudge's rejection of the idea "that human beings have some mysterious part that cannot die" (p. 23). In fact, the Bible does teach that a part of us will not die. This is evident in Revelation 6:9-11 where deceased human beings are referred to as "the souls of those who had been slain" (v. 9). They cry out to God asking how long they must wait until God takes vengeance upon their enemies (vv. 10-11). Plainly, these people are dead, they continue to exist, and their status is intermediate—they long for the end when God will set wrongs right. Here departed human beings are called souls.

They are called spirits in Hebrews 12:23-24, where the writer argues for the superiority of the new covenant over the old: "You have come to God, the judge of all men, to the spirits of righteous men made perfect, to Jesus the mediator of a new covenant." The expression "the spirits of righteous men made perfect" refers to believers who have died and gone to be with the Lord. They have not ceased to exist at death. They exist as disembodied spirits who experienced entire sanctification when they died.

The most famous passage on the intermediate state is 2 Corinthians 5:6-9.

> Therefore we are always confident and know that as long as we are at home in the body we are away from the Lord. We live by faith, not by sight. We are confident, I say, and would prefer to be away from the body and at home with the Lord. So we make it our goal to please him, whether we are at home in the body or away from it.

Paul contrasts being "at home in the body" and "away from the Lord" with being "away from the body and at home with the Lord." As long as the apostle lives in the body, he is away from the immediate presence of Christ in glory. He therefore prefers to depart the body and enjoy his Savior's immediate presence. Here Paul teaches that there is a disembodied existence in an intermediate state.

There is therefore abundant evidence for the fact that human beings are composed of two parts: a material one, the body, and an immaterial one, the soul. Although the normal state of affairs is for us to exist as holistic persons with body and soul united, at death a separation occurs between our material and immaterial parts.

Fudge ignores this evidence and states that the idea of natural immortality is pagan in origin and has misled Christians to teach immortality and eternal hell. He thereby uses one theological error (denying our survival in the intermediate state) to try to prove another theological error, annihilationism.

An argument from Christ's atonement. Fudge employs another theological argument for annihilationism, this time related to the doctrine of the atonement. Fudge correctly teaches that Jesus suffered the pains of hell on the cross. But since Fudge is convinced that hell means annihilation, he teaches that Jesus was annihilated when he died. Fudge argues from his conviction that Jesus was annihilated to reach the conclusion that annihilationism is the correct view of hell.

> However, we do not have to wait until the end to see what God's wrath
> means, for God has revealed it in the death of Jesus. The cross of Christ por-
> trays the divine wrath against sin more vividly than any apocalyptic descrip-
> tion of the end ever could, no matter how imaginative or vivid its terms.
> What the cross shows us is a picture of total destruction and death from
> which God alone can deliver.[22] (p. 55)

Because I respond to this argument on pages 174-79, here I will only offer
a few comments. First, Fudge by implication compromises the doctrine of
Christ. To hold that Jesus was annihilated when he died means either that
his whole person (deity and humanity) was annihilated or that his human
nature alone was annihilated. Either conclusion is disastrous. To hold that
the person of Christ ceased to exist in death is to explode the biblical doctrine of the Trinity. It is to assert that the second person of the Godhead
went out of existence. It is to assert that the resurrection was a re-creation of
the second person of the Trinity so that henceforth one person of the Trinity
is a creature, not the Creator.

The second alternative leaves the Trinity intact but destroys the unity of
the person of Christ. If Christ was annihilated in his death, but his whole
person (deity and humanity) was not destroyed, then only his humanity
met its end. This means that his natures became separated when he died.
Furthermore, this implies that the resurrection of Jesus involved God's re-
creating Jesus' human nature in what amounted to a second incarnation.

Therefore, when Fudge argues for annihilationism from Christ's atonement, he runs afoul of the biblical teaching concerning the person and work
of Christ. It is hard to conceive of teaching that strikes more directly at the
vitals of the Christian faith. Readers may want to believe that annihilationism is true because it is more comfortable to believe in and because it fits
better with modern ideas about God's love and justice. But annihilationism
is not true, and subjecting it to the test of systematic theology only illumi-
nates its deficiencies. God's truth coheres. The Bible doesn't give us a complete system of truth that offers answers for every question that we might
ask. But the Bible teaches truth and biblical teaching coheres with itself.
Fudge's attempts to prove annihilationism from the doctrines of humanity
and the atonement do not achieve his desired effect. Indeed, they have the

opposite effect. His effort to prove his point of view on the basis of these key doctrines occasions serious questions about his teachings, teachings that adversely affect our understanding of the person and work of the Redeemer.

Arguments from Scripture

Fudge argues against traditionalism and for conditionalism on the basis of history, hermeneutics, linguistics and theology, but he preeminently seeks to make his case from Scripture. How well does he accomplish this task? I cannot reiterate all the answers from previous sections, but I must examine Fudge's handling of two key passages: Jesus' most extensive teaching on eternal destinies, Matthew 25:31-46, and Scripture's last word on the subject, Revelation 20:10-15. What is most remarkable about Fudge's treatment of these two critical passages is that he does not explain them in their contexts. Instead, he uses an array of methods to claim that these texts are compatible with annihilationism.

Matthew 25:41, 46. Fudge correctly says that Matthew 25:41, 46, contains "perhaps the most famous of all of Jesus' words concerning final punishment" (p. 44). Fudge quotes Jesus' statement, "Depart from me, you who are cursed, into the eternal fire prepared for the devil and his angels," but offers no comment on this verse (Mt 25:41), thereby failing to do what he often calls upon his readers to do—to let Scripture interpret Scripture.

Matthew 25:41 records Jesus' teaching that unsaved human beings will suffer the same fate as the devil and his angels. This text prompts the question: Does the Bible indicate what that fate will be? It does, in Revelation 20:10. There we read that "the devil" will be "thrown into the lake of burning sulfur," where he "will be tormented day and night for ever and ever." To summarize: Jesus says that the unsaved will go into "the eternal fire prepared for the devil." John says that the devil will be cast into the lake of fire and will suffer eternal conscious torment there. The conclusion is irresistible. Unsaved human beings also will suffer eternal conscious torment. This is the meaning of Jesus' words in Matthew 25:41 interpreted in the context of the New Testament. But Fudge employs a strategy of avoidance and skips this crucial verse.

However, Fudge does not dodge the single most important text in the Bible concerning final destinies: "Then they will go away to eternal punishment, but the righteous to eternal life" (Mt 25:46). In fact, he works hard to make this verse seem compatible with annihilationism by employing seven strategies.

First, he emphasizes the contrast between the two fates in order to play down the obvious symmetry between "eternal" punishment and "eternal" life. "The Lord emphasizes the contrast between these two destinies: life or fiery punishment" (p. 45). This is indeed curious. Fudge avoided the mention of "eternal fire prepared for the devil" in verse 41. Here, where "eternal punishment" is mentioned, he talks about "fiery punishment." The result is the same: in both cases he avoids the obvious meaning of the words in the text at hand.

Second, Fudge studies the word *punishment* and implies that since "the worst punishment of all is capital punishment," so annihilation would be a worse fate than eternal conscious torment (p. 45). But this is absurd. Although most prisoners would prefer life imprisonment to capital punishment, who would prefer having to endure the eternal pains of hell over being annihilated?

Third, Fudge appeals to Augustine to show that we regard as punishment not only the execution but also the victim's removal from the earthly community that results from the execution. This is true but beside the point. We are debating not civil punishments, but eternal ones. The conclusion of the last paragraph, therefore, applies here as well.

Fourth, Fudge summarizes a study of the word translated "punishment" in Matthew 25:46 ("eternal punishment"). I examine this word study on pages 99-101, where I demonstrate the failure of Fudge's attempt to argue that *punishment* in Matthew 25:46 means "cutting short" (annihilation). This word study is another device to avoid the meaning of the phrase "eternal punishment" when it is juxtaposed with the phrase "eternal life."

Fifth, Fudge explains what "eternal" punishment means: "First, it is the punishment of the age to come, not a punishment in this present life. Second, and more importantly, it is called 'eternal' because it will last forever" (pp. 45-46). Of course eternal punishment and eternal life properly pertain to the age to come. And Fudge is correct to say that eternal punishment will last forever, but incorrect in the sense he attributes to those words. According to Fudge eternal punishment will last forever because the annihilation of the wicked will never be undone. Their extinction of being is forever. Here Fudge violates his own principles of "letting Scripture interpret itself," "taking the simple sense" and so on. Fudge avoids the fact that Jesus uses the same adjective, *eternal*, to describe both destinies in a single sentence: "Then they will go away to eternal punishment, but the righteous to eternal life."

Sixth, Fudge jumps to Paul's reference to "everlasting destruction" in 2 Thessalonians 1:9 and argues that "Jesus mentions, in Matthew 25, the fate of the wicked in the most general of terms (eternal punishment), but Paul tells us its specific nature (everlasting destruction)" (p. 46). Once more Fudge moves away from Matthew 25:46 in an attempt to "explain" it. He attempts to interpret "eternal punishment" in Matthew 25:46 on the basis of his annihilationist understanding of 2 Thessalonians 1:9. As a result, Fudge reads annihilationism into Matthew 25:46.

Seventh, Fudge concludes his treatment of Matthew 25:41, 46 by claiming that Jonathan Edwards conceded that "irreversible extinction would properly be called 'eternal punishment.' " I have already responded to this claim on pages 89-90, where I showed Fudge's argument to be fallacious.

Matthew 25:41 and 46 are two verses that have powerfully shaped the church's doctrine of hell, and rightly so, because these verses interpreted with normal hermeneutics in their literary context teach traditionalism. Jesus will consign the wicked to "eternal fire prepared for the devil and his angels." The Savior thereby affirms that unsaved human beings will suffer the same fate as the devil, who, according to Revelation 20:10 will experience everlasting conscious punishment. Five verses later, Jesus contrasts the respective destinies of the lost and saved as "eternal punishment" and "eternal life." No amount of linguistic gymnastics can get around the fact that Jesus uses the same adjective, *eternal*, to describe the fates of the ungodly and the godly. As different as those fates are, they have this in common: they will be experienced forever.

Nevertheless, Fudge doesn't see it this way. Instead, he avoids Scripture's own commentary on Matthew 25:41 in Revelation 20:10 and employs seven techniques in his discussion of Matthew 25:46 that enable him to avoid treating the verse in its literary context by shifting the focus from Matthew's text to something else. Fudge points readers to the obvious contrast between "punishment" and "life," to the difference between life imprisonment and capital punishment, to Augustine on an irrelevant point, to a biased study of the word *punishment*, to an explanation of the word *eternal* that misses its obvious sense in verse 46, to the phrase "eternal destruction" in 2 Thessalonians 1:9 and to an erroneous appeal to Jonathan Edwards.

There is one thing that these seven devices have in common: they all draw attention away from the meaning of Matthew 25:41, 46. The main job of biblical interpreters—and theologians are above all else biblical interpreters—is to explain the meaning of the statements of Holy Scripture within their context. But this is precisely what Fudge has failed to do. He has put forth an appearance of scholarship with references to Augustine and Edwards, appeals to Greek words and so on, but his work does not stand up to scrutiny.

Revelation 20:10-15. Arguably the second most important passage on the doctrine of hell (after Mt 25:41, 46) is Revelation 20:10-15:

> And the devil . . . was thrown into the lake of burning sulfur, where the beast and the false prophet had been thrown. They will be tormented day and night for ever and ever. . . . The sea gave up the dead that were in it, and death and Hades gave up the dead that were in them, and each person was judged according to what he had done. . . . If anyone's name was not found written in the book of life, he was thrown into the lake of fire" (Rev 20:10, 13, 15).

These words are straightforward: the devil, beast and false prophet are cast into the lake of fire where all three will be eternally tormented. In addition, resurrected unsaved human beings are thrown into the lake of fire, where they will suffer the same fate—eternal torment.

Fudge disagrees. The true meaning of this passage is that the devil, beast, false prophet and unsaved human beings will be annihilated! Let us examine Fudge's reasons for this conclusion.

First, Fudge writes that "the fate of the beast and false prophet does not define the final destiny of wicked human beings." That is because some theologians interpret the beast and false prophet as institutions that are incapable of suffering conscious pain. Moreover, even if the beast and false prophet are persons, they "are different from ordinary human sinners," and therefore their fate tells us nothing about the fate of ordinary sinners (p. 78).

However, Fudge fails to mention the devil, who, along with the beast and the false prophet, is cast into the lake of fire. I understand the beast and the false prophet to be individuals capable of suffering pain, but I'll put that to one side for a moment. What about Satan? Fudge, as an evangelical Christian, refuses to depersonalize the devil. So here is one personal being who will suffer everlasting torment. Revelation 20:10 tells us that the devil will be thrown into the lake of fire. Five verses later we read that human beings will be cast into the same lake of fire. Wouldn't normal hermeneutics dictate the understanding that human beings will be heading for eternal torment too? This passage in Revelation underscores what Jesus taught in Matthew 25:41—that lost human beings will suffer the same fate as the devil: "eternal fire."

Second, Fudge appeals to the hermeneutical principle of interpreting unclear passages in light of clear ones (p. 78). Of course that principle is valid, but it is invalid to appeal to it in order to interpret the words "They will be tormented day and night for ever and ever" (Rev 20:10) as signifying annihilation. This is simply another of the ways in which Fudge avoids what the text teaches.

Third, Fudge appeals to the teaching of the whole of Scripture: "If the beast and false prophet stand for some kind of personal beings, their fate is different from that of lost men and women as consistently described throughout the rest of the Bible" (p. 78). It is wrong to suggest that the traditional view of hell is based only on Revelation 20:10-15. In my case for traditionalism I discuss ten passages that teach traditionalism. Fudge's appeal to other Scriptures must be seen for what it really is—an attempt to evade the teaching of this particular passage.

Fourth, Fudge argues that the lake of fire means "the second death," and that the second death stands for annihilation (p. 78-79). Because I respond to this argument later (on pp. 167-68), here I will point out only that Fudge once again attempts to circumvent the text. The lake of fire signifies eternal torment in verse 10. John does not tell his readers that the meaning of the lake of fire is different in verse 15. So annihilationists have no right to change the meaning.

Fifth, Fudge contends that when human beings are thrown into the lake of fire, this signifies annihilation (pp. 78-79). His interpretation flies in the face of the words of Revelation 20:10, 15. Verse 10 says that the devil is thrown into the lake of burning sulfur and is "tormented day and night for ever and ever." Five verses later we read that unsaved human beings share the devil's fate. They too are cast into the lake of fire. If John had intended for readers to understand the casting of human beings into the lake of fire as annihilation, he would have told them so.

Sixth, Fudge reads his annihilationist interpretation of Old Testament passages into Revelation 20, a technique he frequently employs elsewhere as well. In truth, neither Isaiah 25:7-8 nor Psalm 110:6 teaches annihilation. Fudge is correct to say that the latter passage tells of "the heaping up of dead bodies" (p. 79). He is incorrect, however, to interpret this as final punishment. The final punishment, as Revelation 20 insists, involves resurrection and consignment to the lake of fire. Fudge thus commits two errors: reading annihilationism into Old Testament texts and then reading his annihilationist interpretation of those Old Testament texts into New Testament texts.

Seventh, Fudge maintains that the word *death* universally means extinction (p. 79). To the contrary, *death* signifies separation in Scripture, including the separation of Adam and Eve from God's fellowship on the day that they "surely die[d]" (Gen 2:17; 3:4), the separation of living unbelievers from the life of God in spiritual death (Eph 2:1, 5), the separation of body and soul at the first death (Lk 16:22, 23; 23:46), and finally "the second death," that is, the eternal separation of sinners from the joyous presence of God (Rev 2:11; 20:14; 21:8).

Conclusion

It may surprise readers to hear me say that Edward Fudge is a basically sound interpreter of the Bible. I was surprised to reach that conclusion myself, because my first contact with Fudge's biblical interpretation was with his writings in defense of annihilationism. So I was taken aback when I read other things that Fudge has written, including devotional writings in which he handles the Bible in a straightforward manner. How different this is from the methods he uses to affirm conditionalism. In his devotional writings, for example, he interprets passages in the light of their literary contexts. Although I don't agree with everything, overall his exposition is sound. In those works there are no devices to avoid the thrust of various passages, no questionable word studies, no taking the words of historical figures out of context, no contrived linguistic arguments and no use of bad theological arguments.

My analysis of Fudge's handling of Matthew 25:41, 46 and Revelation 20:10-15 enables us to understand why Fudge's case for conditionalism appears formidable at first. It is because of the way he combines many techniques and arguments. I count seven interpretive techniques for Matthew 25 and seven for Revelation 20. Fudge bombards readers with arguments from history, hermeneutics, linguistics, theology and Scripture. The cumulative effect can appear overwhelming. But if we take apart the arguments one at a time, they don't look nearly as formidable. A person may try to carry water in a leaky bucket that is inside another leaky bucket that is inside yet another leaky bucket and so forth. The pile of buckets appears impressive at first, until one learns that each has a leak. No number of leaky buckets will hold water. And no number of weak arguments piled on top of one another will constitute a strong argument.

I therefore conclude that despite Fudge's considerable efforts, his case for conditionalism lacks cogency. I urge readers to uphold the historic view of the Christian faith on the subject of hell because the church's view is based on solid exposition of the Word of God.

Part Two

THE CASE FOR TRADITIONALISM

Robert A. Peterson

THE ROAD TO TRADITIONALISM

History

Two roads diverged in a yellow wood,
And sorry I could not travel both
And be one traveler, long I stood
And looked down one as far as I could
To where it bent in the undergrowth;

Then took the other, as just as fair,
And having perhaps the better claim,
Because it was grassy and wanted wear;
Though as for that the passing there
Had worn them really about the same,

And both that morning equally lay
In leaves no step had trodden black.
Oh, I kept the first for another day!
Yet knowing how way leads on to way,
I doubted if I should ever come back.

I shall be telling this with a sigh
Somewhere ages and ages hence:
Two roads diverged in a wood, and I—
I took the one less traveled by,
And that has made all the difference.

Robert Frost, "The Road Not Taken"

LIKE THE TRAVELER IN ROBERT FROST'S POPULAR POEM "THE ROAD NOT TAKEN," we too will take a road. I invite readers to accompany me on a tour of one of the many roads in church history. In light of the current debate, two roads stand out: the road to conditionalism and the road to traditionalism. We will travel the latter. Along the way we will stop at eleven different sign posts, each one corresponding to a figure in church history. The mile markers indicate the approximate dates when the figures wrote the works that we will examine.

Before we begin our journey, a word of caution is in order. The destination at the end of the road is much more important than the road itself. In this case the destination is a house, the house of traditionalism, the foundations of which we will examine in the next chapter. The house of traditionalism is far more significant than the road that leads to it. I don't believe in eternal punishment merely because these eleven figures do. Rather, I believe in it because I am convinced that Scripture teaches it. Nevertheless, it is to our advantage to consider the witness of church history; we can learn from devout and wise persons who have preceded us.

As we travel, it will become apparent that the leading lights in church history affirm traditionalism. Why do they do so? Because they are vindictive and want to see the damned suffer forever? Because they have been duped and their minds have been taken captive by Greek philosophy? (These two explanations are sometimes advanced by annihilationists.)[1] Or is it because they think the Bible teaches it? We will seek to answer this question on our journey.

An overview of the tour will aid travelers. First, we will study the views of seven of the most distinguished figures in church history: Tertullian, Augustine, Thomas Aquinas, Martin Luther, John Calvin, Jonathan Edwards and John Wesley. Then we will examine the ideas of four notable theologians from our own century: Francis Pieper, Louis Berkhof, Lewis Sperry Chafer and Millard Erickson. These eleven figures were chosen because they exhibit great diversity in place, time and tradition.

Mile Marker 208: Tertullian

Tertullian was a North African theologian who lived in the late second and early third centuries and produced the first significant body of Christian literature in Latin.

About A.D. 208 he writes *On the Resurrection of the Flesh* to affirm the resurrection against heretical (Gnostic) denials. He quotes Jesus' saying in Matthew 10:28: "He is rather to be feared, who is able to destroy both body and soul in hell, not those who kill the body, but are not able to hurt the soul," and then comments:

> If, therefore, any one shall violently suppose that the destruction of the soul and the flesh in hell amounts to a final annihilation of the two substances, and not to their penal treatment (as if they were to be consumed, not punished), let him recollect that the fire of hell is eternal—expressly announced as an everlasting penalty; and let him then admit that it is from this circumstance that this never-ending "killing" is more formidable than a merely human murder, which is only temporal.[2]

Tertullian regards it as a scriptural fact that eternal punishment lasts forever; it is "expressly announced as an everlasting penalty." He therefore instructs his readers to understand the word *destroy* in Matthew 10:28 as indicating a "never-ending 'killing'"—rather than an extinction of being.

In his *Apology,* in which he argues for Christianity's superiority over heathen philosophy, Tertullian affirms eternal life and eternal punishment, "The worshippers of God will be with God for ever, clothed with the proper substance of eternity; but the profane and all who are not wholly devoted to God, in the punishment of fire which is just as eternal."[3]

Here Tertullian draws a parallel between the eternity of bliss for the righteous and the eternity of sorrow for the unrighteous. In so doing, this early church father endorses as biblical the understanding that the punishment of the wicked will be eternal. This is significant in light of Tertullian's suspicion of philosophy epitomized in his oft-quoted saying "What does Jerusalem have to do with Athens?" It would be unwise for annihilationists to claim that Tertullian believes in eternal punishment under the influence of Greek philosophy. Rather, Tertullian himself maintains that he believes in it because he regards it as the teaching of the Word of God.

Mile Marker 400: Augustine

Augustine of Hippo in North Africa (354-430), the most illustrious father of the early church, exerted incalculable influence on subsequent Christianity.

He devotes a section of *The City of God,* his most famous work, to the fate

of the wicked. As usual, his primary support for his position is biblical. He
regards Jesus' teaching in Matthew's Gospel as especially clear and convincing. When Jesus says, "Out of my sight, accursed ones, into the eternal
fire which is prepared for the Devil and his angels" (Mt 25:41), he gives "a
clear indication that the Devil and his angels are to burn in eternal fire."
And by comparing Scripture with Scripture we can know the destiny of the
devil, his angels and unsaved human beings, for the book of Revelation tells
us: "The Devil, who seduced them, was consigned to the lake of fire and
sulfur. . . . and they will be tortured day and night for ever and ever" (Rev
20:10).[4]

Referring to the two passages just cited, Augustine concludes:

"Eternal" in the first passage is expressed in the second by "for ever and
ever", and those words have only one meaning in scriptural usage: the exclusion of any temporal end. And this is why there cannot conceivably be found
any reason better founded or more evident for the fixed and immutable conviction of true religion that the Devil and his angels will never attain to justification and to the life of the saints.[5]

Remember, in Matthew 25:41 Jesus likens the fate of the "accursed"
humans to that of the devil and his angels. Augustine's conclusion, therefore, is compelling: unrepentant sinners will suffer everlasting condemnation.

Augustine finds more proof for eternal punishment in Matthew 25.
Indeed, he points out that "Christ, in the very same passage, included both
punishment and life in one and the same sentence when he said, 'So those
people will go into eternal punishment, while the righteous will go into
eternal life' " (Mt 25:46). Augustine reasons:

If both are "eternal", it follows necessarily that either both are to be taken as
long-lasting but finite, or both as endless and perpetual. The phrases "eternal
punishment" and "eternal life" are parallel and it would be absurd to use
them in one and the same sentence to mean: "Eternal life will be infinite,
while eternal punishment will have an end." Hence, because the eternal life
of the saints will be endless, the eternal punishment also, for those condemned to it, will assuredly have no end.[6]

Augustine cautions us against following the example of those who,
"while not slighting the authority of the sacred Scriptures, . . . nevertheless

interpret them wrongly and suppose that what is to happen will be not what the Scriptures speak of, but what they themselves would like to happen."[7]

Mile Marker 1270: Thomas Aquinas

Thomas Aquinas (1224-1274) was the greatest philosopher and theologian of the medieval church. His two most famous works are the *Summa contra Gentiles* and the *Summa Theologiae*. In both of these he affirms that the suffering of the wicked in hell will know no end.

From 1261 to 1264 Aquinas wrote the *Summa contra Gentiles* as a manual designed to equip missionaries to understand and defend the faith. He addresses the topic of punishments in chapters 140 to 146: Because God is just, he responds to people's actions with the correct degree of punishment or reward. Here Thomas affirms the endless punishment of the wicked: "We set aside the error of those who say that the punishments of the wicked are to be ended at some time."[8]

Aquinas began the *Summa Theologiae*, his most outstanding work, in 1265 and was still not finished writing at the time of his death in 1273. In a section dealing with guilt he again argues for eternal punishment. To those who claim that it is unjust for God to render everlasting punishment for sins committed during the limited time span of a person's life, he replies, "The duration of a punishment does not match the duration of the act of sin but of its stain; as long as this lasts a debt of punishment remains. The severity of the punishment matches the seriousness of the sin."[9]

This prompts another question from Aquinas's imaginary partners in debate: What makes sins committed in this life so serious that they deserve a never-ending penalty? Once more (this time borrowing from the eleventh-century theologian Anselm) Thomas has a ready response:

> Further, the magnitude of the punishment matches the magnitude of the sin. . . . Now a sin that is against God is infinite; the higher the person against whom it is committed, the graver the sin—it is more criminal to strike a head of state than a private citizen—and God is of infinite greatness. Therefore an infinite punishment is deserved for a sin committed against him.[10]

Mile Marker 1535: Martin Luther

Martin Luther (1483-1546) is the father of the Reformation and one of the most important figures in history. When asked his opinion of certain artists' conceptions of hell, Luther replies (in his exposition of Jonah 2:3) that hell's torments will be worse than anyone can imagine. "It is of little importance whether a person holds hell to be what men now paint or picture it to be. No doubt it now is, and will be, far worse than anyone is able to describe, picture, or think it to be." In fact, Luther preaches, "This punishment" was so terrible "no one understands but the damned, who feel it." He therefore warns his unrepentant hearers, "You will suffer more than words can tell and thoughts can grasp."[11]

Luther agrees with Tertullian, Augustine and Aquinas that the future destiny of the wicked involves eternal punishment, as we learn from Luther's commentary on Psalm 21.

> The fiery oven is ignited merely by the unbearable appearance of God and endures eternally. For the Day of Judgment will not last for a moment only but will stand throughout eternity and will thereafter never come to an end. Constantly the damned will be judged, constantly they will suffer pain, and constantly they will be a fiery oven, that is, they will be tortured within by supreme distress and tribulation.[12]

In one sense hell is so terrible because it entails separation from God. This is the meaning of the biblical image of darkness used to describe the fate of the lost. As Luther explains in a sermon preached in his home in 1533, those who have heard the gospel but have not believed "must lie in darkness, cut off from God's light, that is, from all comfort, in eternal torment, anguish, and sadness, so that they will nevermore see one spark of light."[13]

Yet in another sense it is God's very presence that makes hell so dreadful. Although he is not present in grace and blessing, he is present in holy wrath. As Luther warns the readers of his *Commentary on the Psalms:* "Not as though the ungodly see God and His appearance as the godly will see Him; but they will feel the power of His presence, which they will not be able to bear, and yet will be forced to bear." Indeed, "This chief and unbearable punishment God will inflict with His mere appearance, that is, with the revelation of His wrath."[14]

Mile Marker 1559: John Calvin

John Calvin (1509-1564), the key leader of the Reformed branch of the Reformation, is best known for his systematic theology, *The Institutes of the Christian Religion*. In the *Institutes* Calvin recognizes that Scripture uses figurative language to describe the terrible suffering of the damned:

> Now, because no description can deal adequately with the gravity of God's vengeance against the wicked, their torments and tortures are figuratively expressed to us by physical things, that is, by darkness, weeping, and gnashing of teeth (Mt 8:12; 22:13), unquenchable fire (Mt 3:12; Mk 9:43; Is 66:24), an undying worm gnawing at the heart (Is 66:24). By such expressions the Holy Spirit certainly intended to confound all our senses with dread.[15]

And even worse, the wicked never will know relief: "What and how great is this, to be eternally and unceasingly besieged by him?" Calvin holds to the everlasting damnation of the lost.[16] In fact, he insists (in his commentary on 2 Thess 1:9) that the eternity of hell's sufferings corresponds to the eternity of Christ's glory.

> The phrase which he adds in apposition ["eternal destruction from the face of the Lord"] explains the nature of the punishment which he had mentioned— it is eternal punishment and death which has no end. The perpetual duration of this death is proved from the fact that its opposite is the glory of Christ. This is eternal and has no end. Hence the violent nature of that death will never cease.[17]

Mile Marker 1730: Jonathan Edwards
Jonathan Edwards (1703-1758), America's greatest philosopher-theologian, embodied the union of a consecrated "head" and "heart." God used his powerful preaching to help generate the Great Awakening in the American colonies.[18]

Although Edwards cringes at the horror of hell, he is constrained to preach the truth that "the bodies of wicked men as well as their souls will be punished forever." Here is hell's worst feature—its duration. In fact, "eternity is the sting of the doctrine of hell torments whereby chiefly it is that it stings the consciences of wicked men and there is no other way to avoid the torment of it but to deny it." Edwards plainly defines hell's eternity: "It is that duration that has no end."[19]

Meditating on the endlessness of hell moves Edwards to warn his congregation in love: "This doctrine is indeed awful and dreadful. It is dreadful to think of it, but yet 'tis what God the eternal God who made us and who has us soul and body in his hands has abundantly declared to us, so that so sure as God is true there will absolutely be no end to the misery of hell."[20]

It is no surprise, therefore, that Edwards attacks annihilationism. The Bible teaches eternal condemnation, using the same word for eternal life as it does for eternal punishment (in Mt 25:46). And this punishment involves pain. But, Edwards contends in a sermon on Revelation 6:15-16, annihilation is the end of pain: "Wicked men will hereafter earnestly wish to be turned to nothing and forever cease to be that they might escape the wrath of God." Moreover, "the Scripture [Edwards cites Matthew 25:46] is very express and abundant in this matter that the eternal punishment is in sensible misery and torment and not annihilation."[21]

Mile Marker 1756: John Wesley

John Wesley (1703-1791) was one of Christendom's greatest evangelists and the founder of Methodism.[22] As a lover of people's souls he was deeply impressed by the attention Jesus paid to the fate of the lost. As a result he too gave it a place in his gospel preaching. How then is hell best described? Wesley answers by appealing to a distinction that goes back at least to Augustine: Hell involves the punishment of loss and the punishment of sense.[23] The former is banishment from God's good presence and consequently, the loss of every joy. The latter is the infliction of torments in body and soul, communicated in Scripture by the images of worm and fire. Thomas Oden accurately summarizes Wesley's understanding of this biblical imagery: "In death, whether buried or cremated, we face either worm or fire. In either case the worm dies or the fire goes out. But hell is posited as a place where this desolation does not end, where the worm does not die and the fire is not quenched. He is rather to be feared, who is able to destroy both body and soul in hell, not those who kill the body, but are not able to hurt the soul."[24]

Oden's summary anticipates Wesley's answer to the question of how long the wicked will suffer in hell. The evangelist's reply is unambiguous. The wicked will endure future punishment of both body and soul, and "the eternity of these punishments is revealed as plainly as words can express" in Scripture.[25] The most concise summary of Wesley's views on future things appears in his "Letter to a Roman Catholic":

I believe God forgives all the sins of them that truly repent and unfeignedly believe his holy gospel; and that, at the last day, all men shall arise again, everyone with his own body. I believe that, as the unjust shall after their resurrection be tormented in hell forever, so the just shall enjoy inconceivable happiness in the presence of God to all eternity.[26]

Mile Marker 1924: Francis Pieper

Franz August Otto Pieper was born in Germany and emigrated to the United States where, after graduating from seminary and engaging in pastoral work, he served first as theology professor (1878-1887) and then as president (1887-1931) of Concordia Theological Seminary in St. Louis, Missouri. Of his fifteen theological works his most famous is the three-volume *Christian Dogmatics*, which serves as a doctrinal standard in conservative Lutheran seminaries to this day.

Pieper is knowledgeable of the objections raised against everlasting punishment, yet he remains unswayed by them: "But all objections are based on the false principle that it is proper and reasonable to make our human sentiments and judgments the measure of God's essence and activity."[27] To the contrary, Pieper urges, we are bound to the Word of God to learn such things. And he regards eternal damnation as a doctrine so clearly taught in Scripture that "one cannot deny it without at the same time rejecting the authority of Scripture."[28]

What is the purpose of such a shocking doctrine? It "is to warn against unbelief and carnal security and thus to save from eternal damnation." In Pieper's estimation this purpose is thwarted by all who substitute for the doctrine of everlasting punishment doctrines that are supposedly "more worthy of God," such as annihilationism. Such "mercy theologians," he insists, "are actually most merciless," because they cause people to underestimate the sufferings of hell.[29]

Mile Marker 1938: Louis Berkhof

Louis Berkhof taught theology at Calvin Theological Seminary in Grand Rapids, Michigan, for thirty-eight years. His most famous book, *Systematic Theology*, is still used in evangelical Reformed seminaries around the world. Berkhof opposes "an evident tendency in some circles to rule out the idea of eternal punishment." In response to those who show this tendency Berkhof insists that "there can be no reasonable doubt as to the fact that the Bible teaches the continued existence of the wicked."[30] He exercises caution on such truly debatable points as whether the flames of hell are to be taken literally or figuratively. But of this he is sure: hell is everlasting. Indeed, "the question of the eternity of future punishment deserves more special consideration . . . because it is frequently denied." It is easy to discern why he affirms the traditional position; he is persuaded by the teaching of Scripture passages such as Matthew 25:46; Mark 9:43, 48; and Luke 16:26.[31]

Mile Marker 1948: Lewis Sperry Chafer

Lewis Sperry Chafer was the founder and first president of Dallas Theological Seminary, where he served as professor of systematic theology for twenty-eight years. He is perhaps best remembered as the author of the eight-volume *Systematic Theology*. Because of his biblical and theological convictions Chafer is persuaded of the truth of eternal perdition. He stresses the clarity of the Bible's testimony to this truth: "It . . . is as clearly set forth in the Scriptures as it is possible for language to serve in the expression of ideas."[32] Chafer understands the tendency "to entertain the hope that this distress of the lost is not eternal, or everlasting." Nevertheless, fidelity to the Word of God and not human opinion must be the final arbiter in matters theological. As a result Chafer teaches that hell involves never-ending torment for the wicked. He is not swayed by the annihilationist argument that the Greek word *aionios* often translated "eternal" should be rendered "of long duration." On the contrary, "One passage alone—'and these shall go away into everlasting punishment: but the righteous into life eternal' [Mt 25:46]—demonstrates the truth that the word *aionios* means unending condition for one class as much as for the other."[33]

Mile Marker 1985: Millard Erickson

Millard Erickson is a contemporary Baptist theologian who has written more than twenty-five books, including the highly acclaimed doctrinal textbook *Christian Theology*. In this book he states his position on the matter under debate when he affirms "the doctrine of everlasting punishment . . . is clearly taught in Scripture."[34] Furthermore, he expressly rejects all "the forms of annihilationism." Why? Because "they contradict the teaching of the Bible." The most important point to notice is that Erickson believes in everlasting punishment because he is convinced that the Bible unambiguously teaches it. After examining Isaiah 66:24 and Mark 9:43-48 for teaching concerning hell, he summarizes, "These passages make it clear that the punishment is unending."[35]

Conclusion

We have completed our tour of the road to traditionalism and are ready to draw some conclusions. First, note that it would be difficult to find seven more influential thinkers than Tertullian, Augustine, Aquinas, Luther, Calvin, Edwards and Wesley. These are among the weightiest figures in church history. And although it is too soon to evaluate the lasting significance of the four twentieth-century figures, each wrote a major systematic theology that has influenced a generation of students.

Second, there is a consensus among these eleven key historical figures. They all believe that the wicked will suffer eternal punishment. In other ways, however, the figures exhibit diversity. They hail from various locales: North Africa (Tertullian and Augustine), Italy (Aquinas), Germany (Luther and Pieper), the Netherlands (Berkhof), France (Calvin), Great Britain (Wesley) and the United States (Edwards, Chafer and Erickson). They inhabit diverse periods in church history: the early church (Tertullian and Augustine), the Middle Ages (Aquinas), the Reformation (Luther and Calvin), the eighteenth century (Wesley and Edwards) and the twentieth century (Berkhof, Pieper, Chafer and Erickson). They represent major branches of the church: Roman Catholicism (Augustine and Aquinas) and the leading Protestant traditions, Lutheran (Luther and Pieper), Reformed (Calvin, Edwards and Berkhof), Baptist (Erickson) and Anglican (Wesley). It is significant, then, that in spite of their great diversity in place, time and tradition, these theologians agree on the subject of hell's duration. Their writings constitute the majority report of the church historic.

This consensus leads us to ask an important question: Is it possible that these eleven figures are wrong on the topic debated in this book? It is possible but highly unlikely! In fact, I cannot think of even *one* doctrinal issue in which they *all* are in error. It is not that they agree on every detail of theol-

ogy; they differ in their understanding of baptism and of the millennium, to
choose two examples. But on basic aspects of the Christian faith they are
united—and one of those aspects is eternal punishment. This unified confession of traditionalism is impressive, and it is not to be set aside lightly.

It is time to return to the question with which this chapter began: Why
do these eleven figures unanimously believe in everlasting punishment? By
now readers can see that it is ludicrous to argue as some annihilationists
have done that only vindictive people believe in the orthodox view of hell.
And equally absurd is the idea that all eleven are deceived by pagan philoso-
phies. Rather, if we take their own words seriously, we must understand
that they unanimously believe in everlasting punishment because they are
convinced that the Bible teaches it. Thus the road to traditionalism leads to
the house of traditionalism—a house whose foundation is set in the solid
bedrock of Scripture. It is to an examination of this foundation that our
attention now turns.

8

THE FOUNDATION
OF THE HOUSE
Scripture

WHEN SHOPPING FOR A HOUSE SEVEN YEARS AGO, OUR FAMILY WAS greatly helped by a realtor named Betty McCracken. She led us to our dream home and wisely insisted that we pay for a house inspection. In retrospect this was $190 well spent. For that price Mark Abeln gave our prospective home a going over, inside and out. Although his inspection report recommended that we make minor repairs, it concluded, "The overall condition of this home appears to be good." He wrote this after checking the grounds; the roof and attic; the exterior; the plumbing; the electrical, heating and cooling systems; the interior; and the foundation. It is, of course, the last of these that is the most important part of a house—the foundation.

When Jesus contrasts the houses built on stone and sand (Mt 7:24-27), he affirms that a house is only as solid as its foundation. In the last chapter we traveled the road to traditionalism. In this chapter we will inspect the foundation of the house of traditionalism. We usually think of a foundation as consisting of a concrete slab that braces the foundation walls. Actually, underneath the ground, supporting the slab, are footings. A dictionary defines a footing as "an enlargement at the lower end of a foundation wall . . . to distribute the load."[1]

The foundation of a theological doctrine consists of the reasons for believing that the doctrine is true. Here some of the most compelling reasons are pictured as the footings supporting the foundation. Readers are invited to become house inspectors who test the house of traditionalism's foundation. Come, inspect the footings, the ten biblical passages that I believe teach that the wicked will suffer eternal conscious punishment.

I will follow this outline for each footing:

☐ Passage
☐ Time frame
☐ Setting
☐ Teaching
☐ Annihilationist interpretation

After quoting each passage I will establish that it speaks of the final destiny of the unsaved (time frame). This is important because sometimes annihilationists make appeals to texts that do not pertain to the topic of hell. Next, to promote accurate interpretation, I will place the passage in its context (setting). Then I will consider what the text teaches about the nature and duration of hell, drawing the teaching out of the passage. Finally, I will interact with annihilationist interpretations of the passage.

The First Footing: Undying Worm and Unquenchable Fire (Old Testament)

Passage. The first footing supporting the foundation of the house of traditionalism is Isaiah 66:22-24.

> "As the new heavens and the new earth that I make will endure before me," declares the LORD, "so will your name and descendants endure. From one New Moon to another and from one Sabbath to another, all mankind will come and bow down before me," says the LORD. "And they will go out and look upon the dead bodies of those who rebelled against me; their worm will not die, nor will their fire be quenched, and they will be loathsome to all mankind."

Time frame. The first words of the passage point readers to the "the new heavens and the new earth." Here at the end of his prophecy Isaiah looks toward the distant future and the final destinies of human beings. The prophet sees many people bowing down before the Lord in worship; others, however, will forever be "loathsome to all mankind" (Is 66:24).

Setting. Isaiah 66:22-24 harks back to Isaiah 65:17: "Behold, I will create new heavens and a new earth. The former things will not be remembered, nor will they come to mind." God will replace his people's sorrow with "joy" (Is 65:18). They will rejoice over his accomplishments, especially his vanquishing of the foes of his humble people (Is 66:1-5).

God will bless his own but show "his fury" to his foes. The prophet boldly paints the divine warrior's punishment of the wicked:

> See, the LORD is coming with fire,
>   and his chariots are like a whirlwind;
> he will bring down his anger with fury,
>   and his rebuke with flames of fire.
> For with fire and with his sword
>   the LORD will execute judgment upon all men,
>   and many will be those slain by the LORD. (Is 66:15-16)

God displays his glory by judging the wicked but more so by spreading his fame among the nations. In addition, he will "gather all nations" to "come and see" his "glory." As a result, redeemed Jews will worship God, and even Gentiles will be brought to "Jerusalem as an offering to the LORD" (Is 66:18-21). Here in old covenant language is a prediction of the world-wide worship of God that is characteristic of the new covenant.[2]

Teaching. The context, then, speaks of God's creating the new heavens and the new earth. Now, in verse 22 the Lord draws a comparison: "As the new heavens and the new earth that I make will endure before me, so will your name and descendants endure." God promises his people that they will be part of the new order. He will grant them the permanence that belongs to the new heavens and earth.

What will occupy their time? "From one New Moon to another and from one Sabbath to another, all mankind will come and bow down before" the Lord (Is 66:23). Isaiah foretells redeemed Jews' and Gentiles' ongoing adoration of God in the new earth. The prophet uses the language of Old Testament worship to predict the adoration of God in the last days. People from every nation will worship God forever. But not everyone will be among the worshipers; the ungodly will suffer a dreadful fate.

Isaiah says: "And they will go out and look upon the dead bodies of those who rebelled against me" (Is 66:24). The prophet pictures worshipers leaving the temple and gazing on the corpses of the Lord's enemies, probably located in the valley of Hinnom, as a comparison with Jeremiah 7:32—8:3 suggests. In this valley, also called Tophet, human sacrifices were made to the Ammonite god Molech during the reigns of Ahaz and Manasseh, kings of Judah (2 Kings 16:3; 21:6). King Josiah later desecrated the valley of Hinnom (2 Kings 23:10), but it had already gained such an evil reputation that it was still used as a designation for hell during the first century A.D.

Drawing imagery from the battlefield, Isaiah envisions the rebels slain by the divine warrior as suffering dreadful consequences. What does Isaiah mean when he refers to worms not dying and fire not being quenched? In Old Testament times victorious armies sometimes left their foes' bodies unburied as a sign of contempt. For corpses to be publicly exposed was a great disgrace. This accounts for the courageous efforts of the citizens of Jabesh Gilead to recover the dead bodies of Saul and his sons from the Philistines (1 Sam 31:11-13). And it also explains Rizpah's remarkable protection of her sons' dead bodies from the birds and wild animals (2 Sam 21:10). Eventually unburied corpses became food for maggots.

The burning of dead bodies in the Old Testament is sometimes viewed as an act of desecration. The burning of Achan's body (Josh 7:25) and the king of Moab's act of burning the bones of the king of Edom (Amos 2:1) are examples of this.

Keeping in mind these pictures of exposed and burned corpses helps us interpret Isaiah's words: "And they will go out and look upon the dead bodies of those who rebelled against me; their worm will not die, nor will their fire be quenched" (Is 66:24). The prophet uses imagery from his present world to describe the future fate of the wicked. For exposed corpses to be eaten by worms or burned was a disgrace; Isaiah envisions the ultimate disgrace. In all other cases when the maggots had finished their work, they would die. And once the fuel was consumed, the fire would go out. But in the prophet's picture, "their worm will not die, nor will their fire be quenched." The shame of the wicked will have no end; their fate is eternal. Therefore, "they will be loathsome to all mankind" (Is 66:24).

Annihilationist interpretation. Here is Edward Fudge's explanation of Isaiah's words:

The righteous contemplate with satisfaction "the dead bodies" of the wicked. They look at corpses (Heb. *pegerim*) not living people. They view their destruction, not their misery. . . . Because this fire is "not quenched" or extinguished, it completely consumes what is put in it. . . . Both worms and fire speak of a total and final destruction.[3]

Fudge's explanation is not persuasive. He takes the words "dead bodies" literally and on that basis understands the undying worm and unquenchable fire as indicating extinction. But this is impossible. How can the picture of maggots never dying in their act of consuming a dead body indicate the extinction of that body? And how can the image of fire never being extinguished when it burns a dead body signify that body's consumption?

It is vital to see that Isaiah does not teach annihilation here. He does not say that the fire consumes what is put in it; on the contrary, he says that the fire will never be put out. He does not say that the worms symbolize a total and final consumption; rather, he says that the worms never die; that is, their destructive work is never complete.

Fudge, therefore, misconstrues Isaiah's words when he takes the image of corpses literally. Fudge misinterprets the words "dead bodies" by failing to see how they function as part of a larger picture. Instead, we must interpret *as a unit* the image of corpses beset by undying worm and unquenchable fire. Isaiah uses the words "dead bodies" here to refer to lost "human beings." By speaking of corpses beset by unquenchable fire and undying worm, he communicates unsaved human beings' never-ending shame after death. The picture is one of everlasting contempt, not of annihilation. Unlike the greatest shame Isaiah could imagine—having one's dead body abandoned on the battlefield to be consumed by fire or worms—this shame will never come to an end. Thinking through Fudge's handling of Isaiah 66:24, then, confirms my conviction that the traditionalist interpretation of this text is correct.

The Second Footing: Everlasting Life/Everlasting Contempt
Passage. The second foundational passage is Daniel 12:1-2.

At that time Michael, the great prince who protects your people, will arise. There will be a time of distress such as has not happened from the beginning of nations until then. But at that time your people—everyone whose name is found written in the book—will be delivered. Multitudes who sleep in the dust of the earth will awake: some to everlasting life, others to shame and everlasting contempt.

Time frame. It is easy to show that this passage points to the last days. Daniel speaks of an unequaled "time of distress" (v. 1), the time of the resurrection of the dead (v. 2) and "the time of the end" (v. 4). Jesus confirms this conclusion when he connects the unparalleled distress mentioned in Daniel 12:2 with "the Son of Man coming on the clouds of the sky, with power and great glory" (Mt 24:21, 30).

Setting. Daniel predicts a time of unprecedented trouble, the great tribulation spoken of by Jesus. Nevertheless, God promises to deliver his people. The mighty angel Michael will arise to do battle for "everyone whose name is found written in the book" (Dan 12:1). Here Daniel uses the image of the list of citizens of the true Jerusalem (compare Ps 69:28; Mal 3:16) to show that in the last days God will rescue spiritual Israel.

Although the text does not spell out the logical connection between Daniel 12:1 and 2, this seems likely: God will deliver his people in the terrible times foretold by Daniel. Nevertheless, both they and the wicked will suffer casualties. Because God is Lord even over death, however, his conquest extends beyond the grave. He will resurrect the dead—his martyrs to glory and his enemies to shame.

Teaching. The picture Daniel paints in 12:2 of "multitudes who sleep" merits our attention. The Hebrew construction here rendered "multitudes who" most commonly means "many" in the Old Testament.[4] Daniel writes of the resurrection of the martyrs and of their foes who will have died during the distressful times predicted in verse 1. Of course, he is not denying that God will raise *all* of the dead; he is just focusing on a part of that whole in this context.[5]

The prophet uses language from an everyday activity—awakening people who are asleep—to depict the bodily resurrection of the last day: "Multitudes who sleep . . . will awake." God rouses the deceased bodies of the dead from the "slumber" of death as easily as we awaken someone from sleep. Before his power, death is only a temporary state of "sleep" from which people "awake."

Furthermore, those who are slumbering are said to "sleep in the dust of the earth." Here is an allusion to the divine Potter's original work: "The LORD God formed the man from the dust of the ground and breathed into his nostrils the breath of life, and the man became a living being" (Gen 2:7). God's words to Adam after his fall are also pertinent:

By the sweat of your brow
  you will eat your food
until you return to the ground,
  since from it you were taken;
for dust you are
  and to dust you will return. (Gen 3:19)

The Creator who made Adam from the dust of the earth and who turns human bodies to dust at death will raise the bodies of those who have died.

The resurrected will be divided into two groups heading for opposite fates: "Multitudes who sleep in the dust of the earth will awake: some to everlasting life, others to shame and everlasting contempt." This is the only time the words "everlasting life" appear in the Old Testament, although the idea appears several times of God's people enjoying life in his presence after death (see Job 19:26; Ps 73:23-24; Is 26:19). The word *everlasting* (Hebrew *olam*) is used here to describe the fates of the just and unjust (Dan 12:2). This word deserves careful study. It is an adjective signifying long duration with limits set by the context. For example, it describes the period of time a willing bondslave could choose to serve his master: "Then he will be his servant for *life*" (Ex 21:6).

When used of God, however, as in Psalm 90:2, "from *everlasting* to *everlasting* you are God," it means "eternal." In this case the limits of the long duration indicated by *olam* are set by the eternal life of God himself. This use of the word happens frequently in the Old Testament, in which it is used to speak of the eternal name (Ex 3:15) of the eternal God (Gen 21:33), of his eternal attributes (love, 1 Kings 10:9; glory, Ps 104:31; faithfulness, Ps 117:2; righteousness, Ps 119:142), of his eternal reign (Ex 15:18), of eternal salvation (Is 51:6, 8), of eternal covenants (Gen 9:16; 17:7, 13, 19), of God's eternal word (Is 40:8) and of the eternal praise due God (Ps 89:53; 135:13).

In Daniel 12:2 this word describes the destinies of both the righteous and the wicked. It is incorrect to limit either of these destinies; they are both "everlasting."[6] As we will see when we study the New Testament, the state of affairs after the resurrection of the dead is characterized by the life of God himself; the age to come lasts as long as he does—forever. In sum: we see that even though *olam* does not always mean eternal, in this context it must.

The godly will be raised to "everlasting life." *Life* is used in the Old Testament to speak of welfare and happiness in the presence of the king (Prov 16:15, contrasted with the king's wrath in v. 14). At the time described in Daniel 12:2, being in the presence of the great King brings never-ending "life," that is, true welfare and happiness. The wicked, however, are not raised to life; they are raised to "shame and . . . contempt." The first of these two words speaks of "reproach," "shame" and "disgrace" (see 2 Sam 13:13; Lam 5:1; Dan 9:16). The second occurs only here and in Isaiah 66:24, where, as we saw, it is used to describe the wicked at the end as "*loathsome* to all mankind."

Daniel assures his believing readers that God will not abandon them, even in death. He will raise them to their reward, as the Lord later promises Daniel: "As for you, go your way till the end. You will rest, and then at the end of the days you will rise to receive your allotted inheritance" (Dan 12:13). God will raise his people to eternal life. The wicked, however, will suffer a terrible fate: they will be raised to eternal disgrace.

Annihilationist interpretation. Edward Fudge interprets Daniel 12:2 as involving "total destruction" and writes, "It is an 'everlasting' contempt because the state is irreversible."[7] That is, God will annihilate the wicked whose "everlasting contempt" involves their never again coming into existence. The unsaved will exist no more, but their shame will never end.

Surely this is a mishandling of Daniel 12:2. The prophet says nothing of annihilation. Instead, after foretelling God's raising the righteous and unrighteous, he uses the same adjective, *everlasting (olam)*, to describe the fate of both groups. Just as the "everlasting life" will be experienced by believers forever, so the "shame and everlasting contempt" will be experienced by unbelievers forever. Listen to Daniel's words again: "Multitudes . . . will awake: some to everlasting life, others to shame and everlasting contempt." Does a resurrection "to shame and everlasting contempt" mean annihilation? No indeed. Instead it indicates a never-ending conscious existence that corresponds to the never-ending conscious existence of the righteous. In fact, Daniel 12:2 marks the beginning of a pattern in Scripture of parallels between the destinies of the righteous and wicked (compare Mt 25:46; Jn 5:28-29).

The Third Footing: Eternal Fire/The Fire of Hell

Passage. The third footing beneath the house of traditionalism is Matthew 18:6-9.

> But if anyone causes one of these little ones who believe in me to sin, it would be better for him to have a large millstone hung around his neck and to be drowned in the depths of the sea. Woe to the world because of the things that cause people to sin! Such things must come, but woe to the man through whom they come! If your hand or your foot causes you to sin, cut it off and throw it away. It is better for you to enter life maimed or crippled than to have two hands or two feet and be thrown into eternal fire. And if your eye causes you to sin, gouge it out and throw it away. It is better for you to enter life with one eye than to have two eyes and be thrown into the fire of hell.

Time frame. This passage deals with eternal destinies. Jesus speaks twice of "entering life" (vv. 8, 9), that is, of experiencing eternal life in its final dimension. Jesus also refers to the final fate of the wicked, when he warns of "eternal fire" (v. 8) and "the fire of hell" (v. 9).

Setting. Responding to the disciples' question "Who is the greatest in the kingdom of heaven?" Jesus summons a little child to serve as an object lesson. "Unless you change and become like little children, you will never enter the kingdom of heaven. Therefore, whoever humbles himself like this child is the greatest in the kingdom of heaven" (Mt 18:1-4). Not a desire for greatness but childlike humility is precious in God's sight. Jesus calls his disciples to repent of their selfish ambition and adopt instead the submissive attitude of God's true children.

After asking his hearers to consider their inner lives, Jesus turns their attention outward. They must watch their influence on others. Someone who receives "a little child" in Jesus' name receives Jesus. On the other hand, someone who causes "one of these little ones" to sin is headed for God's judgment (Mt 18:5-6). When he speaks of children, Jesus means those who humble themselves, true disciples.

With a graphic picture Jesus compares God's punishment of sinners to the drowning of a person. A huge millstone, the kind pulled by a donkey, is hung about someone's neck, and he is submerged in the Mediterranean Sea until he dies.

Next Jesus exclaims, "Woe to the world because of the things that cause people to sin!" The Savior condemns the wickedness of sin and warns of the terror of God's wrath. Nevertheless, because he believes that all matters are under God's control, even sin, he says, "Such things must come," and he underscores human responsibility when he continues, "but woe to the man through whom they come!" (Mt 18:7).[8]

Jesus, like many preachers, recycles his illustrations. This passage is a restatement of the hyperbole of Matthew 5:29-30, where he also speaks of cutting off an offending hand or gouging out an offending eye. He means that his hearers should take drastic action rather than sin and face the horrors of hell.

Teaching. In this passage Jesus contrasts heaven and hell. First, he distinguishes entering life from being thrown into "eternal fire" (Mt 18:8). Then he juxtaposes entering life with being cast into "the fire of hell" (v. 9). Here are opposite destinies. The righteous will enter eternal life in God's joyous presence. The unrighteous, however, will be cast by God into hell. Jesus paints a picture of hellfire to warn his listeners of the pain of God's judgment. When he speaks of "eternal fire," he means that the torments of hell will have no end. The Savior compassionately warns his hearers of the dreadfulness of eternal punishment at God's hands.

Annihilationist interpretation. Although this explanation of Matthew 18:8-9 seems straightforward, annihilationists contest it. They use various strategies to handle passages that historically have been understood to teach everlasting punishment. At times they gloss over such passages rather than studying them in detail. That is what Fudge does when he treats verses 8-9:

> Gehenna here is called the "eternal fire." In another place Jesus says the "eternal fire" was prepared for the devil and his angels (Mt 25:41). This is paralleled by reference to the kingdom, which was "prepared since the creation of the world" (v. 34). By implication the "fire" seems to be at least as old as creation; it is clear that it will extend beyond the Present Age. It is therefore said to be "eternal," since it neither begins nor ends with the Present Age. The phrase does not convey what "eternal fire" will do to those thrown into it.[9]

Fudge fails to deal with Matthew 18:8-9 in context. Instead, he appeals to Matthew 25, inferring that hell, like heaven, must have been prepared before creation. He then concludes that *eternal* in the expression "eternal fire" in Matthew 18:8 need not mean everlasting but simply lasting beyond this age into the age to come.

Is this an accurate handling of Jesus' words in Matthew 18:8-9? Certainly not. It is a way of avoiding the import of those words. When Jesus speaks of eternal fire, he does not mean fire that annihilates but fire that never ends. This is the sense readers would arrive at by reading his words in context. They would understand "eternal fire" as the opposite of "life" in verse 8 and the "fire of hell" as the opposite of "life" in verse 9. When Jesus refers to life here, he means "eternal life." It is natural, then, to understand the eternal hellfire that is twice contrasted with eternal life as being eternal in the same way that life is eternal, that is, as everlasting.

Fudge, in another attempt to leave the door open for annihilationism, mentions that Jesus does not say what "eternal fire" will do to those thrown into it. Again, however, Fudge errs. Scripture repeatedly explains the effect of hellfire on those cast into it; it brings great pain. Jesus teaches this twice in Matthew 13, where he speaks of the unsaved being thrown "into the fiery furnace, where there will be weeping and gnashing of teeth" (vv. 42, 50). According to Jesus, hellfire brings anguish.

Jesus will send the lost into "the eternal fire prepared for the devil and his angels" (Mt 25:41). John instructs us about that fire: "And the devil . . . was thrown into the lake of burning sulfur . . . [and] will be tormented day and night for ever and ever" (Rev 20:10). Here fire denotes unspeakable torment.

The use of fire imagery in the parable of the rich man and Lazarus confirms our conclusion. The deceased rich man found himself "in hell where he was in torment." He begged for relief because he was in agony in the fire (Lk 16:23, 24). Fire here symbolizes the agony that one suffers in the "place of torment" (Lk 16:25, 28).

In Revelation, John says that the wicked "will be tormented with burning sulfur. . . . And the smoke of their torment rises for ever and ever" (Rev 14:10-11). The lake of fire, the site of the devil's endless torment (Rev 20:10), is where sinners too are cast (Rev 20:14) and therefore will suffer forever.

Plainly the imagery of burning conveys eternal torment for the damned.

In the light of this biblical evidence that the fire of hell signifies awful suffering, it is an evasion for Fudge to say that Matthew 18:8-9 doesn't specify the effects of the fire of hell on sinners. The New Testament need not specify every time it uses the imagery of fire in connection with hell. It specifies many times and uses shorthand in others.

The Fourth Footing: Eternal Punishment/Eternal Life

Passage. The fourth footing under the foundation of traditionalism is Matthew 25:31-46, historically the most important biblical passage on hell.

> When the Son of Man comes in his glory, and all his angels with him, he will sit on his throne in heavenly glory. All the nations will be gathered before him, and he will separate the people one from another as a shepherd separates the sheep from the goats. He will put the sheep on his right and the goats on his left.
>
> Then the King will say to those on his right, "Come, you who are blessed by my Father; take your inheritance, the kingdom prepared for you since the creation of the world." . . .
>
> Then he will say to those on his left, "Depart from me, you who are cursed, into the eternal fire prepared for the devil and his angels." . . .
>
> Then they will go away to eternal punishment, but the righteous to eternal life.

Time frame. Three factors prove that this passage deals with the end. First, it begins with a reference to Christ's glorious second coming (v. 31). Second, Jesus speaks of the final separation of the human race into two groups: the saved and the lost (v. 32). And third, at issue are the ultimate destinies of heaven and hell (vv. 34, 41, 46).

Setting. Jesus speaks of the Last Judgment following his return in glory. Matthew presents Jesus, in Old Testament fashion, as a shepherd-king who separates the human race into sheep and goats. The sheep are blessed by God the Father with the inheritance of the kingdom of God (v. 34). By contrast, the goats are cursed by God and cast into eternal fire (v. 41). The passage ends with Jesus succinctly contrasting the two destinies: "eternal punishment" and "eternal life" (v. 46).

Teaching. This passage exhibits the symmetry that we observed in Daniel

12:2, which contrasted "eternal life" with "shame and everlasting contempt." In Matthew 25:31-46 the symmetry is even more pronounced, for it structures the passage as a whole. Verse 32 foretells King Jesus' separation of the sheep from the goats. The next verse places the sheep on Jesus' right and the goats on his left. The pattern of sheep/goats continues, as Jesus invites the sheep to take their inheritance and banishes the goats to hell (vv. 34, 41). At the end of the passage Jesus reverses the order and tells of the fate of the goats first and then that of the sheep: "Then they will go away to eternal punishment, but the righteous to eternal life" (v. 46). We can diagram the pattern in this way, labeling the sheep A and the goats B:

Separation of sheep (A) and goats (B) (vv. 32-33)

Sheep (A) enter kingdom (v. 34)

Goats (B) enter hell (v. 41)

Summary: destinies of goats (B) and sheep (A) (v. 46)

This pattern underscores the symmetry of fates of the saved and lost. Above all it points to verse 46, where the order of sheep/goats is reversed. This reversal arrests the hearers' attention. Jesus' words "eternal punishment" and "eternal life" are left ringing in their ears. The overall structure of the passage and the emphatic last verse highlight the fact that the destinies of the godly and ungodly are alike in this respect—they are both everlasting.

It is difficult to improve upon Augustine's logic when he comments on the parallelism of "eternal punishment" and "eternal life" in verse 46:

> Is it not folly to assume that eternal punishment signifies a fire lasting a long time, while believing that eternal life is life without end? For Christ, in the very same passage, included both punishment and life in one and the same sentence when he said, "So those people will go into eternal punishment, while the righteous will go into eternal life" (Mt. 25:46). If both are "eternal," it follows necessarily that either both are to be taken as long-lasting but finite, or both as endless and perpetual. The phrases "eternal punishment" and "eternal life" are parallel and it would be absurd to use them in one and the same sentence to mean: "Eternal life will be infinite, while eternal punishment will have an end." Hence, because the eternal life of the saints will be endless, the eternal punishment also, for those condemned to it, will assuredly have no end.[10]

Augustine's conclusion agrees with Jesus' choice of words; he labels the fate of the damned "eternal *punishment*." The translation of the Greek word *kolasis* as "punishment" is correct according to the standard dictionary *A Greek-English Lexicon of the New Testament*. The correctness of this translation can be seen from its usage in various contexts. It is used in early Christian literature outside of the New Testament to mean "long-continued torture." The dictionary correctly says that it is used within the New Testament and elsewhere of "divine retribution" and "eternal damnation." An instructive parallel is found in 1 John 4:18: "There is no fear in love. But perfect love drives out fear, because fear has to do with *punishment*." Here God's love removes fear of punishment after death.[11] I remain unconvinced by annihilationists' claims that the extinction of being constitutes "eternal punishment." On the contrary, annihilation is relief from punishment; the damned in hell would love to be annihilated, for this would deliver them out of their terrible suffering.

Furthermore, the cursed are banished into "eternal fire" (v. 41). This speaks of never-ending suffering, as Jesus' words describing the fire indicate. He says the "eternal fire" is "prepared for the devil and his angels" (v. 41). Where does Scripture tell us about this fire? In Revelation 20:10. That passage reads, "And the devil, who deceived them, was thrown into the lake of burning sulfur. . . . They will be tormented day and night for ever and ever." Comparing Scripture with Scripture, specifically Matthew 25:41 with Revelation 20:10, Augustine concludes:

> "Eternal" in the first passage is expressed in the second by "for ever and ever", and those words have only one meaning in scriptural usage: the exclusion of any temporal end. And this is why there cannot conceivably be found any reason better founded or more evident for the fixed and immutable conviction of true religion that the Devil and his angels will never attain to justification and to the life of the saints. There can be, I say, no stronger reason than this: that the Scriptures that never deceive, say that God has not spared them.[12]

Once again Augustine's logic is compelling. In Matthew 25:41 Jesus likens the fate of "accursed" human beings to that of the devil. In Revelation 20:10 we learn that the devil's fate is to be "tormented day and night for ever and ever." Lost sinners therefore will suffer everlasting condemnation.

Annihilationist interpretation. Edward Fudge offers a competing interpretation of Matthew 25:41, 46. Here is his summary:

> In this apocalyptic picture the wicked are banished into eschatological fire prepared for the satanic angels. There they will eventually be destroyed for ever, both body and soul, as the divine penalty for sin. The process may well involve a period of conscious pain involving body and soul, but the "eternal punishment" itself is the capital execution, the everlasting loss of existence, the everlasting loss of the eternal life of joy and blessing in the company with God and the redeemed.[13]

How does Fudge reach this conclusion? He employs at least three strategies. First, he defines the key words *eternal* and *punishment* in ways that are compatible with annihilationism. Fudge studies the word *eternal (aionios)* and concludes that "eternal punishment" in Matthew 25:41, although it does not exclude penal suffering, "consists primarily of the total abolition and extinction of the person for ever."[14] Eternal punishment (according to Fudge) does not mean that the wicked suffer forever in hell, but that God annihilates them with no possibility of their being recreated.

I have already evaluated the linguistic argument that lies behind Fudge's conclusion (pp. 96-98); now I will explain why I reject his conclusion. The parallelism between "eternal punishment" and "eternal life" in Matthew 25:41 speaks volumes. The two destinies of human beings—punishment and life—are both modified by the same adjective *eternal* in the same sentence. Fudge would do well to heed his own words, "Whatever *aionios* [eternal] means, one should have good cause for not translating it the same way when it appears twice in one verse!"[15] I heartily agree. But that is precisely what Fudge does when he understands "eternal life" to speak of never-ending bliss and "eternal punishment" to mean irreversible annihilation. The import of Jesus' words is rather that both the wicked and the righteous will experience their respective destinies for all eternity.

Fudge also defines *punishment (kolasis)* in a manner compatible with annihilationism. He studies the word and concludes, " 'Punishment' may certainly include conscious pain, as in all the examples above, but it does not have to." His evidence for this conclusion is one occurrence of *kolasis* where it is used to describe something that happens to an idol of stone or wood. Next, Fudge places side by side the judgment passages in Matthew

25, John 5:29, Daniel 12:2 and Isaiah 66:24 and concludes that "eternal punishment" means annihilation.[16] Here Fudge combines faulty linguistic work
with avoidance of the text in question (Mt 25:46). The fact that *kolasis* can be
used to speak of an idol (in a personification!) tells us nothing about occasions when it is used to speak of human beings. If we study occurrences
when it is used of human beings, we find that it means "punishment," as
for example, in 1 John 4:18. Furthermore, Fudge's appeal to Isaiah 66:24 is
an attempt to avoid the teaching of Matthew 25 by turning to a passage
with which Fudge feels more comfortable. He must explain Matthew 25:41,
46 in context, and that he does not do.

Fudge's second strategy is to employ an emotional argument. He warns:

> We must be careful in pressing the parallel between "eternal" life and "eter-
> nal" punishment that we do not fall into any spirit of vindictiveness at the
> fate of the wicked. Since Augustine, traditionalists have argued that unless
> "eternal punishment" means endless torment, we have no assurance that
> "eternal life" secures our endless joy. Many have cautioned against taking
> delight in the fate of the lost, a sure sign that some have done just that.[17]

Fudge implies that one is liable to vindictiveness who understands Matthew 25:46 as teaching endless punishment. This is an *ad hominem* argument, meaning an argument directed *to the man*. An *ad hominem* occurs,
according to Irving M. Copi, "when, instead of trying to *disprove the truth* of
what is asserted, one attacks the man who made the assertion."[18]

The ad hominem argument belongs in the category of irrelevant arguments. The premises of such arguments "are logically irrelevant to, and
therefore incapable of establishing the truth of, their conclusions."[19] This is
true of Fudge's argument here: whether traditionalists are vindictive or not
has nothing to do with the meaning of Matthew 25:46. In fact, the defenders
of the orthodox doctrine of hell have often demonstrated compassion for
the lost. But whether they are compassionate or vengeful does not help us
understand Jesus' words in this passage.

Fudge, by arguing in this way, seeks to persuade by "the psychological
process of transference," to use Copi's description. Copi explains, "Where
an attitude of disapproval toward a person can be evoked, it may possibly
tend to overflow the strictly emotional field and become disagreement with
what the person says."[20]

Fudge's third strategy is to avoid an argument that is difficult for his position. He fails to correlate Matthew 25:41 with Revelation 20:10. Jesus' words suggest this correlation when he speaks of "the eternal fire prepared for the devil and his angels" (Mt 25:41). Readers naturally ask, Does the Bible describe that fire? The answer is yes, in Revelation 20:10. There John explains that the devil will be "thrown into the lake of burning sulfur," where he "will be tormented day and night for ever and ever." Traditionalists from ancient to modern times have regarded this as a strong argument for endless punishment.[21] How does Fudge deal with this argument? He simply does not address it. But a strategy of avoiding one's opponents' best arguments is surely an unsuccessful one.

Here then are the three ways that Fudge attempts to explain Matthew 25:41, 46, as harmonizing with annihilationism: he redefines key words, appeals to readers' emotions and avoids a key argument. These three strategies fail; in fact, they actually serve to highlight the correctness of my exposition of the passage. I conclude this exposition the way I began it—by reminding readers that this is the single most important passage in the history of the doctrine of hell. In fact, even if Matthew 25:41, 46, were the only verses to describe the fate of the wicked, the Bible would clearly teach eternal condemnation, and we would be obligated to believe it on the authority of the Son of God.

The Fifth Footing: Undying Worm and Unquenchable Fire (New Testament)
Passage. The fifth passage supporting the foundation for belief in the traditional view of hell is Mark 9:42-48.

> And if anyone causes one of these little ones who believe in me to sin, it would be better for him to be thrown into the sea with a large millstone tied around his neck. If your hand causes you to sin, cut it off. It is better for you to enter life maimed than with two hands to go into hell, where the fire never goes out. And if your foot causes you to sin, cut it off. It is better for you to enter life crippled than to have two feet and be thrown into hell. And if your eye causes you to sin, pluck it out. It is better for you to enter the kingdom of God with one eye than to have two eyes and be thrown into hell, where "their worm does not die, and the fire is not quenched."

Time frame. Jesus speaks of eternal destinies in this passage. He contrasts entering life, or the kingdom of God, with going into hell, or being thrown into hell (vv. 43, 45, 47).

Setting. Jesus warns his hearers to weigh carefully their influence on others. Woe to those who cause Jesus' followers, described as "little ones," to stumble! In fact, the fate of such evildoers will be worse than being forcibly drowned in the sea (v. 42). What could be worse than that? Being thrown into hell by almighty God!

In light of the terrible consequence of sin—being thrown into hell—Jesus urges drastic action. Rather than indulge in sin, his listeners should perform spiritual "surgery" on themselves (vv. 43, 45, 47). It is better to "cut off" the sinning hand or foot and to "pluck out" the offending eye than to be whole and go to hell.

As is Palestinian custom Jesus does not "refer to an abstract activity that would cause someone to be condemned but to the specific member of the body which is responsible for it."[22] Jesus is not commanding bodily mutilation. Such action would insult the Creator. And it would not be an effective remedy against sins of the heart: a blind person can still covet or lust in the mind. Jesus does not command mutilation; rather, he instructs his hearers to impose severe limitations upon themselves in order that they might avoid sin and not end up in hell.

Teaching. Jesus speaks of both the positive and negative destinies of human beings. Positively, he twice tells of the desirability of entering "life" (vv. 43, 45); he means eternal life with God on the new earth. In addition, to those who heed his message he promises the joy of entering the final stage of the kingdom of God (v. 47).

Jesus, however, also speaks negatively; he warns of hell three times (vv. 43, 45, 47). In so doing he teaches both divine sovereignty and human responsibility. When he warns of being "thrown into hell" (vv. 45, 47), he points his hearers to God's control of everything, even the fate of the damned. For it is God alone who casts people into hell. But when Jesus warns of going into hell (v. 43), the accent falls on human accountability. Anyone who sows sin with abandon in this life will reap God's wrath in the next.

Jesus offers a vivid description of hell. In verse 44, alluding to Isaiah 66:24, he teaches that it is a place "where the fire never goes out." He thereby distinguishes the fires of hell from those on earth. Colossal forest fires, spread for miles by raging winds, may burn for weeks or even months. But eventually they will burn out, as do all fires in this world. But not the fire in the world to come; hellfire never will be snuffed out.

Along with the majority of evangelical interpreters, I understand hellfire figuratively rather than literally. It was not Jesus' intention to teach concerning the chemistry of hell. Instead, he sought to alert us of its terrible eternal reality that we might believe in him and be saved. No one interprets all the biblical pictures of hell literally. Jesus speaks of hypocrites' being "cut to pieces" before being cast into hell (Mt 24:51). Should we understand that the resurrected wicked will be drawn and quartered? Of course not. Rather, God employs images taken from our earthly life to teach us about the pains of hell.

The key thing to note is that Jesus describes hell as a place "where the fire never goes out." Jesus paints a picture of inextinguishable hellfire to depict unbearable and enduring pain. We have all had the experience of being burned. Jesus and his apostles use this common experience to warn their hearers of a far worse fate. There are many New Testament verses in which the fire of hell signifies suffering (Mt 13:42, 50; 25:41 [compare Rev 20:10]; Lk 16:23-25, 28; Rev 14:10; 20:10, 15).

Jesus reinforces this point at the end of the passage when he again warns of being cast "into hell, where 'their worm does not die, and the fire is not quenched' " (vv. 47-48). He does not merely allude to Isaiah 66:24, as he did in Mark 9:43, but quotes from that passage, with minor variations: "their worm will not die, nor will their fire be quenched." Jesus changes the tense from future to present, as is fitting. The Old Testament prophet foretells the eternity of hell; the Savior describes it in eternal—and present—terms.

According to Jesus, hell is "where 'their worm does not die, and the fire is not quenched' " (Mk 9:48). Jesus' words are not obtuse. Most people in Jesus' day, like people in our own, have seen maggots infesting decaying matter and burning fire consuming its fuel. Jesus' words point beyond common experience, however, for he says in hell the worm does *not* die and the fire is *not* quenched. Hell, then, is a place unlike any with which human beings are familiar. Who has ever heard of worms not dying after they have consumed their host? Or of a fire continuing to burn after it has depleted its fuel? Jesus thus uses the familiar to teach his hearers about the unfamiliar. They have all seen maggots and fires. Yet none of them has ever seen undying maggots or unquenchable fire. That is precisely Jesus' point. Hell is a place where the destruction of the wicked never ends.

Annihilationist interpretation. Listen to Edward Fudge's explanation of Jesus' words:

> The "worm" here *(skolex)* is the kind that feeds on dead bodies; we have already examined this figure. . . . This is a devouring worm, and what it eats—in Isaiah's picture here quoted without amendment—is already dead.
>
> The devouring worm is aided by a consuming fire. This understanding is supported, not only by the biblical references already noted to "unquenchable fire", but also by Homer's reference to "unquenchable fire" used by the Trojans against the Grecian ships *(Iliad* 16.123.194; 1.599) and the church historian Eusebius' "unquenchable fire" which burns a martyr to ashes *(Eccl. Hist.* 6.41). By his repeated use of the phrase, Jesus clearly implies that God's final decision concerning each person "is irreversible and entails eternal consequences."[23]

Fudge's explanation contains at least four errors. First, it suffers from faulty word-study methodology. Appealing to Homer and Eusebius to understand words used in the Gospel of Mark is not very helpful because Homer wrote six centuries before and Eusebius at least two-and-a-half centuries after Mark was written. More promising are Fudge's appeals to the usage of words in Scripture, although even these can be misleading. Such appeals are helpful, but only in establishing a word's range of meaning. The way a word is used elsewhere does not tell us the way it is used in a particular context. In fact, the single most important factor in understanding a word's meaning in a given context is that very context, and this is the very thing Fudge often minimizes. His word-study work suffers from an atomistic tendency to consider meanings apart from the contexts being studied. Here, for example, Fudge doesn't explain in Mark's context Jesus' description of hell as a place where "their worm does not die and the fire is not quenched."

Second, Fudge reverses the proper relation between the Old and New Testaments. Correct theological method involves studying New Testament texts in the light of their Old Testament background. This involves allowing the New Testament writers to move beyond the Old Testament in accordance with the progress of revelation. This is what I attempted to do above. Instead, Fudge errs by reading his annihilationist understanding of Isaiah 66:24 into the New Testament texts, where it does not fit.

Third, Fudge misuses an authority. The quotation above concluded with Fudge's words, "By his repeated use of the phrase, Jesus clearly implies that God's final decision concerning each person *is irreversible and entails eternal consequences.*' " Here Fudge quotes from William L. Lane's commentary on Mark.[24] Readers could get the impression that Lane agrees with Fudge on the matter under discussion. In fact, however, the opposite is true, as the following quotation two pages after the first one reveals, "As the final word of the prophecy of Isaiah the passage was thoroughly familiar to the disciples as a vivid picture of a destruction which continues endlessly."[25]

Fourth, by these means Fudge avoids interpreting Jesus' words in their own context. The principle stated above for the study of words is true for interpretation in general: the most important factor in interpreting a biblical passage is the immediate context of that passage. I fault Fudge, therefore, for omitting an exposition of Mark 9:42-48 from the second edition of *The Fire That Consumes*. It is one of the most notable passages on hell in church history. Nevertheless, although the index to biblical literature at the end of Fudge's book includes entries to more than one hundred passages, Mark 9:42-48 is not among them.

The Sixth Footing: Everlasting Destruction
Passage. The sixth foundational passage undergirding the house of traditionalism is 2 Thessalonians 1:5-10.

> All this is evidence that God's judgment is right, and as a result you will be counted worthy of the kingdom of God, for which you are suffering. God is just: He will pay back trouble to those who trouble you and give relief to you who are troubled, and to us as well. This will happen when the Lord Jesus is revealed from heaven in blazing fire with his powerful angels. He will punish those who do not know God and do not obey the gospel of our Lord Jesus. They will be punished with everlasting destruction and shut out from the presence of the Lord and from the majesty of his power on the day he comes to be glorified in his holy people and to be marveled at among all those who have believed.

Time frame. This passage foretells the second coming of Christ followed by his judgment of the wicked and the saints' worship and awe before his majesty.

Setting. Paul is proud of the Thessalonians' persistence while suffering persecutions (v. 4). Because of this persistence their assurance of salvation is strengthened (v. 5). Moreover, the apostle reminds them that God is just and will show his justice in two ways. First, in retribution he will give the believers' oppressors the punishment they deserve. Second, he will deliver his people in Thessalonica (vv. 6-7).

Paul anticipates that his readers will ask when God will do these things, and replies, "This will happen when the Lord Jesus is revealed from heaven in blazing fire with his powerful angels" (v. 7). At Christ's second coming he will give relief to Christians and punish their persecutors. Paul describes those heading for judgment as "those who do not know God and do not obey the gospel of our Lord Jesus" (v. 8). The wicked are condemned for their ignorance of God, manifested in rejection of the message of salvation.[26]

Teaching. Within this context Paul describes the fate of the lost: "They will be punished with everlasting destruction" (v. 9). The word *destruction*, considered by itself, could mean annihilation. In this setting, however, it signifies eternal punishment. I say this for two reasons.

First, the expression "*everlasting* destruction" denotes the never-ending devastation of the unsaved in hell. Contrary to annihilationist claims, "*everlasting* destruction" is a cumbersome way to denote the obliteration of the wicked. If extinction were meant, why not just say "destruction?"[27] The everlasting destruction of 2 Thessalonians 1:9 is not to be taken as indicating extinction of being. Instead, as Leon Morris notes, it expresses "the loss of all that is worthwhile, utter ruin."[28] And the adjective *everlasting* qualifies the "destruction" indicating that it will not end.[29]

Second, the latter part of 2 Thessalonians 1:9 supports traditionalism rather than annihilationism. Paul writes: "They will be punished with everlasting destruction and shut out from the presence of the Lord and from the majesty of his power on the day he comes to be glorified in his holy people and to be marveled at among all those who have believed" (vv. 9-10). Here we learn what "everlasting destruction" entails—the wicked being forever excluded from the gracious presence of the Lord. This cannot be annihilation, for their separation presupposes their existence. I will amplify this point in the following section.

Annihilationist interpretation. According to Fudge, 2 Thessalonians 1:9 teaches annihilationism for three reasons: "everlasting destruction" means obliteration, the verse does not require conscious unending torment, and Paul has Old Testament background in mind. Let's examine these three reasons.

Fudge seeks to explain the adjective *everlasting* in Paul's expression "everlasting destruction" (2 Thess 1:9):

> The punishment is *aionios* in both senses. It is "eternal" in quality since it belongs to the Age to Come. It is "everlasting" in quantity since it will never end. It is not only inescapable; having once occurred, it is also irreversible. . . . We suggest that this "everlasting destruction" also is the unending result of an action or process of destroying, not the process or action itself. However short or long may be the time of the destroying, a point on which Scripture maintains an awesome and mysterious silence, its results are clear. The wicked, once destroyed, will never be seen again.[30]

Fudge appeals to word study in an attempt to reconcile this passage with annihilationism. His attempt fails for two reasons. First, he claims that "everlasting destruction" signifies an irreversible annihilation. But as stated above it trivializes Paul's words to understand "everlasting destruction" as meaning that once God exterminates the ungodly, he will never recreate them.

Second, Fudge's explanation founders on the second part of verse 9. Paul writes concerning the lost, "They will be punished with everlasting destruction and shut out from the presence of the Lord and from the majesty of his power." How does Fudge explain these words? He writes that everlasting destruction "will also remove the wicked away from his presence for ever." In a footnote Fudge explains:

1. God's presence will fill all that is, in every place.
2. The wicked will not be in his presence.
3. Therefore the wicked will no longer exist.[31]

That is, because God is everywhere, to be separated from his presence means to be nonexistent.

This argument is based on a faulty understanding of God's presence in

2 Thessalonians 1:9-10. The presence of God referred to there is not his general omnipresence. If it were, separation from his omnipresence would mean nonexistence. Rather, the verse refers to Christ's revealing to his people his special presence as King. That is why Paul says that the unsaved are "shut out from the presence of the Lord and from *the majesty of his power.*"

Scot McKnight correctly interprets "everlasting destruction" and "shut out from the presence of the Lord":

> The emphasis here is on the nature of that final judgment: it is eternal, it is destructive, and it excludes one from the presence of God. Eternal separation from God is the essence of God's punishment on the wicked, as eternal fellowship with God is the essence of God's final deliverance of the faithful. But separation from God's presence must be defined as nonfellowship, not annihilation. In other words, it could be argued that since God is omnipresent, then banishment from his presence means extinction. It is more likely, however, that Paul has in mind an irreversible verdict of eternal nonfellowship with God. A person exists but remains excluded from God's good presence.[32]

Fudge advances two more reasons why he understands 2 Thessalonians 1:9 as teaching annihilationism:

> Nothing in the language here requires conscious unending torment. Repeatedly, however, Paul's words, inspired by the Holy Spirit, send us to the former Scriptures, where the doom of sinners is made clear. They will perish, be destroyed, be burned up, be gone for ever.[33]

Fudge's second reason for maintaining that 2 Thessalonians 1:9 teaches annihilationism is that "nothing in the language" of that verse "requires conscious unending torment." This is simply a statement of denial and not an explanation of the verse. And I strongly disagree with his conclusion. The verse, taken in its context, requires eternal conscious punishment, as I have shown.

Fudge's third reason is to claim that Paul (in 2 Thess 1:9) points his readers to Old Testament texts that teach the annihilation of the ungodly. This is a favorite strategy of annihilationists. Confronted by a New Testament passage difficult to reconcile with their theology, they say that the passage points to the Old Testament, which, they maintain, clearly teaches annihilationism. But this doesn't explain the meaning of 2 Thessalonians 1:9; instead it diverts readers' attention away from the passage at hand. Moreover, as I have shown earlier in this chapter and elsewhere, the Old Testament does not teach annihilationism.[34]

I conclude that when Paul writes that the unsaved, "will be punished with everlasting destruction and shut out from the presence of the Lord and from the majesty of his power," he means that they will endure never-ending ruin in separation from the joy of King Jesus.

The Seventh Footing: The Punishment of Eternal Fire

Passage. The seventh footing under the foundation of the house of traditionalism is Jude 7.

> In a similar way, Sodom and Gomorrah and the surrounding towns gave themselves up to sexual immorality and perversion. They serve as an example of those who suffer the punishment of eternal fire.

Time frame. Jude speaks of human beings' final condemnation (v. 4), even "the punishment of eternal fire" (v. 7), and of evil angels' "judgment on the great Day" (v. 6). Plainly, these words pertain to the Last Judgment and beyond.

Setting. Jude starts his letter by stating that although he wanted to write about salvation, he was compelled to exhort his readers to fight for the Christian faith (Jude 3). Why did Jude change his purpose for writing? Because false teachers had "secretly slipped in among" his audience and were spreading heresy and promoting ungodliness (v. 4).

In this charged atmosphere Jude assures his readers that the heretics will not escape God's judgment but will suffer condemnation. He points out three examples of God's act of punishing rebels in the Old Testament. First, Jude recalls that after God delivered the Israelites from Egyptian bondage, he destroyed in the wilderness those who were disobedient (see Num 26:64-65).

Second, Jude reminds his audience that God has incarcerated the rebellious angels.[35] "These he has kept in darkness, bound with everlasting chains for judgment on the great Day" (v. 6). These angels, now imprisoned, await a worse fate on judgment day: the fire of Gehenna (see Mt 25:41).

Third, Jude cites the classic Old Testament case of God's judgment—that of Sodom and Gomorrah. The inhabitants of these cities practiced the "per-

version" of homosexuality. In response God made an "example" of them
(Jude 7). Genesis provides the details: "The LORD rained down burning sulfur on Sodom and Gomorrah. . . . Thus he overthrew . . . all those living in
the cities—and also the vegetation in the land." This judgment was so thorough that the next morning Abraham looked down toward the cities and
"saw dense smoke rising from the land, like smoke from a furnace." Thus
"God destroyed the cities of the plain" (Gen 19:24-29).

Teaching. Recalling God's destruction of the people of Sodom and
Gomorrah, Jude explains, "They serve as an example of those who suffer
the punishment of eternal fire" (Jude 7). Jude regards eternal fire as a punishment, even as the Lord Jesus had when he warned of the "eternal punishment" of "eternal fire" (Mt 25:41, 46).

What does Jude mean when he says Sodom and Gomorrah "serve as an
example of those who suffer the punishment of eternal fire"? Contrary to
annihilationist claims, Jude does not mean that the wicked will be literally
destroyed, as the ancient cities were. He does not intend for us to look to his
three examples of God's punishment of rebels to learn the mode of punishment. We are not to insist that the Israelites' death in the wilderness (v. 5),
the evil angels' imprisonment (v. 6) or the people of Sodom and Gomorrah's
incineration with fire from heaven (v. 7) serve as exact models of the final
fate of the lost. Rather, these are instances of temporal judgment that illustrate the inevitability of God's punishing the ungodly.

Jude teaches that God's judgment of Sodom and Gomorrah furnishes an
earthly, temporal example of the final fate of the damned. The destruction
of Sodom and Gomorrah "became a proverbial object-lesson of God's vengeance on sin: Is 1:9; Jer 23:14; Ezek 16:48-50; Amos 4:11; . . . Mt 10:15; 11:24;
Rom 9:29."[36] Even as God poured out his wrath on the rebellious cities of
old, so will he condemn to hell all who, like the heretics in Jude's day, are
finally impenitent. The fire from heaven that destroyed the cities prefigures
the "punishment of eternal fire," that is, the fire of hell that will forever torment the wicked.

British biblical scholar Richard J. Bauckham concurs:

> The idea is that the site of the cities, . . . a scene of sulfurous devastation, pro-
> vided ever-present evidence of the reality of divine judgment. . . . According
> to Philo [a first-century Jewish writer] "even to this day the visible tokens of

the indescribable disaster are pointed out in Syria—ruins, cinders, brimstone, smoke and murky flames which continue to rise from the ground as from a fire still smoldering beneath." Jude means that the still-burning site of the cities is a warning picture of the eternal fires of hell.[37]

Annihilationist interpretation. Fudge understands Jude 7 ("they serve as an example of those who suffer the punishment of eternal fire") differently. For at least two reasons he thinks Jude portrays the fate of Sodom and Gomorrah as an example of final annihilation. First, he argues that the word translated "example" (Greek *deigma*) here means "sample." God's judgment of the ancient cities is a sample of the judgment of hell; as they were consumed by fire, so the wicked will be consumed in hell.

This is an unlikely understanding of Jude's words. The word *example* (*deigma*) in Jude 7 and words related to it do not consistently mean "sample" in the New Testament. Let's examine a few of the instances Fudge cites. Paul teaches that Jesus' cross "*made a* public *spectacle* of" the demons (Col 2:15). The word *deigmatizo* here means "expose, make an example of, disgrace," according to Bauer, Arndt and Gingrich's *A Greek-English Dictionary of the New Testament,* and does not connote "sample."[38] The meaning of the same verb in Matthew 1:19 is very similar. There Joseph plans to quietly divorce pregnant Mary because he "did not want *to expose her to public disgrace.*" *Example* here doesn't mean "sample."

Some of Fudge's examples may fit his thesis. One illustration: After washing his disciples' feet and telling them to do the same, Jesus says, "I have set you an *example* that you should do as I have done for you" (Jn 13:15). Some churches understand Jesus' word *example* as "sample" and practice foot washing. Most, however, take *example* in a more general sense and conclude that Jesus was telling us we should practice acts of humble service.

These New Testament usages of words related to the word *example* in Jude 7 do not always bear the sense of "sample." Still Fudge summarizes: "Nor does Jude say that Sodomites are a vague and general example of those who actually will suffer the punishment of eternal fire, but that they themselves exemplify that very punishment."[39] In fact, Jude says neither that the Sodomites are a "vague and general example" nor that they are a specific sample. He simply says that they are an example. A more natural interpretation than Fudge's, then, is that Jude uses Sodom and Gomorrah as an example of God's judgment of the wicked, parallel to the examples of the Israelites in the wilderness and the rebellious angels. Jude doesn't focus on the details of the judgment that these groups experienced; instead, he stresses the *fact* of God's judgment of them. He parallels the fire that God rained on the rebellious cities and the fire of hell, but he doesn't intend for us to go beyond that.

Fudge holds that Jude 7 teaches annihilationism for a second reason. He appeals to a parallel passage in 2 Peter 2:6, writing:

> The passage [Jude 7] defines "eternal fire." It is a fire from God which destroys sinners totally and for ever. . . . Peter makes the same point unequivocally: God condemned these cities "by burning them to ashes, and made them an example of what is going to happen to the ungodly" (2 Pet 2:6).[40]

Taken in isolation it is possible to understand Peter's words as teaching annihilationism. Nevertheless, we ought not to do so. It is better to take Peter's words as more generally predicting the downfall of the wicked than to understand them as foretelling their precise fate—reduction to ashes. In fact, when we examine this passage alongside Jude 13 and the other nine passages that we have studied or will study, I am certain that Fudge overreaches by insisting on a literalistic interpretation of the words of Jude 7 and 2 Peter 2:6. Instead, we should allow the message of all ten passages to inform our view of the fate of the wicked. When we do, we conclude that as God brought cataclysmic judgment of fire upon the ancient cities, so will he terribly punish the wicked on the Last Day. Their fate is not annihilation but rather "the punishment of eternal fire," that is, never-ending torment in hell.

The Eighth Footing: Blackest Darkness Reserved Forever

Passage. The eighth passage upon which the traditional doctrine of hell is based is Jude 13: "They are wild waves of the sea, foaming up their shame; wandering stars, for whom blackest darkness has been reserved forever."

Time frame. At the beginning of his epistle Jude warns of false teachers "whose condemnation was written about long ago" (v. 4). "Woe to them!" he cries in verse 11. In the present passage he likens the heretics to "wandering stars, for whom blackest darkness has been reserved *forever*" (v. 13). He speaks of the final fate of the ungodly—their banishment from God's presence "forever" (v. 13).

Setting. Jude likes triads (groups of three). He starts his epistle by describing believers with a triad; they are "called . . . loved . . . and kept" (v. 1). He concludes it by pointing to God the Father's worthiness to receive praise through the Son "before all ages, now and forevermore" (a temporal group of three, v. 25). In between he frequently uses triads, including two in verses 12-13, in which he condemns the heretics.

In the triad of verse 12 Jude likens the false teachers to blemishes (or hidden reefs; there is debate over the word's meaning), shepherds and clouds. The apostates are out of place at Christian love feasts, since they are not Christians. In spite of their claiming to be shepherds of the flock, actually they care only for themselves, similar to the false shepherds of ancient Israel (compare Ezek 34:2). Additionally, "they are clouds without rain"; that is, they make big boasts but don't make good on them (v. 12).

In the second triad Jude compares the apostates to trees, waves and stars. They are trees that ought to produce great quantities of fruit but instead are "without fruit and uprooted" and therefore are "twice dead." This picture of trees means the same thing as the clouds metaphor: The heretics fail to deliver on their promises.

Next, Jude depicts the false teachers as "wild waves of the sea, foaming up their own shame." He probably has Isaiah 57:20 in mind: "But the wicked are like the tossing sea, which cannot rest, whose waves cast up mire and mud." Jude points to the fact that a stormy ocean churns up debris and deposits it in foam on the shore. In a similar way "the false teachers spread everywhere traces of their corruption and impurity."[41]

Teaching. Finally, when Jude calls the false teachers "wandering stars" (v. 13), he means they are, "stars which go astray from their God-ordained courses . . . misleading those who look to them for guidance."[42] Although the teachers claim to be spiritual luminaries who bring great light to the congregation, they are really blind guides. They do not know the way to eternal life themselves, and consequently they lead astray all who follow their spiritual counsel.

At the Last Judgment, however, God will put an end to their masquerade and will consign them to "the blackest darkness" (v. 13). How their fate differs from that of the righteous who "will shine like the brightness of the heavens . . . like the stars for ever and ever" (Dan 12:3)!

In spite of the heretical teachers' audacious claims, their destiny is certain. This is what Jude means when he says that the darkness of hell "has been reserved" for them (v. 13). Their fate is fixed. Furthermore, since it "has been reserved *forever,*" their being deprived of God's grace will know no end.

This conclusion is confirmed by a study of the expression translated "forever" here. It and its near equivalent occur twenty times in the New Testament.[43] When applied to the age to come these expressions mean "without temporal end." Representative examples will demonstrate this. The one guilty of blasphemy against the Holy Spirit "will *never* be forgiven" (Mk 3:29). Those who believe in Christ will live *"forever"* (Jn 6:51, 58; 1 Jn 2:17). God's righteousness (2 Cor 9:9) and word (1 Pet 1:25) endure *"forever."* Because the risen Christ "lives *forever"* (Heb 7:24), he is a high "priest *forever"* in the order of Melchizedek (Heb 5:6; 6:20; 7:17, 21). Plainly, when speaking of the coming age, these words mean "forever." This is also true in Jude 13. Instead of eternity in God's light, the destination of the false teachers is "blackest darkness . . . forever."

As in his use of fire imagery (v. 7), when Jude portrays hell in terms of darkness (v. 13), he follows Jesus' example (see Mt 8:12; 22:13; 25:30). Moreover, Jude not only uses these two images to describe hell; he also employs them both to teach that hell is endless. In verse 7 he speaks of "eternal fire," and in verse 13 he says that condemnation has been reserved for the heretics "forever." In emphasizing the eternity of hell, Jude again walks in the footsteps of Jesus who spoke of "eternal fire" (Mt 18:8; 25:41) and "eternal punishment" (Mt 25:46).

Annihilationist interpretation. In *The Fire That Consumes,* when discussing Jude 13 Fudge points his readers to his comments on 2 Peter 2:17. There he says:

> "Blackest darkness is reserved for them" (v. 17). Jude completes the simile, comparing the spurious teachers to "wandering stars, for whom blackest darkness has been reserved for ever" (Jude 13). Like the comparison with Sodom and the death of brute beasts, this figure also suggests and harmonizes with the idea of final, total extinction.[44]

When Fudge asserts that Jude's words suggest and harmonize with annihilationism, he errs. "Blackest darkness" is not a figure for extinction of being. Jesus uses the figure of darkness to depict hell, as I noted above. Each time Jesus uses it, he follows it with the same words:

> But the subjects of the kingdom will be thrown outside, into the darkness, where there will be weeping and gnashing of teeth. (Mt 8:12)

> Then the king told the attendants, "Tie him hand and foot, and throw him outside, into the darkness, where there will be weeping and gnashing of teeth." (Mt 22:13)

> And throw that worthless servant outside, into the darkness, where there will be weeping and gnashing of teeth. (Mt 25:30)

Consistently, the darkness imagery describes hell as a place "where there will be weeping and gnashing of teeth," that is, terrible suffering. Nowhere in the Bible does the image of darkness when applied to hell signify extinction of being. Fudge is incorrect when he claims that Jude 13 "suggests and harmonizes with the idea of final, total extinction." This is an attempt to persuade one's hearers by merely affirming one's position; no proof is given. An examination of the facts leads readers to the opposite conclusion. Being consigned forever to darkness does not indicate cessation of existence but existence away from God who is light and whose gracious presence alone is the source of eternal joy.

The Ninth Footing: "The Smoke of Their Torment Rises for Ever and Ever"
Passage. The ninth support for the foundation of the doctrine of everlasting hell is Revelation 14:9-11.

> If anyone worships the beast and his image and receives his mark on the forehead or on the hand, he, too, will drink of the wine of God's fury, which has been poured full strength into the cup of his wrath. He will be tormented with burning sulfur in the presence of the holy angels and of the Lamb. And the smoke of their torment rises for ever and ever. There is no rest day or night for those who worship the beast and his image, or for anyone who receives the mark of his name.

Time frame. The angel who flies in midair announces, "Fear God and give him glory, because the hour of his judgment has come" (Rev 14:7). This refers to the Last Judgment, because the punishment of the wicked described three verses later lasts forever: "The smoke of their torment rises for ever and ever. There is no rest day or night" (v. 11).

Setting. Two of the three most revealing biblical passages on hell are found in the last book of the Bible: Revelation 14:9-11 and 20:10-15 (the third is Mt 25:31-46). In Revelation 14:10 an angel announces the doom of idolaters: They will drink from the cup of God's wrath. This is a picture borrowed from the Old Testament. It is found, for example, in Jeremiah 25:15-16, where God commands the prophet: "Take from my hand this cup filled with the wine of my wrath and make all the nations to whom I send you drink it. When they drink it, they will stagger and go mad because of the sword I will send among them." This graphic image foretells God's judgment on the wicked nations: as strong drink causes people to stagger and fall, so God will bring down those who oppose him (cf. v. 27).

John paints a similar picture in Revelation 14:10. Idolaters "will drink of the wine of God's fury, which has been poured full strength into the cup of his wrath." That is, they will experience God's fierce anger. John's vocabulary (*fury, full strength* and *wrath*) points to the terror of falling into the hands of the living God.

Again John uses Old Testament language to describe hell; this time he appeals to God's judgment of Sodom and Gomorrah: the damned "will be tormented with burning sulfur" (Rev 14:10; see Gen 19:24). The annihilationists' claim that the main purpose of fire in judgment is to consume the wicked does not stand up to scrutiny in the light of this passage. To the contrary, fire's purpose is to inflict pain, as this text shows. This does not mean, however, that we must insist that hell consists of literal fire. Rather, "such language . . . must be taken as symbolical of a fearful and final reality which no man can describe."[45]

Furthermore, hell's torment takes place "in the presence of the holy angels and of the Lamb" (Rev 14:10). Although not many Christians conceive of Christ's being present in hell, he is there, as the word *Lamb* suggests. In fact, in twenty-seven of the twenty-eight times that John uses the word *lamb* in Revelation, it is a symbol denoting Christ (in Rev 13:11 it occurs in a simile). However, Christ does not bring grace and peace to hell, but "the wrath of the Lamb" (6:16).

Teaching. After describing the fate of the lost in terrible terms—they "will be tormented with burning sulfur" (Rev 14:10)—John extends that imagery: "The smoke of their torment rises for ever and ever" (v. 11). What is the import of these words? That the sufferings of the damned in hell are endless. I say this for two reasons.

First, the fact that John extends the fire imagery is significant. He speaks of "burning sulfur" in verse 10 and of "smoke" in verse 11. It is crucial to note that both the fire and smoke are tied to the pains of hell. The burning sulfur is God's instrument for punishing the wicked. And the smoke is "the smoke *of their torment.*" The fire and smoke, therefore, are parts of one picture depicting the suffering of the lost.

The smoke of the torment "rises for ever and ever." There is no mistaking the meaning of these words. The expression "for ever and ever" occurs thirteen times in Revelation and each time denotes eternity. The occurrences fall into several categories: God (either the Father, the Son or both) is to be praised "for ever and ever" (Rev 1:6; 5:13; 7:12); the risen Christ is alive "for ever and ever" (Rev 1:18); God the Father lives "for ever and ever" (Rev 4:9, 10; 10:6; 15:7); Christ will reign "for ever and ever" (Rev 11:15); the smoke of the burning city Babylon goes up "for ever and ever" (Rev 19:3); the devil, beast and false prophet will be tormented "for ever and ever" (Rev 20:10); and the saints will reign "for ever and ever" (Rev 22:5). In Revelation 14:11, therefore, when John writes, "the smoke of their torment rises for ever and ever," he means that the sufferings of the lost in hell will never end.

The second reason why I conclude that Revelation 14:11 teaches eternal torment is that this conclusion is confirmed by the rest of the verse. The text reads, "He will be tormented with burning sulfur. . . . And the smoke of their torment rises for ever and ever. There is no rest day or night" (vv. 10-11). In contrast to those "who die in the Lord" and "will rest from their labor" (Rev 14:13), the wicked will know no rest. They will suffer endlessly and never know the sweet repose afforded by the bosom of the Lord.

Annihilationist interpretation. Fudge isolates four images in this passage: 1) drinking from the cup of God's wrath, 2) being tormented with burning sulfur, 3) the smoke rising for ever, and 4) having no rest day or night. He contends, "The first three figures in the passage all either indicate or are agreeable to the idea that the suffering [of hell] finally ends in total extinction or desolation." He thinks that the fourth "possibly does as well."[46]

I will summarize and refute his arguments. Fudge insists that the image of "drinking from the cup of God's wrath," examined against its Old Testament background, signifies annihilation. Those who drink from this cup often experience "total and irreversible extinction." Furthermore, according to Fudge, John uses the image in the same way in Revelation 19:15-18. After Jesus treads the winepress of God's wrath, the birds of prey feast on the carcasses of God's vanquished foes.[47]

These arguments are not cogent. It is true that in the Old Testament God's enemies are sometimes destroyed after drinking the cup of his wrath. But this destruction is a premature physical death on earth, not annihilation in hell. Fudge's citation of Revelation 19:15-18 is no more convincing. The birds' eating of the corpses of God's foes, slain by the returning Christ, predates the wicked being cast into hell. In John's chronology the unsaved will be raised and consigned to hell after the Last Judgment (Rev 20:11-15). In short, Fudge tries to prove annihilationism by appealing to passages in both Testaments that speak of God's destruction of the wicked on earth rather than his punishment of them in hell. The image of drinking the cup of God's wrath is employed in Revelation 14:10 to teach neither annihilation nor eternal suffering. The verse simply says that the wicked drink from that cup, thereby indicating that they will experience God's wrath.

The second image that Fudge examines is that of "being tormented with burning sulfur." Fudge claims that "in the Bible the symbol derives its meaning from the annihilation of Sodom and Gomorrah, and the Old Testament uses it often to signify complete and total desolation."[48] He implies that it signifies the same thing in Revelation 14:11. My answer is similar to that for the last figure of speech. The inhabitants of Sodom and Gomorrah, along with other Old Testament characters who suffered a similar fate, were not annihilated after being raised from the dead and punished in hell. Their annihilation occurred on the earth. That is, God punished them with physical death; the passages do not speak of spiritual death in hell. John does not use the image of being tormented with burning sulfur to teach annihilation—quite the opposite, as a study of the next image reveals.

The third image, that of the smoke rising forever, also indicates annihilation, according to Fudge. He points to the function of the smoke after God's destruction of Sodom and Gomorrah, and in John's vision of the fall of Babylon (Rev 18). In both cases the smoke signifies that "the conscious torment is past; the reality of its destruction continues; the smoke is its silent but powerful witness (cf. Rev 19:3)."[49] Although this is the customary way in which annihilationists handle this image, their argument is not sound. First, the destruction of Sodom is not annihilation in hell; it is a case of God's wiping out the lives of the ungodly on earth. Second, Revelation 19:3 does say of burned Babylon, "The smoke from her goes up for ever and ever." This differs from Revelation 14:11 in two ways. Revelation 19:3 pictures God's burning of a city *on earth* (similar to Sodom). Revelation 14:11 pictures God's tormenting of unsaved individuals *in hell* with burning sulfur. The second difference is that Revelation 14:11 says something that 19:3 does not: "And the smoke *of their torment* rises for ever and ever." This is not smoke testifying to the obliteration of the wicked. It is "the smoke of their torment" rising eternally, denoting that their being "tormented with burning sulfur" will never cease.

Fourth, Fudge argues that "having no rest day or night" (v. 11) is compatible with annihilationism. He approvingly quotes an annihilationist writer who holds that these words suggest that there will be "no break or intermission in the suffering of the followers of the Beast, while it continues; but in themselves they do not say that it will continue for ever."[50] This quotation is technically true if we consider the words in isolation from the sentence that precedes them. But surely this is no way to interpret the Bible. Here, once again, is the text of verse 11 in full:

He will be tormented with burning sulfur in the presence of the holy angels and of the Lamb. And the smoke of their torment rises for ever and ever. There is no rest day or night for those who worship the beast and his image, or for anyone who receives the mark of his name.

It is illegitimate to sever the words "There is no rest day or night" from their context. And in context their meaning is plain. The unsaved in hell will suffer punishment at the hands of God—they "will be tormented with burning sulfur" (v. 10). This suffering will never end—"the smoke of their torment rises for ever and ever" (v. 11). And the wicked will have no relief from this torment—"There is no rest day or night" (v. 11).

I conclude then that Revelation 14:9-11 teaches that hell entails eternal conscious torment for the lost.

The Tenth Footing: The Lake of Fire

Passage. The tenth foundational passage for traditionalism is Revelation 20:10, 14-15.

> And the devil, who deceived them, was thrown into the lake of burning sulfur, where the beast and the false prophet had been thrown. They will be tormented day and night for ever and ever. . . . Then death and Hades were thrown into the lake of fire. The lake of fire is the second death. If anyone's name was not found written in the book of life, he was thrown into the lake of fire.

Time frame. These verses surround the most famous Last Judgment passage in the Bible: Revelation 20:11-13. Here God sits on his great white throne and assigns resurrected human beings to their eternal destinies. Verse 10 depicts the devil being thrown into the lake of fire to suffer eternal torment (v. 10). Verses 14-15 speak of unsaved human beings suffering the same fate.

Setting. The lake of fire, which plays a prominent part in this passage, is first mentioned in Revelation 19:20. There the returning Christ strikes down the human armies ranged against him and incapacitates two of his three major foes: "But the beast was captured, and with him the false prophet." We next learn of their fate, "The two of them were thrown alive into the fiery lake of burning sulfur."

Teaching. When we turn to Revelation 20:10, we find the beast and the false prophet still in the lake of fire. Now, however, God's third major foe, the devil, joins them. "And the devil, who deceived them, was thrown into the lake of burning sulfur, where the beast and the false prophet had been thrown." God's three enemies, then, have been cast into hell. How long will their punishment last? John specifies, "They will be tormented day and night for ever and ever." This text unequivocally teaches that the devil, the beast and the false prophet will endure eternal torment.

Next John sees God seated as king and judge on "a great white throne." John creates a mood of awesome majesty by painting a picture of the earth and sky running away from God. The vision continues with "the dead,

great and small, standing before" the majestic One (Rev 20:11-12). That
these are the resurrected dead is plain from the following verse in which
John says that the sea, death and Hades gave up the dead that were in them
(v. 13). Because the Bible never speaks of the sea containing departed souls,
this must be a reference to the resurrection of the bodies of those who died
at sea. In addition, "death and Hades gave up the dead that were in them."
Since Hades here signifies the grave, John means that God will raise those
who were buried. The term *death* covers any omitted from the categories of
those dying at sea or buried. John therefore means that God will raise *all* of
the dead.

Notice that John speaks of hell from the vantage points of divine sovereignty and human responsibility. God's sovereignty is evident in the concept of "the book of life." This is the register of the city of God in which all
of God's elect are enrolled. John explains, "If anyone's name was not found
written in the book of life, he was thrown into the lake of fire" (v. 15). John
also speaks in terms of human responsibility: "The dead were judged
according to what they had done. . . . Each person was judged according to
what he had done" (vv. 12, 13). God's justice is manifest when the wicked
reap the wrath of God for the sins they have sown.

John declares that the intermediate state gives way to the final one:
"death and Hades were thrown into the lake of fire" (v. 14). He reinforces
this idea when he equates the lake of fire with "the second death" (v. 14). As
death means the separation of the soul from the body, so the second death
denotes the ultimate separation of the ungodly from God's love. God
reunites the souls of the unsaved dead with their bodies to fit them for eternal punishment. Eternal life consists of knowing the Father and the Son for
ever (John 17:3); its converse, the second death, involves being deprived of
God's fellowship for ever.

A summary is in order. In the span of six verses John teaches that wicked
human beings will share the devil's fate. This fate, here called "the lake of
fire" and "the second death," entails being "tormented day and night for
ever and ever" (Rev 20:10).

Annihilationist interpretation. Fudge advances four arguments to show
that Revelation 20:10, 14-15 teaches annihilationism. First, the fact that the
beast and false prophet are cast into the lake of fire and are tormented there

(Rev 19:20; 20:10) signifies their annihilation. Because they are institutions and not persons, they are incapable of suffering "conscious, sensible pain." For them, therefore, the lake of fire does not symbolize eternal punishment but extinction of being.[51]

Fudge's argument will not hold. How does he know the identities of the beast and false prophet? He assumes that they are institutions, even "personal abstractions," and not persons, and concludes that they are incapable of suffering forever.[52] But Revelation 20:10 says that the devil, beast and false prophet "will be tormented day and night for ever and ever." Certainly the devil is a personal being capable of experiencing eternal pain. And it is important to allow Scripture to inform our identification of the beast and false prophet. D. A. Carson does and concludes, "the beast and false prophet are best thought of as *recurring* individuals, culminating in supreme manifestations of their type, rather than mere symbols that cannot experience pain."[53] It is astonishing that Fudge interprets the words "they will be tormented day and night for ever and ever" (v. 10) to indicate annihilation.

Fudge's second argument is that in the case of death and Hades being cast into the lake of fire, the lake means annihilation—indeed, it "can mean nothing else." Fudge explains, "Death itself will die. What sense does it make to say, 'separation will be separated?' But what a powerful thought it is that 'annihilation will be annihilated!' "[54]

This argument on close inspection is also unconvincing. The way to determine the meaning of the expression "death and Hades" (or of any other expression) is to study its usage in context. Let's examine the four occurrences of the expression in Revelation. In the first instance the risen and glorified Christ says, "I hold the keys of death and Hades" (Rev 1:18). He means that he has absolute authority over the realm of death and the grave. The second occurrence concerns the opening of the fourth seal of the scroll of God's judgment. There death and Hades, pictured as a rider on a pale horse, "were given power" to kill "a fourth of the earth" (Rev 6:8). Here again *death* and *Hades* signify "death" and "the grave."

It is the same for the last two occurrences, in Revelation 20:13-14. Death and Hades giving up the dead in them parallels the sea giving up the dead in it (v. 13). This means that all the dead are raised: those who died at sea, those who were buried and those whose bodies were disposed of in any other way. When John says, therefore, that death and Hades are thrown into the lake of fire (Rev 20:14), he means that even death and the grave yield to the final state of affairs. The situation of lost humans' bodies after death and before resurrection now gives way to their final situation—they are raised from the dead and sent to their final doom.

John says nothing about the dead being annihilated. When Fudge speaks of annihilation being annihilated, he commits two errors. First, death and the grave do not constitute annihilation; the Bible teaches the continued existence of the immaterial part of human beings after death and before the resurrection of the body (see Lk 16:22-29; 23:42-43; 2 Cor 5:6-8; Phil 1:21-23; Heb 12:23; Rev 6:9). In this regard death involves separation of the soul (or the spirit) from the body. Fudge's second error is his insistence that being thrown into the lake of fire constitutes final annihilation. To the contrary, for the devil and human beings alike it means eternal torment (Rev 20:10, 14-15).

Third, Fudge argues that when John says that the lake of fire is "the second death" (Rev 20:14; 21:8), he intends for us to allow the second expression to define the first. "In other such expressions throughout Revelation, the second term used interprets the first. . . . On this pattern 'lake of fire' is the expression to be defined; 'second death' is the clearer meaning."[55] And it signifies annihilation.

At times in Revelation expressions that use *is* or *are* employ the term following the verb to define the one preceding. But such expressions do not always constitute definitions. I will cite one example: "the Lord God Almighty and the Lamb *are* its temple" (21:22).[56] It would be incorrect to claim that *temple* defines what God and the Lamb are. The verb *are* (the Greek actually has *is*, the exact form in Rev 20:14; 21:8) here means "constitutes."

Fudge even concedes, "Such a formal observation is not conclusive." It is surprising then that later on the same page he writes:

> Traditionalist authors always read the equation [in] the other direction, as if it said "the second death" (which is indefinite) is "the lake of fire" (which is clear). In fact, however, John says that "the lake of fire" (his symbol) is "the second death" (a clearer reality). Because John's statement is so clear, writers

who hold to everlasting conscious torment are very careful to contradict what
it seems to say.[57]

Fudge thus contradicts himself. Is the pattern "not conclusive" or "so
clear"? In fact, the pattern does not hold in this case because such an interpretation cuts against the grain of the immediate context, the flow of Revelation 20. In verse 10 John foretells the devil's being cast into the lake of fire
and indicates what the lake of fire entails: never-ending torment. Four
verses later he speaks of humans being thrown into the same lake of fire.
This is in keeping with Jesus' words to unsaved people, "Depart from me,
you who are cursed, into the eternal fire prepared for the devil" (Mt 25:41). I
conclude that Fudge's appeal to word order in the expression, "The lake of
fire is the second death," to make it fit annihilationism is an evasion of the
teaching of Revelation 20.

Fourth, Fudge urges in defense of annihilationism the argument that
Revelation 20:14-15 never says that human beings are tormented for ever
and ever.[58] Technically, this is correct, but it is a case of straining out the gnat
and swallowing the camel. The devil's banishment into the lake of fire
involves eternal punishment (Rev 20:10). When four verses later human
beings are cast into the same lake of fire, does it mean annihilation for
them? If so, then why hasn't John informed his readers of the change in
meaning? Because there is no change in meaning; the lake of fire means
everlasting torment for them too.

Conclusion

This concludes our inspection of the ten footings supporting the foundation
of the house of traditionalism. That foundation proves to be solid for at least
four reasons. First, all ten passages speak of hell and not just of temporal
punishments as do many passages used in annihilationist arguments. Second, contextually considered, the passages teach eternal conscious punishment. We did not jump from text to text to avoid the thrust of these ten
passages. Instead, we examined them in their contexts. Third, we endeav-
ored to draw the teachings about hell out of each passage rather than reading ideas into the texts. As a result, we saw that the case for traditionalism is
very strong—passage after passage interpreted in normal fashion teaches
that hell consists of endless torment. Fourth, in each passage we contrasted

traditionalism with Fudge's conditionalism. Repeatedly, Fudge's arguments were shown to be weak. Consequently, evaluated biblically, traditionalism looks like a house built on rock and annihilationism like one built on sand.

In the light of this overwhelming evidence we are not surprised that the leading thinkers in church history were traditionalists, as we saw in the last chapter. And we won't be surprised to learn (in the next chapter) that traditionalism's correctness is confirmed by studying the ways it fits with other important biblical themes. By contrast, embracing annihilationism easily leads to other doctrinal errors, as we will see.

9

SEEING
THE BIG PICTURE
Theology

H*ELLISH OFFSPRING OF URBAN EARTHQUAKES, FIRE RAVAGES KOBE'S* Nagata Ward as darkness falls on the disaster's first day."[1] So ran a caption to a *National Geographic* photograph depicting the devastation of the great Hanshin earthquake that struck Kobe on January 17, 1995, the worst quake to hit Japan in seventy-two years. The article spelled out in two ways what took place that day. First, it took a detailed look at the effects of this awful tremor on the port city of Kobe: fifty-five hundred lives lost, three hundred thousand people displaced, and at least 100 billion dollars worth of damage. Second, complementing this detailed picture, the article took a broader view of the quake. A two-page layout illustrated how plates of the earth's crust collided to cause the movement of the Nojima Fault that in turn produced the earthquake. The inclusion of detailed and larger views helped readers see the whole picture.

At least in this case what is true for seismology is also true for theology: looking at detailed and broader views yields a fuller picture than is obtainable by observing either one alone. Thus far we have traveled the road to traditionalism and have inspected the foundation of the house of traditionalism. In so doing we have zoomed in on the doctrine of eternal conscious punishment in isolation from other beliefs. Now it is time to consider the bigger picture and view the house of traditionalism in its setting. It is time to study hell in relation to other doctrines.

One way to confirm truth and expose error is to consider theological ramifications of various beliefs. I will, therefore, offer further evidence that traditionalism is true and annihilationism false by discussing the implications of both for the Bible's teachings concerning human beings, Christ and last things.

Human Beings

It is customary for theologians to distinguish the present, intermediate and final states of human beings. The present state involves living in the body now. The intermediate state concerns the status of people after death and before resurrection. The final state follows the resurrection of the dead. When the writers of the Bible speak of heaven and hell, they deal mainly with the final state. The great hope for believers is the resurrection and subsequent bliss with God on the new earth. Overwhelmingly, when the Bible describes the fate of the lost, it speaks of their final situation—never-ending torment after resurrection.

Nevertheless, Scripture also teaches the existence of an intermediate state for both the just and the unjust. Human beings do not cease to exist when they die. Rather, death marks the unnatural separation of their material and immaterial parts. Their bodies decay in the grave, while their immaterial parts continue to exist. The New Testament affirms that at death souls go immediately to an interim heaven or hell awaiting the resurrection and Last Judgment.

For believers death means being "away from the body and at home with the Lord" (2 Cor 5:8). That is why our Lord said at his death, "Father, into your hands I commit my spirit" (Lk 23:46). That is why he promised the penitent dying thief, "Today you will be with me in paradise" (Lk 23:43). That is why Paul described departing the body to be with Christ as "better by far" than remaining in the body (Phil 1:23). And that is why Scripture speaks of deceased human beings as souls "under the altar" (Rev 6:9) and as "the spirits of righteous men made perfect" (Heb 12:23).

For unbelievers, however, death means being away from the body and

absent from the Lord, experiencing conscious suffering. The clearest biblical
passage on this subject is the parable of the rich man and Lazarus in Luke
16:19-31. Here Jesus depicts the reversal of fortunes in the next world of a
godly poor man named Lazarus and an ungodly rich man. In the present
world the rich man "was dressed in purple and fine linen and lived in luxury every day" (v. 19). By contrast the poor man lay at the rich man's gate
"covered with sores and longing to eat what fell from the rich man's table"
(vv. 20-21).

At death, however, their lots were reversed. The godly poor man found
repose at "Abraham's side," a Jewish way of referring to heaven (v. 22). But
the ungodly rich man found himself "in hell, where he was in torment" (v.
23). Abraham, speaking for God, summarizes the reversal of fortunes when
he says to the lost man, "In your lifetime you received your good things,
while Lazarus received bad things, but now he is comforted here and you
are in agony" (v. 25). Jesus leaves no doubt as to the terrible sufferings of the
deceased unsaved man. In the parable the man himself pleads for relief
because, in his words, "I am in agony in this fire" (v. 24). He fears for his
unsaved brothers, lest they too "come to this place of torment" (v. 28).

Plainly, Jesus uses the parable of the rich man and Lazarus as a vehicle to
teach that death involves separation of soul (or spirit) from body, with the
righteous and wicked immediately experiencing bliss or pain, respectively.
In *Interpreting Parables*, the most significant book on parables penned by an
evangelical scholar in recent years, Craig Blomberg wisely counsels that
readers should derive one point for each major character in a parable. His
summary of the teaching of the parable of the rich man and Lazarus merits
quotation:

> (1) Like Lazarus, those whom God helps will be borne after their death into
> God's presence. (2) Like the rich man, the unrepentant will experience irre-
> versible punishment. (3) Through Abraham, Moses, and the prophets, God
> reveals himself and his will so that none who neglect it can legitimately pro-
> test their subsequent fate.[2]

In this parable, therefore, Jesus affirms the existence of an intermediate
state after death for the people of God and for the wicked. After death the
latter endure torment and agony (Lk 16:23-25, 28).

Edward Fudge, because of his view of the way in which human beings are constituted, denies the existence of the intermediate state. It is helpful at this juncture to consult the best recent book treating the Bible's teaching on life after death, John Cooper's *Body, Soul and Life Everlasting*. Cooper lists three views held by evangelicals as to what happens to human beings after death, only two of which concern us: the intermediate state/resurrection view and the extinction/re-creation view.[3]

The first is the view that I affirmed above: there is an intermediate state into which the immaterial parts of human beings pass at death, only to be reunited with their resurrected bodies at the last day. This, because of Scripture's clear teaching, is the historic view of the Christian church. The second, the extinction/re-creation view, holds that at death human beings cease to exist and that the resurrection of the dead involves their re-creation. Although he uses different terminology, it is evident from his book *The Fire That Consumes* that Fudge subscribes to this view.

Fudge admits that belief in the immortality of the soul is the main current in church history. He, however, favors another view: "Crisscrossing all of this flows the stream of Christian mortalism. . . . This understanding appears as the sparkling water of pristine Christianity."[4] He defines mortalism as "the belief that according to divine revelation the soul does not exist as an independent conscious substance after the death of the body."[5] This view is reflected on many pages of *The Fire That Consumes*. Indeed, Fudge even claims that Jesus' human nature ceased to exist when he died on the cross, as we will see in the next section.

Fudge denies that there is any connection between annihilationism and belief in mortalism. He can show that there is not a necessary connection between the two, since not all annihilationists are mortalists. But normally the two beliefs go together. Fudge himself argues for annihilationism on the basis of mortalism. He does this when he comments on John's words, "Then death and Hades were thrown into the lake of fire. The lake of fire is the second death" (Rev 20:14). Traditionalists have committed a double error, according to Fudge. They have understood physical death as meaning separation of soul from body and the second death as involving eternal conscious separation from God. Instead, when commenting on death being thrown into the lake of fire, Fudge insists, "What a powerful thought it is that 'Annihilation will be annihilated'!"[6]

Fudge remarks regarding Jude 7, "There is no biblical hint that Sodom and Gomorrah's inhabitants presently endure conscious torment; several passages, in fact, make a point of their abiding extinction."[7] Because they are a sample of "those who suffer the punishment of eternal fire," Fudge concludes that ultimately the lost will be annihilated. To summarize, Fudge argues for annihilationism (in Rev 20:14 and Jude 7) on the basis of his view that death means extinction of being rather than separation of soul from body.

But this is an error. I say this because the seven passages cited above teach the survival of the soul after death (2 Cor 5:8; Lk 23:44, 46; Phil 1:23; Rev 6:9; Heb 12:23; Lk 16:19-31). Study of these texts should give annihilationists pause. And further theological reflection should do the same. The intermediate state/resurrection view demonstrates the continuity of personal identity. The same person who dies lives on without the body and will one day be reunited in body and soul in the resurrection of the dead. The extinction/re-creation view, however, encounters serious difficulties in maintaining personal identity at the resurrection. In what sense is a human being who dies and ceases to exist the same person as the one who is re-created by God at the resurrection? As John Cooper shows, advocates of the extinction/re-creation view do not claim to be able to prove continuity of personhood between the person who dies and the one who is raised; the best they can do is argue for the possibility of continuity of personal identity.[8]

Christ

Second, traditionalism correctly correlates orthodox belief in Christ's person and work with belief in hell. Advocates of annihilationism who claim that Christ was annihilated when he died on the cross, however, commit a grave christological error.

The traditional understanding of the punishment of hell includes two elements: separation from God (*poena damni*, the punishment of the damned) and the positive infliction of torments in body and soul (*poena sensus*, the punishment of sense). Jesus suffered the punishment of hell for sinners. That he endured separation from the Father's love is evidenced by his cry, "My God, my God, why have you forsaken me?" (Mt 27:46). On Calvary's cross Jesus also endured God's wrath. In Gethsemane Jesus was deeply grieved at the prospect of drinking the cup of God's wrath (Jer 25:15). This is why he thrice asked the Father, "If it is possible, may this cup be taken from me" (Mt 26:39; compare Mt 26:42, 44). On the cross, then, the Son of God suffered the pains of hell: separation from God and the positive infliction of torments in body and soul.

Scripture presents Christ in his death as making a substitutionary atonement for his people (Rom 3:25-26; Gal 3:13; Col 2:13-14). This means he died in their place and bore the punishment that they deserved. This does not mean, however, that he literally endured never-ending punishment. If he had, he would be on the cross forever and wouldn't be able to save anyone. Instead, he suffered the equivalent of eternal punishment; his temporal anguish was equal to the eternal condemnation due sinful human beings. How can this be? Perhaps the most obvious starting point for solving this difficulty is the observation that the Christ who suffered was neither sinful nor merely a human being. When Jesus endured the wrath due sinful humanity, it was as the incarnate God-man; when by virtue of his human nature he suffered separation from his Father's love, it was as the eternal Son of God who had become human; when he bore the penalty of our sins, it was as the sinless substitute, whose own life merited the exact opposite of God's wrath. In light of such considerations it is not surprising that Jesus could have borne on the cross what sinful, rebellious human beings can only bear in hell forever. In other words, because of the infinite dignity of Christ's person, his sufferings, though finite in duration, were of infinite weight on the scales of divine justice (much as his righteousness, though displayed during his incarnation over a finite period, is of infinite weight). As God incarnate, Jesus was capable of suffering in six hours on the cross what we can suffer only over an infinite period of time.[9]

By contrast, Fudge holds that Jesus was annihilated in his death. In fact, Fudge devotes a three-page discussion in his book to the thesis: "Jesus' Death Involved Total Destruction."[10] Here he quotes approvingly James Dunn's statement, "Man could not be helped other than through his [Jesus'] annihilation."[11] Fudge marshals what he regards as impressive biblical evidence for the conclusion that Jesus was annihilated:

The Bible exhausts the vocabulary of dying in speaking of what happened to
Jesus. He "died for our sins" (1 Cor 15:3). He laid down his "life [psyche]" (Jn
10:15). He was destroyed (Mt 27:20, KJV) or killed (Acts 3:15). Jesus compared
his own death to the dissolution of a kernel of wheat in the same passage that
mentions losing one's life (psyche) rather than loving it in order to find life
eternal (Jn 12:23-26). Jesus "poured out his life [psyche] unto death" and was
thus "numbered with the transgressors" (Is 53:12).[12]

None of these verses teaches that Jesus was annihilated. Fudge has to
cite the KJV to find even one verse that uses the vocabulary that, according
to annihilationists, teaches extinction. Matthew 27:20 (KJV) says, "But the
chief priests and elders persuaded the multitude that they should ask for
Barabbas, and destroy Jesus." The text doesn't say that Jesus was destroyed;
instead it indicates the Jewish leaders' intention to do away with him. Compare the way other translations render the end of the verse: "to put Jesus to
death" (NASB), "to have Jesus executed" (NIV) and "to have Jesus killed"
(NRSV). The only way Fudge finds annihilationism in these texts is by reading it into them. He concludes:

> Every scriptural implication is that if Jesus had not been raised, he—like
> those fallen asleep in him—would simply have perished (1 Cor 15:18). Scrip-
> tures such as 2 Timothy 1:10; Hebrews 2:14; Revelation 20:14 affirm that his
> resurrection reverses every such estimation of affairs, assuring us instead of
> the death of Death.[13]

Fudge, therefore, seeks to strengthen his case for annihilationism by
arguing that Jesus endured final punishment by being annihilated on the
cross. The systemic implications of such a view are enormous. Nothing less
than orthodox Christology is at stake. It is possible to understand Fudge's
claim that Jesus was annihilated in one of two ways: either the God-man
ceased to exist or his human nature ceased to exist. I have tried to be fair to
Fudge by asking him twice in private correspondence to explain his understanding of Jesus' annihilation. He refuses to endorse or deny either of the
two possibilities above. He affirms that Jesus truly died and was annihilated but won't specify if he believes that Jesus' humanity was annihilated
or that his whole person, deity and humanity, was annihilated. Fudge says
that he does not attempt to explain Jesus' annihilation but leaves it in the
realm of mystery. I confess astonishment that Fudge will not deny that the

God-man ceased to exist for three days. If Jesus the God-man was annihilated and thus ceased to exist between his death and resurrection, then the Trinity only consisted of two persons during that period of time. The Trinity would have been reduced to a Binity, or the resurrection of Jesus meant the re-creation of the second person of the Trinity. In that case, the second person of the Trinity would be a created being. Such conclusions are ruinous for the Christian faith because they compromise the doctrine of the Trinity. For the rest of this section I will assume that Fudge, although he is unwilling to say so, concurs with Edward White, who held that when Jesus died in crucifixion, his humanity was annihilated but not his divinity. Fudge approvingly cites White on this matter in the first edition of *The Fire That Consumes*.[14]

The definitive statement on the Bible's teaching concerning the person of Christ was made by the Council of Chalcedon in 451 in this formal confession of faith:

> In agreement, therefore, with the holy fathers, we all unanimously teach that we should confess that our Lord Jesus Christ is one and the same Son, the same perfect in Godhead and the same perfect in manhood, truly God and truly man, the same of a rational soul and body, consubstantial with the Father in Godhead, and the same consubstantial with us in manhood, like us in all things except sin; begotten from the Father before the ages as regards His Godhead, and in these last days, the same, because of us and because of our salvation begotten from the Virgin Mary, the Theotokos [bearer of God], as regards His manhood; one and the same Christ, Son, Lord, only-begotten, made known in two natures without confusion, without change, without division, without separation, the difference of the natures being by no means removed because of the union, but the property of each nature being preserved and coalescing in one prosopon [person] and one hypostasis—not parted or divided into two prosopa [persons], but one and the same Son, only-begotten, divine Word, the Lord Jesus Christ, as the prophets of old and Jesus Christ Himself taught us about Him and the creed of our fathers has handed down.[15]

The major ideas in this confession are a good summary of the Bible's teaching about Christ in John 1:1-18; Colossians 1:15-19; 2:9; Philippians 2:6-11; and Hebrews 1—2. The Word of God declares that as a result of the incarnation Jesus Christ is both truly God and truly man. He is one person with two natures, one divine and one human. These natures are not mixed together and are not separable. But if Fudge is right and Jesus was annihilated, then the conclusion of the Council of Chalcedon is wrong and Christ's natures were separated. John Cooper points out the disastrous implications of holding that Jesus was annihilated in his death:

> Now if the extinction—re-creation account of Jesus' resurrection is true, then the teaching of Chalcedon is false. The two natures of Christ are separable and were in fact separated between Good Friday and Easter Sunday. The human being Jesus completely ceased to exist. . . . So the divine-human person Jesus Christ did not exist for the interim. Only the nonincarnate Word, the wholly divine Son, the Second Person of the Trinity, existed during that time.[16]

Moreover, if Jesus were annihilated on the cross and his natures separated because his humanity ceased to exist, then his resurrection must involve another incarnation. This incarnation would differ from the first in that this time the Word would take to himself resurrected flesh. Notwithstanding, it would be a second incarnation.

I conclude then that traditionalism, not annihilationism, correctly integrates Christology with the doctrine of hell. Fudge's argument that Christ was annihilated does not strengthen the case for annihilationism; rather, it weakens it considerably. Indeed, to hold either that the God-man was annihilated on the cross or that Jesus' humanity was annihilated there brings one into conflict with orthodox Christology. Such a prospect ought to cause annihilationists to reexamine their views, for the Bible teaches that Christ did suffer the pains of hell, but not as they are conceived by annihilationists.

To provide a helpful vantage point from which to view the matters addressed so far in this chapter, I have adapted the following chart from the notes of my colleague, Professor David Clyde Jones:

A	B	C	D	E
truth	mistaken opinion	isolated error	systemic error	heresy

The chart illustrates that not all theological mistakes are of the same severity. All Christians hold some mistaken opinions. I would put into this category quibbles about minor details pertaining to church government and eschatology. At the other end of the spectrum is heresy—error so serious that holding it leads one to damnation. Heresy is denial of the cardinal doctrines of the faith, such as the deity of Christ. Between mistaken opinions and heresies are errors. These can be subdivided into a whole range from less to more serious errors. For our present purposes, however, one division will suffice: that between isolated errors and systemic ones. An isolated error is a theological mistake that does not affect other matters of faith. John Stott's tentative defense of annihilationism is a case in point. To the best of my knowledge, Dr. Stott does not combine belief in annihilationism with a denial of the intermediate state of human beings or with the view that Jesus was annihilated when he died.[17] Unfortunately, Edward Fudge does. So Fudge, unlike Stott, is involved in systemic error. His annihilationism adversely affects his stand on other points of Christian doctrine.

Unfortunately, both Stott and Fudge underestimate the rigor of God's punishment of the wicked, as the following section shows.

Last Things

The truthfulness of traditionalism is confirmed by the fact that it coheres with other biblical teachings. We have examined the doctrines of the intermediate state and of the person and work of Christ. Finally, we consider eschatology. Traditionalism teaches the historic Christian view of last things. By contrast, Fudge mixes annihilationism with a traditional Christian eschatology and thereby creates an unstable compound.

From the beginning the church has agreed on a general picture of end-time events, each element of which is plainly biblical: the second coming (2 Thess 1:6-10; Rev 19:11-16), the resurrection of the dead (Dan 12:2; Jn 5:28-29), the Last Judgment (Mt 25:31-46; Rev 20:10-15) and the eternal destinies of heaven and hell (Dan 12:2; Rev 20-22). I will refer to this order of future events as the biblical scenario of the end.

Evangelical annihilationists have a difficult task: they must try to combine two elements that do not go together: annihilationism and the biblical scenario of the end. They accept the final extinction of the wicked but must reject the annihilationism of someone like Bertrand Russell. Listen to Russell:

> I believe that when I die I shall rot, and nothing of my ego will survive. I am not young, and I love life. But I should scorn to shiver with terror at the thought of annihilation. Happiness is none the less true happiness because it

must come to an end, nor do thought and love lose their value because they are not everlasting.[18]

Russell's annihilationism, like that of the Jehovah's Witnesses, entails that human beings cease to exist at death. Fudge rejects this version of annihilationism because it precludes the biblical scenario of the end, described above.

However, by appending the obliteration of the wicked onto the biblical scenario of the end, Fudge creates severe theological problems. In the traditional scenario at the Last Judgment people are assigned to their destinies of heaven and hell. This is true for Fudge's scenario too, although he modifies the traditional picture when he defines hell as annihilation preceded by suffering. Fudge explains in his comments on the phrase "eternal destruction" in 2 Thessalonians 1:9:

> In keeping with the rest of the teaching of both Old and New Testaments, we suggest that this "eternal destruction" will be the penal suffering exactly suited to each degree of guilt by a holy and just God, but the penal suffering is not itself the ultimate retribution of punishment. There will be an act of destroying, resulting in a destruction that will never end or be reversed. The act of destroying includes penal pains, but they will end. The result of destruction will never be reversed and will never have an end.[19]

In other words, according to Fudge hell is penal suffering followed by the ultimate punishment, annihilation. But this is exactly where the problem creeps in. When this view of hell is affixed to the end of the biblical scenario of last things, annihilation does not constitute the ultimate punishment. Rather, annihilation would constitute the end of punishment. It would mean relief for the wicked in hell who are suffering for their sins.

Fudge skillfully presents annihilationism so as to satisfy many biblical requirements. He accepts the traditional eschatological scenario, right up to the point of eternal destinies. He affirms suffering for the unsaved in hell and thus upholds the biblical principle that there will be degrees of punishment in hell. But when he makes annihilation the caboose, he derails the whole train. For in spite of his claim to the contrary that cessation of being is the worst possible punishment, annihilation would bring an end to punishment. The wicked would be delivered from their terrible suffering and would experience the pains of hell no more. The ungodly in hell would like for annihilationism to be true, as Jonathan Edwards noted more than two centuries ago: "Wicked men will hereafter earnestly wish to be turned to nothing and forever cease to be that they might escape the wrath of God." Edwards further spoke the truth when he declared, "the Scripture is very express and abundant in this matter that the eternal punishment is in sensible misery and torment and not annihilation."[20]

Conclusion

In previous chapters we were tourists on the road to traditionalism and inspectors of the foundation of the house of traditionalism. In this chapter we have been spectators who viewed the house of traditionalism in its surroundings. We exchanged the zoom lens of our camera for a wide-angle lens. Instead of studying hell in isolation from other biblical teachings, we have connected the doctrine of hell with those teachings. Specifically, we studied hell in relation to the doctrines of human beings, Christ and last things. In so doing we saw that traditionalism "fits" with scriptural teachings on the intermediate state, the inseparability of Christ's two natures and the characteristics of final punishment. By contrast, Fudge's annihilationism introduces serious problems into each of these areas of theology. Fudge denies the intermediate state, which is so clearly taught in Scripture. He runs afoul of traditional Christology when he teaches that Jesus was annihilated. And he takes the sting out of the pains of hell by maintaining that they will come to an end.

This completes the presentation of my case for traditionalism. It is the historic view of the Christian church—and for good reason because it is abundantly taught in Scripture. And as we might expect of one aspect of God's truth, it coheres well with other biblical teachings. I plead with readers to carefully and prayerfully consider the evidence for traditionalism before they jettison this part of the Christian faith for the seemingly kinder and gentler view known as annihilationism.[21]

A Conditionalist Response to Traditionalism

Edward William Fudge

R OBERT PETERSON NOW HAS DONE HIS BEST TO DEFEND THE NOTION THAT God will keep sinners alive in hell forever to torture them without end. I have no doubt that he has done so as well as anyone of his persuasion might do. His case has three parts: (1) an endorsement by eleven other theologians, (2) an appeal to ten passages of Scripture, and (3) three rationalistic arguments involving other areas of systematic theology.

As for the first part of Peterson's case, I admit that these eleven theologians agree with his position. If he searched long enough, he might even find eleven hundred theologians on his side. His theory is not called the "traditionalist" view for nothing. It has been the majority opinion in most denominations for at least fifteen hundred years. I take that fact very seriously. It is not easy to step out away from such a crowd. Nor is it safe to do so—without sufficient biblical warrant.

I also grew up on the traditionalist view, and I fully expected to die holding it as well. It took a yearlong, exhaustive examination of the entire Bible on this subject to convince me that the majority is simply mistaken. If we ever begin to suppose that ecclesiastical tradition outweighs scriptural teaching in authority, Protestants ought all to line up and apologize to the pope of Rome. Evangelicals in particular claim to honor the final authority of Scripture. How we handle the topic of final punishment just might show whether we really mean those words or whether they are simply pious talk.

It was not my intention when we began writing this book to discuss the origin and history of the everlasting torture view. In my own presentation I simply walked with you through the Bible, asking what each portion of Scripture says about final punishment. We examined each section of biblical literature in turn, paying attention to its genre (history, poetry, prophecy and so on), context, message and use by writers of Scripture who came later. Since Peterson has appealed to the theologians, however, we must now take a quick stroll through church history.

The "road to traditionalism" is paved with many kinds of stones. Among those paving stones are pagan Greek philosophy, overreaction to theological error, Augustinian presuppositions, medieval caste-consciousness, Reformation politics and blind creedalism. In a moment I will invite you to look briefly at these various building materials that went into the road Peterson claims we all should take.

As for the second part of Peterson's case, I have already discussed his ten Scripture passages in the first part of this book—along with dozens of other biblical texts about which he is stone silent. Here too Peterson stands in the long train of traditionalist authors who for centuries have focused on a handful of proof texts, never letting the Bible interpret itself and completely ignoring the multitude of Scripture passages from Genesis through Revelation that flatly contradict their view. Peterson admits that several of his own proof texts seem to say that the wicked will truly perish, just as I have argued. Because he rules out that possibility to begin with, however, he has to engage in creative mental gymnastics to avoid their plain meaning. Although I see no need to repeat my earlier presentation, I will respond to some false charges, foolish accusations and other red herrings Peterson has scattered throughout his second section.

With regard to the third part of Peterson's case, I remind us all that systematic theology properly *follows* biblical exegesis; it does not *determine* it in advance. Although his rationalistic arguments from systematic theology can never establish what we ought to believe on the topic of final punishment, they might confuse some readers and prevent them from hearing what the Bible actually says. I will therefore respond briefly to the three issues Peterson raises and point out some theological implications of his view, including the way it distorts our understanding of the character of God.

The Road to Traditionalism

The writings of several second-century Christians have survived.[1] These Christians, sometimes referred to as the apostolic fathers, either knew the apostles or knew people who had known them. Interestingly, when the apostolic fathers wrote about the final destiny of the wicked, they almost always expressed themselves in biblical terminology. The unknown author of the *Didache*, for example, contrasts the way of "life" and the way of "death."[2] The *Epistle of Barnabas* contains a warning about "eternal death and punishment,"[3] stating that wicked people will "perish" along with the "Evil One."[4] Clement of Rome writes that transgressors "will be cut off," using the same Greek word Peter uses in Acts 3:23.[5] The author of 2 *Clement* quotes various warnings from Jesus as well as Isaiah's final prophecy about the worms and fire. He speaks of "eternal punishment"[6] and warns concerning "dreadful tortures in unquenchable fire."[7]

Ignatius of Antioch writes concerning "the wrath that is to come"[8] and the "unquenchable fire."[9] He contrasts the final fates of "life" and "death."[10] The martyr Polycarp, perhaps the best known of the apostolic fathers, repeats Scripture's warnings that the wicked will be raised and judged, but he goes no farther than that. A later work quotes Polycarp as speaking of "that fire of the coming judgment and eternal punishment."[11] The *Address to Diognetus* urges its pagan recipient to adopt the Christian attitude toward faith and suffering and to fear the "real death" that awaits those "condemned to the eternal fire which will punish unto the end those delivered to it."[12] All of this language mirrors the vocabulary of the Bible itself.

If the later church fathers had also confined themselves to biblical terms on this subject, we would probably not be having this discussion. Unfortunately, that is not what happened. Soon after the time of the apostolic fathers, certain converts from Greek philosophy, known as the apologists, brought into the church the pagan doctrine of the immortality of the soul.

The writers of the Bible never speak of the "immortality of the soul." Rather, Paul says that only God has inherent immortality (1 Tim 6:16) and that in the resurrection he will give bodily immortality to those who are saved (Rom 2:6-7; 1 Cor 15:53-54). According to the Genesis account God breathed the "breath of life" into Adam's nostrils of dust, and Adam *"became* a living soul" (Gen 2:7). The pagan theory of the immortality of the soul says that every human being has an invisible, immaterial part called the *psyche* or "soul," which can never die but will live forever. The traditionalist notion of everlasting torture in hell springs directly from that nonbiblical teaching.[13]

The converted Christian philosophers who brought this idea into the church did modify it somewhat in the process. Where their pagan counterparts said that the soul had always existed, the Christian philosophers said that God had created the soul. But when it came to the *destruction* of the soul, the apologists often spoke out of both sides of their mouths, just as many of their traditionalist descendants do today. They acknowledged that since God *created* the soul, he also had the power to *destroy* it if he wished to do so. Yet while they conceded that point in talking about humans, when they turned to discuss final punishment, they seemed to forget the concession they had already made. When explaining Jesus' warning that God "can destroy both body and soul in hell" (Matt 10:28), traditionalist authors from the beginning have reasoned as if God were *not* able to do that very thing, although when pressed on the point, they admit that he is able to do it.

It does no good for Peterson to deny that the traditionalist doctrine is built on the notion of the immortality of the soul. When we look at the writings of the first Christians to teach the traditionalist view, we see that they clearly based their doctrine on that very assumption. Peterson cannot avoid that fact by saying that the authors quoted Scripture to support their view. Yes, they quoted Scripture. They used such scriptural terms as *die, perish* and *destroy.* Then they denied that the soul would ever truly die, perish or be destroyed; they said instead that souls are immortal and will never die. So they interpreted the word *die* to mean that the wicked would never really die. They explained that *perish* means that the lost will never truly perish.

And they defined *destroy* in a way that would signify that the damned will never actually be destroyed but will live forever in torments that will never end.

This kind of logic is not simply an oddity of ancient history. As recently as the late nineteenth century, traditionalist authors unashamedly argued that souls are immortal and cannot be destroyed. William G. T. Shedd boldly writes:

> But irrepressible and universal as it is, the doctrine of man's immortality is an astonishing one, and difficult to entertain. For it means that every frail finite man is to be as long-enduring as the infinite and eternal God; that there will no more be an end to the existence of the man who died today than there will be of the Deity who made him. God is denominated "The Ancient of Days." But every immortal spirit that ever dwelt in a human body will also be an "ancient of days." ... Yes, man *must* exist. He has no option. Necessity is laid upon him. He cannot extinguish himself. He cannot cease to be.[14]

Although Shedd's statement contradicts numerous biblical affirmations and exhibits a human hubris that borders on blasphemy, Shedd is simply being true to his traditionalist heritage.

The stones of pagan Greek philosophy. The first Christian writer to expressly deny the final annihilation of the lost was Athenagoras (127-190), a Platonic philosopher who later became a Christian. Athenagoras writes that after this life, the wicked will live another life, "a worse one and in fire," for God has not made us "that we should perish and be annihilated."[15] But note carefully the basis on which Athenagoras reaches this conclusion. His conclusion is not based on Scripture, which he learned as a Christian. Rather, it is based on a pagan doctrine that he had learned earlier as a philosopher: the notion that every person has a soul that is inherently immortal and that can never die.[16] God "made man of an immortal soul and a body."[17] Therefore "man, who consists of the two parts, must continue for ever."[18]

It was Tertullian, the subject of one of Peterson's theological mile markers, who most successfully taught Christians to accept the immortality of the soul and who popularized the notion of everlasting torment based on that foreign doctrine. So zealous was Tertullian for the immortal soul that he devoted his second longest work, *De Anima,* to the subject.

Tertullian, who was born about A.D. 160, argues that when God breathed the "breath of life" into Adam, he gave humankind an immortal soul. More than that, claims Tertullian, a sister in his church actually saw a soul during a supernatural vision. "Not, however, a void and empty illusion," she reported, "but such as would offer itself to be even grasped by the hand, soft and transparent, and of an ethereal colour, and in form resembling that of a human being in every respect."[19]

Some things "are even known by nature," Tertullian writes, and "the immortality of the soul is held by many. . . . I may use, therefore, the opinion of a Plato when he declares, 'Every soul is immortal.'" [20] The soul does not even need saving, Tertullian argues, for it is "'safe' already in its own nature by reason of its immortality."[21] Because the soul is immortal, he concludes, it cannot be destroyed. Therefore, when Jesus warns that God is able to "destroy" both body and soul in hell, we should not think he means that God will actually destroy the soul, says Tertullian, but rather that God will torment it forever.[22] "We, however, so understand the soul's immortality as to believe it 'lost,' not in the sense of destruction, but of punishment, that is, in hell."[23] Tertullian thus denies that the soul can be destroyed, the very fate of which Jesus sternly warns. In this way the stones of pagan Greek philosophy began to pave the road to today's traditionalism.

The stones of over-reaction to theological error. Clement of Alexandria, like Tertullian of Carthage, based his arguments about the nature of hell on the supposed immortality of the soul. In his *Recognitions* Clement reasons like this:

> But if any persist in impiety till the end of life, then as soon as the soul, which is immortal, departs, it shall pay the penalty of its persistence in impiety. For even the souls of the impious are immortal, though perhaps they themselves would wish them to end with their bodies. But it is not so; for they endure without end the torments of eternal fire, and to their destruction they have not the quality of mortality.[24]

In another work Clement affirms that God's punishments in this life are intended to teach and to correct, and he raises the question of whether the punishments of hell might serve the same positive purposes.[25] Clement did not come right out and say that hell's fire purges souls and fits them for heaven, but he opened the door for his pupil Origen to raise that possibility.

Origen believed in the immortality of the soul, as had Clement, Tertullian and Athenagoras before him. God is just and good, Origen reasoned, and rational beings have absolute free will. Might not human souls therefore live and die and be purged time after time through a succession of eons, learning and improving as they go, until they finally are cleansed of sin and prepared to live with God?[26] Scholars argue about whether Origen intended to advance this idea as his own belief or whether he simply wanted to raise the question for discussion. However that might be, Origen's suggestion that even hell's fire would serve the constructive purpose of a good God was clearly a reaction against Tertullian's picture of a vengeful God who would create souls that could never die and would then torture some of them in hell forever.

Based on his belief that souls are immortal and cannot be destroyed, Tertullian had turned the Bible's fire that *consumes* into a fire that *tortures forever*. Origen also believed that all souls would live forever, but his view of God's goodness led him to reject Tertullian's theory and to suggest instead that hell's fire would *purify* those immortal souls and fit them to dwell with God. Their preconceived notion that souls must live forever kept both Tertullian and Origen from taking seriously Jesus' plain warning that God can destroy both body and soul in hell. Tertullian and Origen shared a common false assumption that they carried to opposing conclusions. The road to traditionalism was paved in part with stones of Origen's overreaction to Tertullian's theological error.[27]

The stones of Augustinian presuppositions. About A.D. 300 another African philosopher named Arnobius of Sicca wished to become a Christian. The bishop in his area hesitated to accept this man who had been his adversary, so Arnobius wrote *Adversus Gentes*, also called *Adversus Nationes* (*Against the Pagans*), to convince the bishop of his sincerity. In this work Arnobius devotes himself to a refutation of the pagan doctrine of the immortality of the soul. The very idea reeks with improper pride, Arnobius says. "If men either knew themselves thoroughly, or had the slightest knowledge of God, they would never claim as their own a divine and immortal nature."[28] The truth is that no one "but the Almighty God can preserve souls, nor is there any one besides who can give them length of days and grant to them also a spirit which shall never die, except he who alone is immortal and everlasting, and restricted by no limit of time."[29]

Arnobius's primary goal was neither to counter Tertullian's view of hell as the fire that tortures forever nor to discredit Origen's hypothesis of hell as the fire that purifies and redeems. His chief intention was to demonstrate the falsity of the pagan Greek notion of the immortality of the soul—a theory that took many forms in Arnobius's day just as it does today. Tertullian's and Origen's views of hell, though opposite from each other, both sprang directly from the theory of the immortality of the soul. Arnobius's work used logically destroyed the foundations of both those earlier views of hell. Interestingly, seventeen hundred years ago Arnobius began at the same point to which today's biblical scholars are rapidly moving. They are rediscovering the nonbiblical nature of the ancient teaching that some part of human beings is so inherently "deathless" that it will live forever, even apart from the gracious gift of God.

About fifty years after Arnobius wrote *Adversus Gentes,* Augustine of Hippo, known today as Saint Augustine, was born. His influence on Western Christianity is immeasurable. Traditionalist author Harry Buis says that Augustine's advocacy of the position that hell will be a place of unending conscious torment "tended to cause it to become the accepted doctrine of the church for the centuries that followed."[30] Edward B. Pusey, a leading traditionalist of the nineteenth century, acknowledged that Augustine "has, more than any other, formed the mind of our Western Christendom."[31] And Augustine, as Peterson rightly noted, agreed with Tertullian and others who said that God will keep the wicked alive in hell to torment them forever. Blessed with Augustine's endorsement, this already popular view quickly became unquestioned orthodoxy. This happened despite the fact that Augustine himself had once urged: "Do not follow my writings as Holy Scripture. When you find in Holy Scripture anything you did not believe before, believe it without doubt; but in my writings, you should hold nothing for certain."[32]

We would do well to listen to this advice from Augustine, particularly regarding the subject at hand. For like so many theologians both before him and since, the great Augustine read the biblical warnings about final punishment with another notion firmly implanted in his mind. That notion was the unscriptural doctrine of the immortality of the soul. This is apparent in Augustine's most extensive discussion of final punishment, found in book

21 of his famous work titled *The City of God*.[33]

In *The City of God* Augustine addresses pagan critics who scoff at his preaching concerning final punishment. His opponents have argued that hell cannot involve unending torment, because any human body capable of feeling pain is incapable of enduring pain forever without being destroyed. Augustine replies that there is a reality higher than the body that his critics are failing to take into account. Writes Augustine:

> That reality is the soul, without whose presence there would be neither life nor movement in the body. What is more, it is a reality that is susceptible of pain and *not susceptible of death*. Here, in fact, we have the reality which, conscious as it is of pain, is *immortal*. And it is this capacity for immortality *(already, as we know, inherent in everybody's soul)* which, in the world to come, will be present in the bodies of the damned.[34]

A little later Augustine repeats his underlying assumption in these words:

> If, then, there is any genuine argument connecting pain and death ... this argument would apply, if at all, to the death of the soul, since it is to the soul rather than to the body that pain pertains. But *the fact is that the soul*, which more truly feels pain than the body, *cannot die*. What follows is that there is no basis for arguing that ... because bodies in the future life are to be in pain, we therefore must believe that even in the future life they will die.[35]

Augustine's language concerning immortality differs from that of the Bible on three significant points. Augustine says that immortality belongs to (1) to souls (2) of the wicked (3) by creation. However, when Scripture speaks of immortality in connection with human beings, it always speaks (1) concerning the body, never concerning a separable soul or spirit; (2) of the saved, never the lost; and (3) in terms of resurrection, never concerning the natural or created state. People might wish to argue for the immortality of the lost, or the immortality of the soul, or immortality as a created or natural phenomenon, but they can support such arguments only with something other than the Word of God.

Although Augustine is clearly a mile marker on the road to traditionalism, he inadvertently answers in advance the common traditionalist quibble that says that total irreversible destruction would not constitute "eternal punishment." Augustine recognizes that the duration of punishment is not always determined by the length of time required for its execution. He is speaking about perpetual torment when he writes the following words, but these words apply equally well to the biblical picture of hell as the place where God will "destroy both body and soul" forever.

> Where a very serious crime is punished by death and the execution of the sentence takes only a minute, no laws consider that minute as the measure of the punishment, but rather the fact that the criminal is forever removed from the community of the living. And, in fact, this removal of men from mortal society by the penalty of the first death is the nearest parallel we have to the removal of men from the immortal communion of saints by the penalty of the second death. For, just as the laws of temporal society make no provision for recalling a man to that society, once he is dead in body, so the justice of the eternal communion makes no provision for recalling a man to eternal life, once he has been condemned to the death of his soul.[36]

If Augustine had been able to free his mind of the notion that souls are indestructible and can never die, he could have allowed these words—and so very many words of Scripture—to have their most obvious and common meaning. Instead he remained captive to the thought patterns of his time, and he embedded with his own considerable authority the stones that formed the road to traditionalism.

The stones of medieval caste-consciousness. For six or seven centuries after Augustine, most Western theologians neither developed traditional teaching nor called it into question, but contented themselves with passing it on. Then came Anselm (d. 1117) and Thomas Aquinas (d. 1274) in the high Middle Ages. During this period "the soul's immortality and its adventures after the separation of body and soul came to occupy the center of attention at the expense of the heroic picture of resurrection."[37] Both Anselm and Aquinas assume that the soul is immortal and interpret biblical teaching concerning hell on the basis of that assumption, although Aquinas reasons from Aristotelian rather than Platonic philosophy. The primary contribution of Anselm and Aquinas to traditionalism is the notion, based on feudalistic systems of justice, that finite man can pay for his sins against an infinite God only by suffering torment for an infinite period of time.

Anselm sets out his case for the traditionalist hell in his works *Cur Deus Homo* (bk. 1) and *Proslogion* (chaps. 8-11). Rather than examining scriptural language in light of scriptural usage, Anselm reasons within the framework of his feudal society. In Anselm's world the same crime could carry any one of a number of punishments depending on the rank of the criminal and especially of the victim. A serf might be executed for committing a particular crime, while a person of nobility who committed the same crime might only be assessed a fine. The king, of course, could commit the same deed with impunity. A serf who insulted a fellow serf might go unpunished. Upon insulting a lord, a serf might be jailed. Any serf who insulted the king would likely be beheaded. Taking his cue from such "justice," Anselm reasons that God is worthy of infinite honor and that sin against God therefore deserves infinite punishment. Because humans are finite, Anselm argues, they cannot suffer infinite punishment in a finite period of time. Therefore they must suffer conscious torment forever (infinitely) in hell.

Not only do all civilized nations today reject such feudalistic concepts of justice, Anselm's model actually contradicts a fundamental principle of jurisprudence presented by God in the law of Moses. God demanded that the Jews provide the same justice for every person, regardless of the person's rank or standing in society (Ex 23:3; Lev 19:15; Deut 1:17). This principle of a single standard applicable to all classes of people found clear expression in the law known as the *lex talionis*—an eye for an eye and a tooth for a tooth (Lev 24:19-22). It did not matter whose eye was at stake or whose tooth had been knocked out; the punishment was the same for all. Furthermore, Israel's laws were intended to elicit praise for the justice of God himself (Deut 4:5-8). In this light it should be clear that the arbitrary and discriminatory practices of feudal society provide no reliable starting place for developing Christian theology.

Even if Anselm's model of feudalistic justice does not contradict divine principles of justice, Anselm's argument cannot be proven. Who can say that even the everlasting torture of a finite human being would truly compensate for rebellion against the Creator of heaven and earth? By what measure would one confidently make such a determination? How could we know, for that matter, that all the everlasting torments of all the sinners in hell put together would "measure up" to the enormity of sin against the only infinite God? On the other hand, why wouldn't the *total and everlasting destruction* of a finite being constitute "infinite" punishment for that individual? Such punishment certainly would be without limitation, both in extent (the whole person) and in duration (forever). Anselm's argument for everlasting torture should be rejected as unbiblical, unreasonable and unnecessary.

Thomas Aquinas continued Anselm's argument for unending torment, an argument based on medieval respect of persons. As a disciple of Aristotle, Aquinas differed from his Platonic predecessors in emphasizing the body in relation to the soul. Aquinas reasoned that both good and evil deeds begin with one's soul before one performs them with the body and that the soul therefore should precede the body in receiving eternal reward or punishment. On that basis he argued that retribution begins immediately at death rather than after the resurrection and final judgment. And since even the righteous are stained with sin's impurity, Aquinas reasoned, their souls also must be purged by punishments—in purgatory.[38] In this way the stones of medieval caste-consciousness laid down by Anselm and Aquinas also became part of the mottled and meandering road to traditionalism.

The stones of Reformation politics. If the sixteenth-century powers and players had been arranged a little differently, the Reformation might well have rejected the tradition of everlasting torment. Many of the radical reformers known as Anabaptists rejected the traditional view of hell and its underlying premise that souls are immortal. Instead, they said humans are created entirely mortal and depend completely on God for existence—now and forever. The wicked, who are finally cut off from God in hell, will eventually cease to exist. John Calvin responded ferociously against the Anabaptists, advocating the ancient tradition in these matters. Not wishing to split the Reformation over a point he considered less than major, Luther became quiet regarding those subjects on which he and the Anabaptists shared some common ground. With Calvin and the Catholics on one side, the universally hated Anabaptists on the other and Luther out of the controversy, the road of belief in unending conscious torment crossed the intersection of the Reformation and continued on into Protestant history.[39]

Luther rejected the philosophical proofs for the immortality of the soul, calling them "monstrous fables that form part of the Roman dunghill of decretals."[40] Although he was not always consistent on this point, Luther frequently spoke of death as a sort of sleep—because sleep is a regular bibli-

cal metaphor for death. He often portrayed the dead as lacking consciousness, experiencing instead a sort of sleep from which they will wake in the
resurrection. Then their period of "sleep" will seem to have lasted but a
moment.[41]

In England the Catholic Thomas More attacked Luther's views on "soul-
sleeping," and the great British Reformer William Tyndale came to Luther's
defense. Contrasting the biblical teaching of bodily resurrection with the
unscriptural notion of the immortality of the soul, Tyndale writes:

> The true faith putteth the resurrection, which we be warned to look for every
> hour. The heathen philosophers, denying that, did put that the souls did ever
> live. And the pope joineth the spiritual doctrine of Christ and the fleshly doc-
> trine of philosophers together; things so contrary that they cannot agree, no
> more than the Spirit and the flesh do in a Christian man. And because the
> fleshly-minded pope consenteth unto heathen doctrine, therefore he corrupt-
> eth the scriptures to establish it.[42]

Many Anabaptists, meanwhile, taught that human beings are entirely
mortal, that there is no conscious awareness between earthly death and the
resurrection. The wicked, they said, will finally perish in hell and cease to
exist forever after. John Calvin responded to their teaching with his first
theological book, *Psychopannychia*.[43] In this work Calvin denounces them as
"some dregs of Anabaptists" and a "nefarious herd."[44] Calvin even warns
his readers:

> Remember that the Catabaptists (whom, as embodying all kinds of abomina-
> tions, it is sufficient to have named) are the authors of this famous dogma.
> Well may we suspect anything that proceeds from such a forge—a forge
> which has already fabricated, and is daily fabricating, so many monsters.[45]

Calvin quotes from the Bible throughout this vitriolic work. Yet whenever Scripture speaks of the dead as "asleep" or refers to the final "destruction" of the wicked, Calvin always explains that these words do not mean
what they appear to mean. Like the church fathers who preceded him,
Calvin acknowledges that the soul is created by God and that God is able to
destroy it. But when he encounters Scriptures that appear to say that God
will do just that, Calvin reverts to his traditionalist roots and explains that
the texts mean that the soul will never be destroyed but will suffer pain forever.[46]

When Luther recognized the intensity of Calvin's passion on this subject, he drew back and did not pursue his own reservations concerning the immortality of the soul. The result was predictable.

> Soul sleep lost what small chance it might have had to be considered a debatable doctrine, a thing indifferent. Once it was identified solely with the Anabaptists, there was no hope for a hearing before respectable Protestants. . . . Unchallenged by the doctrine of a Reformation church of comparable stature, the view of the churches of Geneva and Zurich (and of Rome) on the nature of the soul had to prevail in England.[47]

At one of its most important intersections, then, the road to traditionalism was paved with the stones of Reformation politics.

The stones of blind creedalism. Heinrich Bullinger of Zurich wrote much of the Second Helvetic Confession of 1566, into which he incorporated the traditionalist doctrines that Calvin had championed. Bullinger's work was highly regarded in England because of his friendship with British exiles during the reign of the Catholic Queen Mary. From England traditionalism spread to Scotland and eventually to America as well. Unfortunately, many of the earliest Protestant creeds include language concerning hell that is foreign to the Bible and contradicts the apparent teaching of Scripture from first to last. The Augsburg Confession (1530) says the unfaithful will be "tormented without end." The Belgic Confession of Faith (1561) says that the wicked, as well as the righteous, will be made "immortal." The Second Helvetic Confession (1566) states that the wicked will "burn forever." There is no verse in the Bible that says any of those things.

By contrast, the Apostles' Creed says only that Christ "shall come to judge the quick and the dead" and that there will be a "resurrection of the body." The Nicene Creed is similarly reserved, affirming that Christ will "judge the living and the dead" and that there will be a "resurrection of the dead." These universal statements of Christian faith are completely compatible with conditionalism, which may be expressed clearly by quoting the language of the Bible. Evangelicals who use historic creeds always say that the creeds are subject to Scripture. Sometimes, however, actions speak louder than words. Sadly, the road to traditionalism has often been paved with the stones of blind creedalism.

The Foundation of the House

I have set out the case for conditionalism in great detail, pointing to dozens of pertinent passages found from one end of the Bible to the other. From Genesis to Revelation, biblical writers agree that the wages of sin is *death*. There is no disagreement on this point in any portion of Scripture. The wisdom literature shows its necessity. Historical portions of the Old Testament illustrate and prefigure it. Prophets predict it. Jesus affirms it. Acts warns of it. The epistles explain it. Revelation portrays it.

The final choices are eternal life or the second death. Conditionalists can express their view using the unadorned language of Scripture. Biblical writers teach that the wages of sin is death so frequently and so consistently that one can let the Bible fall open almost anywhere and find this doctrine within a few pages. When they find it, conditionalists can express their view in the clear language of Scripture, allowing the Bible to interpret itself. They do not have to assign strange meanings to common words such as *die*, *perish* and *destroy*. The ordinary person may take these words at face value and affirm them with confidence.

It is a different matter for the traditionalist. Peterson can try to prove his case by appealing to theologians throughout his presentation. But he is hard pressed to find support for his position in Scripture. After searching the whole Bible, Peterson can find only ten passages that he believes remotely support his view. Since he has so little to present in favor of everlasting torture, he spends much of his presentation explaining what he believes I teach, filling his pages with quibbles and red herrings concerning index entries and quotations from uninspired authors.

I hope the reader notices this difference in our presentations. I have already covered these ten texts—and several times that many more. I encourage the reader to examine Peterson's analysis and mine with both an open Bible and an open mind. Consider also the wide variety of biblical texts that I discuss from throughout Scripture, texts that Peterson completely ignores. And when we both treat a passage, ask yourself which explanation seems to take the text more seriously.

Refrain from forming an opinion based on one or two passages alone. Consider the cumulative weight of evidence. Remember the difference between Scripture quotations and the mere opinions of uninspired men.

Keep in mind the type of biblical literature involved. Listen with your heart as well as with your head. Not all Scriptures are intended to be understood literally. Sometimes the author uses word pictures to create a mood or to elicit a particular emotional response. As I consider Peterson's argument about each of his "footings" in turn, scrutinize his and my analyses of these texts and consider which of us is assuming something that needs to be proven. Be alert to red herrings—incidental statements that impute motives, erect straw men or send the reader down side trails, thus only confusing the issue.

The first footing: Isaiah 66:22-24. Peterson sets forth the imagery of this passage quite well. Then he turns around and denies that it means anything remotely akin to the scene it pictures. He says that I insist on a literal interpretation, which he believes is impossible. I do no such thing. I do insist that we take Isaiah's picture *seriously* and that we not interpret it in a way that attributes to it a meaning that is the exact opposite of the scene it portrays. I do not say that Jesus or New Testament writers cannot add to this teaching or even change it if they wish. But we should not assume without good reason that they change Isaiah's meaning when they merely quote his words. And surely good interpretation of such New Testament language must begin with a look at the Old Testament passage being quoted.

The second footing: Daniel 12:1-2. Peterson says that it is "incorrect to limit either of these destinies; they are both 'everlasting'" (p. 135). He writes several paragraphs to prove that the Hebrew word translated "everlasting" in this passage means "without end." This is a red herring. I insist that both destinies are everlasting. This verse does not state what happens to the wicked (Isaiah 66 did that), but merely says that they are held in "everlasting contempt." That statement is fully satisfied by the fact that the fate of the wicked is permanent. Their destruction will never be undone or reversed.

The third footing: Matthew 18:6-9. Peterson tells us that when Jesus "speaks of 'eternal fire,' he means that the torments of hell will have no end" (p. 138). That is Peterson's conclusion, to be sure, but where is the evidence to sustain it? The Bible itself defines "eternal fire" as fire that destroys permanently (Jude 7). Peterson asserts that "Scripture repeatedly explains the effect of hellfire on those cast into it; it brings great pain" (p. 139). As proof he refers to Jesus' mention of "weeping and gnashing of teeth." Like all traditionalists, Peterson reads into this language the meaning he needs to prove. He completely ignores the Bible's own usage of "gnashing of teeth"—a phrase consistently indicating great anger. He also ignores the fact that my view allows for all the conscious pain that God might require any sinner to suffer. The second death does not necessarily occur in an instant.

The fourth footing: Matthew 25:31-46. Peterson emphasizes that "the destinies of the godly and ungodly are alike in this respect—they are both everlasting" (p. 141). That is my very point. Jesus warns of "eternal punishment" in this passage, but he does not tell us here what that punishment consists of. Peterson goes to Augustine for the answer to that question. I prefer to go to Paul, who tells us clearly about what Jesus only vaguely mentions here. Paul says that when Jesus comes, he will punish the lost and that they "will be punished with *everlasting destruction*" (2 Thess 1:8-9). The word *punishment* alone can mean very many things, ranging all the way from a reprimand to capital punishment. Paul tells us that in this case it means "everlasting destruction." Peterson says that it means everlasting torment that never ends in complete destruction.

Peterson chafes at my gentle caution expressed in *The Fire That Consumes* against falling into a spirit of vindictiveness at the fate of the lost. I do not suggest that he does that, but I know no other way to characterize the following words of the late John Gerstner, another recent defender of the traditionalist view. Gerstner writes:

> Even *now*, while the evangelical is singing the praises of his Lord and Savior, Jesus Christ, he knows that multitudes are suffering the torments of the damned. He knows that Judas Iscariot has been in unimaginable agony of soul for two thousand years, and that the worst of all torments will be that after his buried body is raised from his bones and ashes he will suffer in body and soul forever and ever. The true Christian, aware of this, is happily, exuberantly, gladly praising the Judge of the Last Day, Jesus Christ, who has sentenced to such merited damnation millions of souls.[48]

The fifth footing: Mark 9:42-48. In this passage Jesus quotes the language of Isaiah 66:24, and the most accurate translations of both passages speak of fire that is "not quenched." If we allow the Bible to interpret itself, we will find that the figure of "unquenchable" fire stands throughout both Testaments for fire that cannot be *resisted*. Humans cannot stop God's judgment fire. It will therefore burn up whatever is put in its way (Mt 3:12). The use of the adjective "unquenchable" does not mean that the fire never goes out. Peterson says that Jesus teaches that hell is "a place where the destruction of the wicked never ends" (p. 148). That is exactly my point. What Peterson really believes is that complete destruction never takes place because the process of destroying goes on forever.

Peterson claims that I "misuse" a quotation from William L. Lane that states that God's judgment "is irreversible and entails eternal consequences" (p. 149). I never suggested or implied that Lane agrees with my view. (I do not know if he does or not.) I simply quoted a statement by Lane with which I fully agree. Traditionalists constantly say that conditionalists do not believe in eternal consequences. That is a misrepresentation that needs to be corrected.

Peterson also complains that I omit an exposition of Mark 9:42-48 from the second edition of *The Fire That Consumes*. The fact is that I discuss this text in both editions in connection with Matthew 18:8ff.[49] Furthermore, I state at the beginning of the chapter concerning Jesus' teachings that I am focusing on texts from Matthew because Matthew reports more of Jesus' teachings on final punishment than any other Gospel and because material from the other Gospels is usually discussed in connection with the teachings found in Matthew.[50] The reason Peterson could not find Mark 9:42-48 in the index of the second edition is that Paternoster Press chose to include in the index only passages used as headings, rather than including all texts discussed as had been done in the first edition of the book.

The sixth footing: 2 Thessalonians 1:5-10. This passage comes right out and says it—the wicked "will be punished with everlasting destruction." This statement is so unequivocal that Peterson confesses it "could mean annihilation" (p. 150). Despite that clear and obvious meaning, his position requires him to conclude that the wicked will never be destroyed at all. Instead, "they will endure never-ending ruin" (p. 153). Peterson's predecessors came to that conclusion because they believed that souls can never be destroyed. Peterson knows better than that, but he cannot bring himself to break with his historic creed and with his tradition of systematic theology. Some traditionalists argue that the wicked are not really separated from God's presence as this passage says, but are only separated from his grace. Peterson has to agree with them because he understands that humans have no independent existence in themselves. He knows that if sinners were truly removed entirely from God's presence, they would cease to exist.

The seventh footing: Jude 7. Jude writes that Sodom and Gomorrah "serve as an example of those who suffer the punishment of eternal fire." Peterson says this does not mean that the wicked will suffer any fate remotely resembling the fate that befell Sodom and Gomorrah. Instead, he concludes that Jude is telling us that the fire that totally destroyed Sodom and Gomorrah prefigures "the fire of hell that will forever torment the wicked" (p. 154). It is like *Alice in Wonderland*—*destroyed* means never destroyed, and fire that totally consumes prefigures fire that never consumes but that tortures throughout eternity instead. Why not simply allow the obvious meaning?

Peterson rightly notes the similarity between Jude 7 and 2 Peter 2:6. Peter says that God "condemned the cities of Sodom and Gomorrah by burning them to ashes, and made them an example of what is going to happen to the ungodly." Again Peterson admits that Peter's words could teach annihilationism. But, he tells us, "it is better to take Peter's words as more generally predicting the downfall of the wicked than to understand them as foretelling their precise fate—reduction to ashes" (p. 156). If Peter could hear the conversation, he would probably scratch his head and wonder how he could have possibly written more plainly.

The eighth footing: Jude 13. Jude compares the wicked to "wandering stars" whose fate will be "blackest darkness." This sounds like the first-century equivalent of what today we call black holes. Peterson turns from the astronomical metaphor, however, to compare this passage with Jesus' description of people who are expelled from a brightly lit celebration and sent into the darkness outside the area that is illuminated by the lamps. The latter passage mentions "gnashing of teeth," an expression that Peterson thinks designates pain, but that Scripture regularly uses to portray anger. Anger cannot change the outcome of God's judgment, however; those who gnash their teeth will finally waste away (Ps 112:10).

The ninth footing: Revelation 14:9-11. I have discussed Revelation 14:9-11 in detail and will not repeat my discussion here. If this passage is talking about hell, it is one of only two texts in the whole Bible that makes hell sound anything like the traditionalist description of it. (The other passage is Revelation 20:10.) If Peterson were arguing some other end-time detail with the late Lewis Sperry Chafer (mile marker 1948 on Peterson's "road to traditionalism"), he would be the first to insist that one ought not build a doctrine on a passage or two in Revelation. He would be correct to argue that.

Examined phrase by phrase, even Revelation 14:9-11 is consistent with conditionalism. Even if I could not explain this passage, however, we would be wrong to build a doctrine on it that flies squarely in the face of dozens of plain passages of Scripture from both the Old and the New Testament. Again Peterson assigns meanings to the biblical metaphors without regard to the meaning of those same metaphors throughout the Scriptures.

The tenth footing: Revelation 20:10, 14-15. Although Peterson insists more than once that traditionalism does not depend on the immortality of the soul, he comes close to arguing that it does when he discusses this passage. Where John says that the "lake of fire" *is* "the second death," Peterson argues that "God reunites the souls of the unsaved dead with their bodies to fit them for eternal punishment" (p. 165). What does he mean by "fit them?" Does he mean that the souls are immortal—something he denies he believes? Or does he mean that God gives immortal bodies to the unsaved—something that the Bible never mentions but that traditionalists have often assumed? The simple truth is that the wicked do not need anything special to "fit them for eternal punishment." They need only to be raised from the dead to the same mortal condition into which they were born. The "lake of fire," remember, *is* "the second death." God is able to "destroy both soul and body in hell" (Mt 10:28). The wicked "will be punished with everlasting destruction" (2 Thess 1:9). The wicked are apparently raised in mortality to experience the second death.

Seeing the Big Picture

After quoting eleven theologians and arguing from ten texts of Scripture, Peterson concludes by advancing three rationalistic arguments involving systematic theology. Here he and I approach the matter from different personal perspectives.

Peterson belongs to and teaches for a denomination that requires him to defend a particular historical creed—the Westminster Confession of Faith. I am not suggesting that Peterson is engaged in any sort of duplicity or that his opinions arise out of any impure motives. Quite the contrary. I am confident that his heart, mind and conscience all agree that "the truth" has already been decided on all major issues of doctrine and that it is preserved for posterity in the great creeds and confessions from earlier times. If someone raises a theological question, Peterson believes that the correct answer is found in a creed. If someone disagrees with the creed, Peterson assumes that the person is wrong. I was raised on a different view.

My church fellowship taught (though it did not always practice) the idea that Scripture is the only and final authority in matters of doctrine. Creeds were viewed with suspicion. All appeals in spiritual matters were supposed to be made to the inspired Word of God.

Even people who are committed to a human creed can rise above the creed's authority and disagree with the creed when the Word of God demands. Surely it is easier, though, for people to admit that they have been mistaken on some point of doctrine when the mistaken position has not been sanctioned by an official church creed and hallowed for centuries. Some people do not commit to a particular human creed, but they are still bound by an unwritten "creed" based on their own church tradition. The enforcers of unwritten creeds are often as diligent and effective protectors of doctrine as are the guardians of written creeds. Even an unwritten creed can exert enormous power. On both sides of this issue the proof is in the pudding.

My own church tradition embraced the majority view concerning everlasting torment. A careful Bible study required me to change my mind—and to stand at odds with many in my own church fellowship as well as with our tradition. My case in this book rests totally on Scripture. Peterson says that Scripture is the final authority also. But when asked to present his case, he begins with eleven theologians and ends with rationalistic arguments involving human creeds. Sandwiched between is his appeal to ten passages of Scripture, most of which he interprets by quoting uninspired theologians. Remember, actions speak louder than words.

Human beings. Peterson becomes quite exercised over the fact that I do not commit myself to the traditional understanding of a conscious intermediate state between death and resurrection. That issue does often arise in discussions of the final punishment of the wicked. But what one believes about the intermediate state—whether the dead are conscious, "asleep" or extinct—does not determine one way or the other how one understands the subject of final punishment. The Creator is fully capable of reuniting the living, waking the sleeping or re-creating the extinct. Because the intermediate state has absolutely nothing to do with the nature of final punishment in hell, I intentionally avoided that issue in my book *The Fire That Consumes*.

Peterson is simply wrong when he says that I deny an intermediate state. I frequently respond to questions on the subject by saying that I am not dogmatic one way or the other. Peterson's fulminations on this issue are nothing but a smoke screen to divert attention from the weakness of his case.

It is true that the biblical view of humans as mortal creatures wholly dependent on God for existence, a view that I present in *The Fire That Consumes*, has implications for thinking about the intermediate state. So, however, might the Christian's faith-union with Christ and "earnest" possession of the Holy Spirit.[51] Conditionalists vary in their views of the intermediate state[52]—as do traditionalists. Calvin writes voluminously in favor of a conscious intermediate state, while Luther often speaks of death as a "sleep" and considers believers in this state to be blissfully unaware of external surroundings. Does Peterson wish to consider Luther a heretic for that reason?

Peterson becomes particularly agitated at some people's opinion that earthly death means complete extinction, a condition that God reverses by raising people from the dead. Calling on another theologian for support, he says that advocates of this view "do not claim to be able to prove continuity of personhood between the person who dies and the one who is raised; the best they can do is argue for the possibility of continuity of personal identity" (p. 174).

Although this is not even our subject, Peterson's statement is so outlandish that it requires a response. The statement goes to the heart of an overwhelming temptation that confronts anyone who tries to think systematically about biblical doctrines or is committed to a human creed. That is the temptation to bend Scriptures to fit their particular doctrinal grid and to reject whatever they cannot explain. "The best they can do," Peterson fumes. In truth, the best any of us can do is to place our confidence in God—God who is faithful to his people and who has promised to raise the dead. Peterson's logic would lead him to criticize the apostle Paul because Paul could not fully explain the nature of the resurrection body. Paul called such rationalism "foolish" (1 Cor 15:35-36).

Finally, Peterson himself admits that the intermediate state and final punishment are not necessarily connected. Yet he devotes several pages, in which he is supposed to be presenting the biblical case for everlasting conscious torment, to quibbling over whether or not I believe people know anything during the time between their death and resurrection. That is nothing but a blatant effort to arouse prejudice, an attempt to confuse the issue, a red herring to distract the reader from the fact that his position lacks any biblical basis.

Christ. Peterson agrees that Jesus "died in the place of" those who are saved and "bore the punishment that they deserved" (p. 175). He also agrees that Jesus' death somehow reveals the nature of final punishment. Yet he acknowledges that Jesus did not suffer what traditionalists claims the lost will all endure—conscious torment in body and soul forever. Peterson even admits that such a scenario would have been impossible, for if Jesus had "literally endured never-ending punishment . . . he would be on the cross forever and wouldn't be able to save anyone" (p. 175).

How does Peterson resolve this difficulty? He resorts to the ancient argument advanced by Anselm and Aquinas about "finite" and "infinite" persons, punishments and periods of time. I have shown already that this argument grew out of medieval caste-consciousness and that it reflects a legal principle that God directly condemned when he gave his law to Israel. Like all traditionalist advocates, Peterson really cannot allow the death of Jesus to teach anything about the nature of the punishment awaiting the lost.

The simple truth is that Jesus *died;* he was not *tortured forever.* Jesus' death for sinners does provide a window into the final judgment awaiting the lost. But the view we see through that window is one of suffering that ends in death—not one of everlasting conscious torment. Jesus suffered and died because he was bearing the sin of others. Unlike sinners in hell, he rose again because his own life was perfectly pleasing to the Father. It was "impossible for death to keep its hold" on the perfectly obedient Son of God (Acts 2:24). The apostle Paul literally says that Jesus died "because of" our sin and that he rose again "because of" our justification (Rom 4:25 NASB).

Perhaps the most extreme of Peterson's red herrings is his argument based on the Council of Chalcedon's statement known as the Definition of the Union of the Divine and Human Natures in the Person of Christ (issued in the year 451). That ecumenical council composed of bishops from East and West attempted to explain the intricacies of the union of Jesus' divine nature and human nature, using common philosophical terms borrowed from the theological debates of the time. The confession of faith that resulted affirms that Jesus' two natures are "without confusion, without change, without division, without separation." Peterson claims that I separate Christ's divine and human nature, in violation of this creed, because I say that Jesus truly died in the place of those he saved and that if he "had not been raised, he—like those fallen asleep in him—would simply have perished" (p. 176; see 1 Cor 15:18). This smoke screen ought to be rejected for the following five reasons.

First, Peterson himself admits that Jesus' prayer in Gethsemane to "let this cup pass" signified deliverance from death and that God answered that prayer by raising Jesus from the dead.[53] Because Jesus' prayer was not an empty mockery, he must have considered it possible that God might not do what he was requesting. If God had not raised Jesus from the dead, he would have remained dead forever. Although Peterson believes that the dead are not truly dead or at least that part of them remains alive, he still faces the same dilemma that he lays on me. If God had not raised Jesus, would Jesus' divine nature have remained dead and would the Trinity have thus been reduced to a Binity? Or would Jesus' human nature have remained dead although the divine nature remained alive—separating the two natures and violating Chalcedon? This is a sword that cuts both ways.

Second, the fact that God did raise Jesus from the dead does not diminish the reality that the Son of God was dead for parts of three days. Even using Peterson's weakened definition of *death*, he acknowledges that Jesus was dead in some sense. Was his divine nature dead or only his human nature? If both, was the Trinity diminished? If only the human nature, does not such an answer contradict Chalcedonian orthodoxy?

Third, Peterson's criticism of me for honestly saying I cannot explain the mysteries involved in the death of the Son of God raises a real concern about his own acknowledgment of the limitations of human wisdom. Is he prepared to affirm that systematic theologians and philosophers can really explain the "secret things" of God, matters that inspired Scripture leaves unexplained (Deut 29:29)? Can he explain how the Creator God could become a creaturely human? Can he line out for us what it means that Jesus "emptied" himself in the humiliation of the incarnation? Does he believe he can make us understand how the God-man could possibly die? The teaching about his death so outraged certain first-century Gnostics that they theorized Jesus only appeared to be human or that the divine "part" of Jesus left before the human "part" of Jesus died on the cross.

Can Peterson—or any of the theologians whose opinions he quotes as authority—explain how Jesus Christ, the Word of God made flesh, could *be sin* (2 Cor 5:21) or how the blessed Son of God could *become a curse* (Gal 3:13)? I make no apologies for saying that I cannot explain such holy mysteries. There is a time to remember that God is in heaven and we are on the earth and to let our words be few (Eccles 5:2). There is a time to hope in God while refraining from intruding into matters too difficult for us to understand (Ps 131:1-3).

Fourth, Peterson's passion on this point requires us to ask again about his standard of authority. Was the Council of Chalcedon infallible in its pronouncements?[54] If we say that it did speak from the Holy Spirit, who shall infallibly interpret what its pronouncements mean? The Council's language, after all, is highly technical and is fifteen hundred years old.

But Peterson goes even farther than that. He determines, using his own wisdom, the logical implications of my supposed view, then decides on his own authority that those implications are inconsistent with his interpretation of the Chalcedonian pronouncements. Concluding that the implications that he draws from my exposition of Scripture are inconsistent with the implications that he draws from the conclusions of the bishops at Chalcedon, he boldly tells the world that "nothing less than orthodox Christology is at stake." Such authoritarianism and allegiance to human councils would be at home in a court of the Inquisition, but what place do they have in a discussion between Protestants and particularly between evangelicals?

Fifth, Peterson's methodology in this section should remind us of our Lord's indictment of the rationalistic scribes and Pharisees of his day: "Thus you nullify the word of God for the sake of your tradition" (Mt 15:6). Even presuming that it were possible to know for certain all of the implications and applications of the pronouncements set out at Chalcedon, if some declaration of Scripture is found to contradict them, faithfulness to Christ requires us to reject the Council's words in favor of language taken from the Word of God. Although we do not face that situation in the present discussion, it is nevertheless a point that evangelicals must always keep in mind.

Last things. Finally, Peterson says he rejects conditionalism because it makes "annihilation . . . the end of punishment." Here he erects a straw man and then tears it down. I am affirming only what Jesus and Paul and other Scripture writers plainly say time and time again: "The wages of sin is death" (Rom 6:23). But this is no mere earthly death, from which all people will be brought back to life again. No, this is "the second death" (Rev 21:8). It is not temporal punishment within our present world of time and space; it is "eternal punishment" (Mt 25:46). Of what does this "punishment" consist? Of "everlasting destruction" (2 Thess 1:9). How inclusive will this destruction be? It will include "both soul and body," according to Jesus (Mt 10:28).

How long will the destroying continue before the destruction is accomplished? The Bible does not say, but it leaves the door open for whatever flexibility God's perfect justice might require in each individual case. What sensible pains will the process of destruction involve? Again the Bible is silent, although it again leaves room for whatever diversity God's absolute fairness will finally determine. Is this punishment truly everlasting? Yes, it is "everlasting destruction" (2 Thess 1:9). From it there will never be redemption, respite, recovery or return. This punishment lasts as long as the saved enjoy eternal life. For these, after all, are the final options—to "perish" or to enjoy "eternal life" (Jn 3:16). In the end, it will be either "eternal life" or "death" (Rom 6:23). Why is that so hard to understand?

A Final Word
Peterson claims that conditionalism is inconsistent with other biblical doctrines, but the truth is exactly the opposite. Conditionalism presupposes the doctrine of God, who alone has immortality. It is rooted in the doctrine of

creation for it sees human beings as mortal creatures, totally dependent on God for life every moment of their existence. It takes seriously the doctrine of sin, for it understands that the wages of sin is death. It appreciates the doctrines of Christ and of redemption, and it proclaims Jesus' death as a substitutionary atonement, the punishment due to sinners in whose place Jesus died. It loves the doctrine of the Holy Spirit, who is the pledge of our redemption. It teaches us to hope in God who raises the dead, rather than to trust in pagan notions of souls that cannot die. It magnifies the love of God but also his justice.

Conditionalism rejoices in the final victory of God—a culmination that will see all evil gone forever, that will see a pure universe composed of new heavens and a new earth in which only righteousness dwells. If conditionalism happens to be kinder and gentler than the alternative view, that is only an incidental benefit.[55] Conditionalism should be accepted because it is taught throughout the Word of God.

Traditionalism, on the other hand, is at odds with all of these great themes. It springs from a denial that God alone is immortal. It says that he is love but claims that he will keep people alive forever just to make them suffer. It says that he is just but that he will punish people forever for deeds done during a few years on earth. It repeats the serpent's lie in the Garden of Eden, telling men and women that they will not surely die. It says that Jesus died in the place of those whom he saves but denies that his death remotely resembles the punishment they otherwise would have suffered. It often hopes in the human soul rather than in God's power to raise the dead.

Traditionalism aborts the final victory of God, envisioning an eternal torture chamber where some traditionalists say God is present and others say he is absent. Instead of proclaiming a clean universe in which only righteousness dwells, traditionalists claim that evil people will live forever, though in misery, and some traditionalists say that the righteous derive pleasure throughout eternity from the knowledge of what is going on.

I plead with readers to carefully and prayerfully consider the evidence for conditionalism and then to jettison the ancient tradition of everlasting conscious torment. It is a horrible doctrine, unworthy of God, foreign to the Bible, spawned by pagan philosophy and preserved by human tradition. It deserves to be rejected once and for all.

Notes

Introduction

[1]The term *traditionalism* means that this view has long been the majority view. The term *conditionalism* means that immortality is conditional and is not given to those finally lost. The term *annihilationism* means that the lost are totally destroyed in hell.

[2]James I. Packer, "The Problem of Eternal Punishment," *Crux* 26, no. 3 (1990): 24-25.

[3]John W. Wenham, "The Case for Conditional Immortality," in *Universalism and the Doctrine of Hell*, ed. Nigel M. de S. Cameron (Grand Rapids, Mich.: Baker, 1992), pp. 187-88, 190.

[4]James I. Packer, "Evangelicals and the Way of Salvation," in *Evangelical Affirmations*, ed. Kenneth S. Kantzer and Carl F. H. Henry (Grand Rapids, Mich.: Zondervan, 1990), p. 126.

[5]Wenham, "Case for Conditional Immortality," pp. 165, 167, 169.

[6]Edward William Fudge, *The Fire That Consumes: The Biblical Case for Conditional Immortality*, rev. ed. (Carlisle, U.K.: Paternoster, 1994); Robert A. Peterson, *Hell on Trial: The Case for Eternal Punishment* (Phillipsburg, N.J.: Presbyterian & Reformed, 1995).

[7]For more biblical evidence see Daniel 12:1-2; Isaiah 66:22-24; Romans 2:6-10; 2 Thessalonians 1:6-10; Revelation 20:11-15.

[8]For arguments in favor of postmortem evangelism, see Gabriel Fackre, *What About Those Who Have Never Heard?* (Downers Grove, Ill.: InterVarsity Press, 1995), pp. 71-95.

Chapter 1: An Introduction to Conditionalism

[1]Jonathan Edwards, quoted with approval in Arthur W. Pink, *Eternal Punishment* (Swengel, Penn.: Reiner Publications, n.d.), pp. 29-30.

[2]Charles H. Spurgeon, Sermon 66, *New Park Street Pulpit*, 2:105, quoted by Emmanuel Petavel, *The Problem of Immortality* (London: Elliot Stock, 1892), p. 266.

[3]Interview with Billy Graham, "Of Angels, Devils and Messages from God," *Time*, November 15, 1993, p. 74.

[4]J. I. Packer, *"Fundamentalism" and the Word of God: Some Evangelical Principles* (Grand Rapids, Mich.: Eerdmans, 1970), p. 70.

[5]Interview with John R. W. Stott, "Basic Stott," *Christianity Today*, January 8, 1996, p. 28.

[6]Early Christian apologists who were converted Platonic philosophers disagreed with their pagan counterparts who said that souls have always existed, and they conceded that God, who created the soul, could also destroy it if he wished. But when they discussed final punishment, they reasoned as if they had not made that concession and argued that souls are immortal and thus require unending conscious torment. Calvin and other more recent theologians have been similarly inconsistent. See Edward William Fudge, *The Fire That Consumes: The Biblical Case for Conditional Immortality*, rev. ed. (Carlisle, U.K.: Paternoster, 1994), pp. 32-40.

[7]Although the word *Sheol* is a Hebrew word, the picture it portrays was known outside Israel, for example, in "The Epic of Gilgamesh." See James B. Pritchard, ed., *Ancient Near Eastern Texts Relating to the Old Testament*, 3rd ed. (Princeton, N.J.: Princeton University Press, 1969), pp. 72-99.

[8]Professor R. Laird Harris, my teacher and Robert Peterson's predecessor more than twenty-five years ago at Covenant Theological Seminary, suggests that *Sheol* is simply a poetic description of the grave. If correct, this explanation completely removes the argument sometimes advanced by advocates of conscious unending torment that conscious torment begins immediately after death in *Sheol*. See R. Laird Harris, "The Meaning of the Word Sheol as

Shown by Parallels in Poetic Texts," *Bulletin of the Evangelical Theological Society* 4 (1961): 129-35; and "Sheol" in *Theological Wordbook of the Old Testament*, ed. R. Laird Harris, 2 vols. (Chicago: Moody Press, 1980), 2:892-93.

Chapter 2: The Old Testament
[1]Such language is also used by the psalmists in Psalm 36:9-12; 49:8-20; 52:5-9; 59; 73; 92.

[2]For the destruction of Sodom and Gomorrah as a prototype of God's judgment, see Deuteronomy 29:23; Job 18:15; Psalm 11:6; Isaiah 30:33; 34:9; Ezekiel 38:22; and Revelation 14:10; 19:20; 20:10; 21:8.

[3]The unquenchable fire is also found in Isaiah 66:24; Jeremiah 4:4; 7:20; 17:27; 21:12; and Mark 9:43, 48. Contrast Psalm 118:12 and Hebrews 11:34.

[4]For more examples see Matthew 15:5; Acts 4:26; 13:33; Hebrews 1:5; 5:5; Revelation 12:5; 19:15.

[5]A partial list of New Testament verses that quote or allude to Psalm 110:1 includes Matthew 22:44; 26:64; Acts 2:34; 1 Corinthians 15:25; Ephesians 1:20; Colossians 3:1; Hebrews 1:13; 10:12-13; 12:2. New Testament authors quote or reference Psalm 110:4 at Romans 8:34 and Hebrews 5:6, 10; 6:20; 7:11, 15, 21.

[6]Isaiah's portrayal is first stood on its head in the book of Judith, when the heroine twists the prophet's language to warn:

> Woe to the nations that rise up against my race;
> The Lord Almighty will take vengeance of them in the
> day of judgment,
> To put fire and worms in their flesh;
> And they shall weep and feel their pain for ever.
> (Judith 16:17)

Many Christian interpreters from the time of the apologists onward have also changed Isaiah's corpses into living beings, his external maggots into internal worms of conscience or remorse and his destructive fire into fire that never finally destroys.

[7]Robert H. Mounce, *The Book of Revelation*, New International Commentary on the New Testament, ed. F. F. Bruce (Grand Rapids, Mich.: Eerdmans, 1977), p. 367.

[8]William G. T. Shedd, *The Doctrine of Endless Punishment* (New York: Charles Scribner's Sons, 1886), p. 14 n. 1; Harry Buis, *The Doctrine of Eternal Punishment* (Philadelphia: Presbyterian & Reformed, 1957), p. 24; Leslie H. Woodson, *Hell and Salvation* (Old Tappan, N.J.: Revell, 1973), p. 43.

[9]For discussions of specific texts on this topic throughout the Apocrypha, the pseudepigrapha and the Dead Sea Scrolls, see Edward William Fudge, *The Fire That Consumes: The Biblical Case for Conditional Immortality*, rev. ed. (Carlisle, U.K.: Paternoster, 1994), pp. 73-92.

[10]Kendall L. Harmon, "The Case Against Conditionalism: A Response to Edward William Fudge," in Universalism and the Doctrine of Hell, ed. Nigel M. de S. Cameron (Grand Rapids, Mich.: Baker, 1992), p. 209 n. 43. Harmon makes too much of the intertestamental literature, to the neglect of earlier canonical literature. So does Fritsch in his claim that "most of the ideas regarding the future life which are found in the New Testament writings had their origin in the apocalyptic writings" (C. T. Fritsch, "Apocrypha," in The Interpreter's Dictionary of the Bible [New York: Abingdon, 1962], 1:164).

[11]However, Strack and Billerbeck, noted authorities on Rabbinic literature, suggest that the pseudepigraphal references to eternal punishment simply denote everlasting annihilation. See Hermann L. Strack and Paul Billerbeck, *Kommentar zum Neuen Testament aus Talmud und Midrasch* (Munchen: C. H. Beck'sche Verlagsbuchhandlung, Oskar Beck, 1928), 2:1096.

Chapter 3: The Teachings of Jesus

[1]Larry Dixon, *The Other Side of the Good News: Confronting the Contemporary Challenges to Jesus' Teaching on Hell* (Wheaton, Ill.: BridgePoint, 1992).

[2]Even John F. Walvoord, who claims to hold a "literal" view of hell, concedes that this parable concerns the "intermediate state" (John F. Walvoord, "The Literal View," in *Four Views on Hell*, ed. William Crockett [Grand Rapids, Mich.: Zondervan, 1992], p. 22). British traditionalist John Blanchard admits the same (see John Blanchard, *Whatever Happened to Hell?* [Durham, England: Evangelical Press, 1993], pp. 81-82). Norval Geldenhuys goes even further, noting that Jesus "related this parable not in order to satisfy our curiosity about life after death but to emphasize vividly the tremendous seriousness of life on this side of the grave" (Norval Geldenhuys, *The Gospel of Luke*, New International Commentary on the New Testament, ed. F. F. Bruce [Grand Rapids, Mich.: Eerdmans, 1951], p. 427). A widely used evangelical theology textbook says it is "probably better" not to look to this story for "details of life after death" at all (see Alan F. Johnson and Robert E. Webber, *What Christians Believe: A Biblical and Historical Summary* [Grand Rapids, Mich.: Zondervan, 1989], p. 426).

[3]Robert Peterson rightly criticizes those who draw such "ridiculous conclusions" from this parable (see Robert A. Peterson, *Hell on Trial: The Case for Eternal Punishment* [Phillipsburg, N.J.: Presbyterian & Reformed, 1995], p. 66).

[4]Hermann L. Strack and Paul Billerbeck, *Kommentar zum Neuen Testament aus Talmud und Midrasch* (Munchen: C. H. Beck'sche Verlagsbuchhandlung, Oskar Beck, 1928), 2:1032-33.

[5]Athenagoras (A.D. 127-190) and Tertullian (born ca. A.D. 160), two of the earliest Christian teachers to argue that the "destruction" of the lost really means unending conscious torment, base their teaching on the supposed immortality of the soul, and that idea has been the mainstay of the doctrine until recent times (see Athenagoras *Resurrection of the Dead* 12-13, 17, 19; and Tertullian *Resurrection of the Flesh* 34). Charles Hodge reasons: "If the Bible says that the sufferings of the lost are to be everlasting, they are to endure forever, unless it can be shown either that the soul is not immortal or that the Scriptures elsewhere teach that those sufferings are to come to an end" (Charles Hodge, *Systematic Theology* [New York: Charles Scribner's Sons, 1884], 3:876).

[6]*The Fathers of the Church: A New Translation*, trans. Gerald G. Walsh and Daniel J. Honan (New York: Fathers of the Church, 1954), pp. 369-70. In the appendix "Augustine's Discussion of Final Punishment" of the first edition of *The Fire That Consumes: A Biblical and Historical Study of the Doctrine of Final Punishment* (Houston: Providential, 1982), pp. 439-48 (now out of print but available in many theological, university and seminary libraries), I present historical, doctrinal, scriptural and logical perspectives on Augustine's treatment of this topic in book 21 of his magnum opus *The City of God*.

[7]Jonathan Edwards, "Concerning the Endless Punishment of Those Who Die Impenitent," in *The Works of Jonathan Edwards*, rev. Edward Hickman, 2 vols. (Carlisle, Penn.: Banner of Truth Trust, n.d.), 2:524.

[8]For examples of "ruin" standing for divine judgment of destruction in the Greek Old Testament, see Exodus 12:13; 30:12; Numbers 8:19; 16:46-47; Joshua 22:17; and Isaiah 8:14.

[9]Even that simple point aroused a storm of emotional response after my article "Putting Hell in Its Place" appeared more than twenty years ago in *Christianity Today*, August 6, 1976, pp. 14-17.

Chapter 4: The Writings of Paul

[1]See Romans 2:7; 1 Corinthians 15:42, 50, 52-54; and 2 Timothy 1:10 for examples of the immortality of bodies of the saved after the resurrection.

[2]Scripture says that Jesus *died* for our sins (1 Cor 15:3); *laid down his life* (Jn 10:15); *poured out his life* (Is 53:12); was *destroyed* (Mt 27:20 KJV); was *killed* (Acts 3:15). He compared his own death to the *dissolution* of a kernel of wheat (Jn 12:23-26). In some sense consistent with his deity, Jesus was totally dependent on God to raise him from the dead (Mk 14:36; Lk 23:46; Heb 5:7; 1 Pet 2:23). On Jesus' death as a revelation of final punishment, see Edward William Fudge, *The Fire That Consumes: The Biblical Case for Conditional Immortality,* rev. ed. (Carlisle, U.K.: Paternoster, 1994), pp. 135-45.

[3]R. F. Weymouth, as quoted from a letter in Edward White, *Life in Christ: A Study of the Scripture Doctrine on the Nature of Man, the Object of the Divine Incarnation and the Conditions of Human Immortality,* 3rd ed. (London: Elliot Stock, 1878), p. 365.

Chapter 5: The Rest of the New Testament

[1]The death angel who exterminated the firstborn sons of the Egyptians in the days of Moses and who wiped out a generation of Israelites in the wilderness is called the "Destroyer," another form of this same Greek word (see 1 Cor 10:10; Heb 11:28).

[2]J. N. Oswalt, *The Book of Isaiah, Chapters 1-39,* New International Commentary on the Old Testament, ed. R. K. Harrison (Grand Rapids, Mich.: Eerdmans, 1986), p. 599.

[3]"It must be understood," writes William Hendriksen, "that the book of Revelation is rooted in and is in full harmony with the rest of the sacred Scriptures and must be explained on the basis of the clear teaching of the Bible everywhere" (William Hendriksen, *More Than Conquerors: An Interpretation of the Book of Revelation* [Grand Rapids, Mich.: Baker, 1960], p. 63). Another evangelical source wisely comments: "Revelation is rooted in the Old Testament. This is where we find the clues to the meaning of the various symbols—comparing scripture with scripture" (David Alexander and Pat Alexander, eds., *Eerdmans' Handbook to the Bible* [Grand Rapids, Mich.: Eerdmans, 1973], pp. 645-46).

[4]Following the excellent advice of J. Julius Scott, "Some Problems in Hermeneutics for Contemporary Evangelicals," *Journal of the Evangelical Theological Society* 22, no. 1 (1979): 74-75.

[5]The cup of God's wrath as a symbol of divine judgment appears in Job 21:20; Psalm 60:3; 75:8; Isaiah 51:17, 22; Jeremiah 25:15-38; Obadiah 16.

[6]Burning sulfur symbolizing absolute and total destruction is found in Genesis 19:24-25, 29; Job 18:15-17; Psalm 11:6; Isaiah 30:27-33; 34:9-11; Ezekiel 38:22; and Revelation 19:20-21; 20:10; 21:8.

[7]The locative case-form signifies *point* of time; the genitive case-form signifies *kind* of time (as here); the accusative case-form signifies *duration* of time. H. E. Dana and Julius R. Mantey, *A Manual Grammar of the Greek New Testament* (New York: Macmillan, 1960), pp. 77-93.

[8]Revelation opens with a vision cast in the mold of Daniel 7 (Rev 1:13-16; Dan 7:9). It should not be surprising if its concluding visions return to borrow imagery from the same passage of Scripture.

[9]Steward D. F. Salmond, *The Christian Doctrine of Immortality,* (Edinburgh: T & T Clark, 1895), pp. 428-29. Such nonsensical and self-contradictory language dates back to John Chrysostom, who said that "the damned shall suffer an end without end, a death without death, a decay without decay" (cited with approval in John Blanchard, *Whatever Happened to Hell?* [Durham, England: Evangelical Press, 1993], p. 154).

A Traditionalist Response to Conditionalism

[1]See pages 31, 34, 39, 40-41, 43-44, 47, 50 and 82 for Fudge's refutation of straw-man arguments for traditionalism.

[2]See pages 30 (two times) 32, 38, 49, 50, 55, 60, 67, 68 and 69 for Fudge's arguments from silence

against traditionalism.

[3]For more on Fudge's claim that the traditional view is pagan in origin, see pages 22, 23, 35, 54 and 62.

[4]John H. Gerstner, *Jonathan Edwards on Heaven and Hell* (Grand Rapids, Mich.: Baker, 1980), p. 75.

[5]Edward Hickman, ed., *The Works of Jonathan Edwards* (London: William Tegg, 1860), 2:524 (italics in original).

[6]Ibid.

[7]Harold E. Guillebaud, *The Righteous Judge* (n.p., 1941), p. 16 (italics in original).

[8]Edward Fudge, *The Fire That Consumes: A Biblical and Historical Study of Final Punishment* (Houston: Providential, 1982), p. 249 n. 36 (note: this is the first edition).

[9]Ibid., p. 304.

[10]See Guillebaud, *Righteous Judge*, pp. 8-11; and LeRoy Edwin Froom, *The Conditionalist Faith of our Fathers* (Washington, D.C.: Review & Herald, 1965-1966), 1:288-91.

[11]D. A. Carson, *Exegetical Fallacies* (Grand Rapids, Mich.: Baker, 1984), pp. 54-55.

[12]Edward William Fudge, *The Fire That Consumes: The Biblical Case for Conditional Immortality*, rev. ed. (Carlisle, U.K.: Paternoster, 1994), p. 17.

[13]Robert I. Bihwick, *Time and the Verb: A Guide to Tense and Aspect* (Oxford University Press, 1991), p. 189.

[14]Carlota S. Smith, *The Parameter of Aspect*, Studies in Language and Philosophy (Boston: Klumer Academic, 1991), p. 7.

[15]Bernard Comrie, *Aspect* (Cambridge University Press, 1976), p. 47.

[16]Henry George Liddell and Robert Scott, *A Greek-English Lexicon* (Oxford: Clarendon Press, 1996), p. 971.

[17]See Carson, *Exegetical Fallacies*, pp. 54-55.

[18]W. Bauer et al., *A Greek-English Lexicon of the New Testament and Other Early Christian Literature*, 2nd ed. (Chicago: University of Chicago Press, 1979), pp. 440-41.

[19]James Hope Moulton and George Milligan, *The Vocabulary of the Greek Testament Illustrated from the Papyri and Other Non-Literary Sources* (Grand Rapids, Mich.: Eerdmans, 1930), p. 352.

[20]Ibid. (italics added).

[21]J. Lust, E. Eynikel and K. Hauspie, *Greek-English Lexicon of the Septuagint* (Stuttgart: Deutsche Bibelgesellschaft, 1996), p. 261.

[22]For more on Fudge's view that Jesus was annihilated on the cross, see pages 61 and 65.

Chapter 7: The Road to Traditionalism

[1]See for example Edward William Fudge, *The Fire That Consumes: The Biblical Case for Conditional Immortality*, rev. ed. (Carlisle, U.K.: Paternoster, 1994), pp. 38-39, and Clark Pinnock, "The Destruction of the Finally Impenitent," *Criswell Theological Review* 4, no. 2 (1990): 246-47.

[23]Tertullian, *On the Resurrection of the Flesh*, in *The Ante-Nicene Fathers*, ed. Alexander Roberts and James Donaldson, 10 vols. (Grand Rapids, Mich.: Eerdmans, 1973), 3:570.

[3]Tertullian *Apology*, in *The Early Christian Fathers*, ed. and trans. Henry Bettenson (London: Oxford University Press, 1976), p. 160.

[4]Augustine *The City of God* (trans. Bettenson) 21.23 .

[5]Ibid., 21.23.

[6]Ibid.

[7]Ibid., 21.27.

[8]Thomas Aquinas *Summa contra Gentiles* (trans. Bourke) 144.8.

[9]Thomas Aquinas *Summa Theologiae* (Blackfriars ed.) 1a2ae.87.5.

[10]Ibid., 1a2ae.87.4.

[11]Ewald M. Plass, *What Luther Says*, 3 vols. (St. Louis: Concordia, 1959), 2:625-27.

[12]Ibid., 2:627.

[13]Ibid.

[14]Ibid., 2:626-27.

[15]John Calvin *Institutes of the Christian Religion* (trans. Battles) 3.25.12.

[16]Ibid.

[17]John Calvin, *The Epistles of Paul the Apostle to the Romans and to the Thessalonians,* Calvin's Commentaries, ed. D. W. Torrance and T. F. Torrance, trans. R. Mackenzie (Grand Rapids, Mich.: Eerdmans, 1961), p. 392.

[18]I give credit to John H. Gerstner, *Jonathan Edwards on Heaven and Hell* (Grand Rapids, Mich.: Baker, 1980), for teaching me Edwards's views on hell.

[19]Ibid., pp. 55, 73.

[20]Ibid., p. 74.

[21]Ibid., p. 75.

[22]I acknowledge a debt to Thomas C. Oden, *John Wesley's Scriptural Christianity: A Plain Exposition of His Teaching on Christian Doctrine* (Grand Rapids, Mich.: Zondervan, 1994).

[23]That is, *poena damni* and *poena sensus.*

[24]Oden, *John Wesley's Scriptural Christianity,* pp. 355-56.

[25]John Wesley, "Letter to William Law," cited in Oden, *John Wesley's Scriptural Christianity,* p. 357 n. 100.

[26]John Wesley, "Letter to a Roman Catholic," cited in Oden, *John Wesley's Scriptural Christianity,* p. 357 n. 102.

[27]Francis Pieper, *Christian Dogmatics,* trans. J. T. Mueller (St. Louis: Concordia, 1953), 3:545.

[28]Ibid., 3:544.

[29]Ibid., 3:548-49.

[30]Louis Berkhof, *Systematic Theology* (Grand Rapids, Mich.: Baker, 1941), p. 735.

[31]Ibid., p. 736.

[32]Lewis Sperry Chafer, *Systematic Theology,* 8 vols. (Dallas: Dallas Seminary Press, 1948), 4:430.

[33]Ibid., 4:431-32.

[34]Millard Erickson, *Christian Theology* (Grand Rapids, Mich.: Baker, 1985), p. 1235.

[35]Ibid., p. 1238.

Chapter 8: The Foundation of the House

[1]"Footing," *Webster's Seventh New Collegiate Dictionary* (Springfield, Mass.: Merriam, 1972), p. 325.

[2]For an exhilarating presentation of the view that "the ultimate goal of God in all of history is to uphold and display his glory for the enjoyment of the redeemed from every tribe and tongue and people and nation," see John Piper, *Let the Nations Be Glad! The Supremacy of God in Missions* (Grand Rapids, Mich.: Baker, 1993), p. 222.

[3]Edward William Fudge, *The Fire That Consumes: The Biblical Case for Conditional Immortality,* rev. ed., (Carlisle, U.K.: Paternoster, 1994), pp. 62-63.

[4]*Rabbim* followed by the preposition *min* normally is partitive according to Gerhard Hasel, "Resurrection in the Theology of Old Testament Apocalyptic," *Zeitschrift für die Alttestamentliche Wissenschaft* 92 (1982): 279.

[5]Some say that *multitudes* here (Hebrew *rabbim*) means "all." God will raise all—not merely some—from the grave. Cited as examples are Isaiah 2:3 and Deuteronomy 7:1. But this is not the most likely meaning of Daniel 12:2. E. J. Young (*The Prophecy of Daniel* [Grand Rapids,

Mich.: Eerdmans, 1973], p. 256) and Joyce G. Baldwin (*Daniel*, Tyndale Old Testament Commentaries [Downers Grove, Ill.: InterVarsity Press, 1978], p. 204) agree.

[6] Edmund F. Sutcliffe, *The Old Testament and the Future Life*, 2nd ed. (Westminster, Md.: Newman Bookshop, 1947), pp. 115-18.

[7] Fudge, *Fire That Consumes*, rev. ed., p. 123.

[8] See Hans Scharen, "Gehenna in the Synoptics: Part 1," *Bibliotheca Sacra* 149 (July-September 1992): 334.

[9] Fudge, *Fire That Consumes*, rev. ed., p. 113.

[10] Augustine *The City of God* (Penguin ed.) 21.23 .

[11] W. Bauer et al., *A Greek-English Lexicon of the New Testament and Other Early Christian Literature*, 2nd ed. (Chicago: University of Chicago Press, 1979), pp. 440-41.

[12] Augustine *City of God* 21.23.

[13] Fudge, *Fire That Consumes*, rev. ed., p. 125.

[14] Ibid., p. 19.

[15] Ibid., p. 121.

[16] Ibid., pp. 122-23.

[17] Ibid., p. 121.

[18] Irving M. Copi, *Introduction to Logic*, 2nd ed. (New York: Macmillan, 1961), pp. 54-55 (italics in original).

[19] Ibid., p. 53.

[20] Ibid., p. 55.

[21] Examples include Augustine, cited on page 141 of this book; Alan W. Gomes, "Evangelicals and the Annihilation of Hell, Part One," *Christian Research Journal* 13, no. 4 (1991): 17-18; and Larry Dixon, *The Other Side of the Good News* (Wheaton, Ill: BridgePoint, 1992), p. 89.

[22] William L. Lane, *Commentary on the Gospel of Mark*, New International Commentary on the New Testament (Grand Rapids, Mich.: Eerdmans, 1974), p. 347.

[23] Fudge, *Fire*, rev. ed., p. 114.

[24] Ibid; Fudge cites William L. Lane, *Commentary on the Gospel of Mark*, p. 347.

[25] William L. Lane, *Commentary on the Gospel of Mark*, p. 349; cf. p. 349 n. 81.

[26] Leon Morris, *The First and Second Epistles to the Thessalonians*, New International Commentary on the New Testament (Grand Rapids, Mich.: Eerdmans, 1959), pp. 204-5; and F. F. Bruce, *1 & 2 Thessalonians*, Word Biblical Commentary 45 (Waco, Tex.: Word, 1982), p. 151.

[27] See Basil Atkinson, *Life and Immortality* (n.p., n.d.), p. 101; Edward Fudge, *The Fire That Consumes: A Biblical and Historical Study of Final Punishment* (Houston: Providential, 1982), p. 242 (note: this is the first edition).

[28] Leon Morris, *First and Second Epistles to the Thessalonians*, p. 205.

[29] Charles A. Wanamaker agrees, saying, "As there is no evidence in Paul (or the rest of the New Testament for that matter) for a concept of final annihilation of the godless, the expression 'eternal destruction' should probably be taken in a metaphorical manner as indicating the severity of the punishment awaiting the enemies of God" (Charles A. Wanamaker, *The Epistles to the Thessalonians: A Commentary on the Greek Text*, New International Greek Testament Commentary [Grand Rapids, Mich.: Eerdmans, 1990], p. 229).

[30] Fudge, *Fire That Consumes*, rev. ed., p. 153.

[31] Ibid., p. 155, text and n. 31.

[32] Scot McKnight, "Eternal Consequences or Eternal Consciousness?" in *Through No Fault of Their Own? The Fate of Those Who Have Never Heard*, ed. William V. Crockett and James G. Sigountos (Grand Rapids, Mich.: Baker, 1991), pp. 155-56.

[33] Fudge, *Fire That Consumes*, rev. ed., p. 156.

34See pages 129-36 of this volume; and Robert A. Peterson, *Hell on Trial: The Case for Eternal Punishment* (Phillipsburg, N.J.: Presbyterian & Reformed, 1995), pp. 21-37.

35For the two main views on the rebellion, see Richard J. Bauckham, *Jude, 2 Peter*, Word Biblical Commentary (Waco, Tex.: Word, 1983), pp. 50-53; and Simon J. Kistemaker, *Peter and Jude*, New Testament Commentary (Grand Rapids, Mich.: Baker, 1987), pp. 377-80.

36J. N. D. Kelly, *A Commentary on the Epistles of Peter and Jude* (Grand Rapids, Mich.: Baker, 1969), p. 259.

37Bauckham, *Jude, 2 Peter*, p. 55.

38Bauer et al., *Greek-English Lexicon*, p. 172.

39Fudge, *Fire*, rev. ed., p. 180.

40Ibid.

41Kelly, *Peter and Jude*, p. 274.

42Bauckham, *Jude, 2 Peter*, p. 92.

43The expression here is *eis aiona*; the addition of the definite article to form *eis ton aiona* does not alter the meaning.

44Fudge, *Fire*, rev. ed., p. 178.

45George Eldon Ladd, *A Commentary on the Revelation of John* (Grand Rapids, Mich.: Eerdmans, 1972), p. 196.

46Fudge, *Fire*, rev. ed., pp. 187, 190.

47Ibid., pp. 186-87.

48Ibid., p. 187.

49Ibid., pp. 188-89.

50Harold E. Guillebaud, *The Righteous Judge* (n.p., 1941), p. 24, quoted in Fudge, *Fire That Consumes*, rev. ed., p. 190.

51Fudge, *Fire*, rev. ed., pp. 192-93.

52Ibid., p. 193.

53D. A. Carson, *The Gagging of God: Christianity Confronts Pluralism* (Grand Rapids, Mich.: Zondervan, 1996), p. 527 (italics in original).

54Fudge, *Fire*, rev. ed., p. 194.

55Ibid.

56Another example is Rev 19:10.

57Fudge, *Fire*, rev. ed., p. 194.

58Ibid., pp. 193, 195.

Chapter 9: Seeing the Big Picture

1T. R. Reid, "Kobe Wakes to a Nightmare," *National Geographic* 188, no. 1 (1995): 115.

2Craig L. Blomberg, *Interpreting the Parables* (Downers Grove, Ill.: InterVarsity Press, 1990), p. 206.

3John W. Cooper, *Body, Soul and Life Everlasting* (Grand Rapids, Mich.: Eerdmans, 1989), pp. 116-19. The third view is the immediate resurrection view.

4Edward William Fudge, *The Fire That Consumes: The Biblical Case for Conditional Immortality*, rev. ed. (Carlisle, U.K.: Paternoster, 1994), p. 39.

5Norman T. Burns, *Christian Mortalism from Tyndale to Milton* (Cambridge, Mass.: Harvard University Press, 1972), p. 13, cited in *Fudge, Fire That Consumes*, rev. ed., p. 26 n. 25.

6Hans Lilje, *The Last Book of the Bible* (Philadelphia: Muhlenberg, 1957), p. 256, cited in Fudge, *Fire That Consumes*, rev. ed., p. 194.

7Fudge, *Fire That Consumes*, rev. ed., p. 194.

8Cooper, *Body, Soul and Life Everlasting*, pp. 185-94.

9I gratefully acknowledge the help of my colleague Jimmy Agan, adjunct professor of New

Testament at Covenant Theological Seminary, with this paragraph.

[10]Fudge, *Fire That Consumes*, rev. ed., pp. 143-45.

[11]Ibid., p. 144.

[12]Ibid.

[13]Ibid., p. 145.

[14]Edward Fudge, *The Fire That Consumes: A Biblical and Historical Study of Final Punishment* (Houston: Providential, 1982), pp. 230-31 (note: this is the first edition).

[15]J. N. D. Kelly, *Early Christian Doctrines*, 2nd ed. (New York: Harper & Row, 1960), pp. 339-40.

[16]Cooper, *Body, Soul and Life Everlasting*, pp. 144-45.

[17]One could argue that Stott is less consistent in his systematic theology at these points than is Fudge.

[18]Bertrand Russell, *Why I Am Not a Christian* (London: Unwin Books, 1967), p. 47.

[19]Fudge, *Fire That Consumes*, rev. ed., p. 18.

[20]Jonathan H. Gerstner, *Jonathan Edwards on Heaven and Hell* (Grand Rapids, Mich.: Baker, 1985), p. 75.

[21]The expression "kinder and gentler view" is taken from the helpful article by Alan W. Gomes, "Evangelicals and the Annihilation of Hell, Part One," *Christian Research Journal* 13, no. 4 (1991): 15. I am appreciative that Dr. Gomes was so kind as to read my manuscript and gently offer suggestions for improvement.

A Conditionalist Response to Traditionalism

[1]In this section of my response I have quoted from *The Apostolic Fathers: An American Translation*, trans. Edgar J. Goodspeed (New York: Harper & Brothers, 1950). Readers who wish to read the original Greek texts might consult Karl Bihlmeyer, ed., *Die Apostolischen Vater*, 2nd ed. (Tübingen: J. C. B. Mohr [Paul Siebeck], 1956).

[2]*Didache* 1.1.

[3]*Epistle of Barnabas* 20.1.

[4]Ibid., 21.1, 3.

[5]Clement of Rome 1 *Clement* 14.4.

[6]Clement of Rome 2 *Clement* 6.7.

[7]Ibid., 17.6-7.

[8]Ignatius of Antioch *To the Ephesians* 11.1.

[9]Ibid., 16.2.

[10]Ignatius of Antioch *To the Magnesians* 5.1.

[11]*Martyrdom of Polycarp* 11.2.

[12]*Address to Diognetus* 10.7-8.

[13]For a detailed investigation of this earliest phase of the traditional doctrine's evolution, see the first edition of my book *The Fire That Consumes: A Biblical and Historical Study of Final Punishment* (Houston: Providential Press, 1982), pp. 313-77. Although the five-hundred-page hardback first edition is now out of print, it is widely available in theological and seminary libraries.

[14]William G. T. Shedd, *The Doctrine of Eternal Punishment* (New York: Charles Scribner's, 1886), p. 490.

[15]Athenagoras *A Plea for the Christians* 31. Note: this and the following quotations from the church fathers through Origen may be found in English translation in the *Ante-Nicene Christian Library: Translations of the Writings of the Fathers Down to A.D. 325*, ed. Alexander Roberts and James Donaldson (Grand Rapids, Mich.: Eerdmans, 1950).

[16]Four decades ago the European scholar Oscar Cullmann published his book titled *Immortality*

of the Soul or Resurrection of the Dead? The Witness of the New Testament (London: Epworth, 1958). In it he clearly demonstrates the difference between the pagan Greek hope for afterlife based on the supposed "immortality of the soul" and the unique Christian hope based on the resurrection of the dead. Since 1958 careful theologians have practically run over each other in their rush to recognize this monumental distinction. Like their ancient counterparts, however, many modern traditionalists verbally acknowledge that Scripture does not teach the immortality of the soul, yet inevitably revert to that notion in defending their view of hell as a place of undying suffering. To his credit, Peterson has suggested that we abandon the phrase "immortality of the soul," correctly noting that "our final state is not a disembodied spiritual life in heaven, but a holistic resurrected one on the new earth" (Robert A. Peterson, *Hell on Trial: The Case for Eternal Punishment* [Phillipsburg, N.J.: Presbyterian & Reformed, 1995], pp. 177-78). However, he reasons as if the wicked will also be given immortality by God in the resurrection, something the Bible never says.

[17]Athenagoras *Resurrection of the Dead* 13.

[18]Ibid., 15.

[19]Tertullian *De Anima* 9.

[20]Tertullian *Resurrection of the Flesh* 3.

[21]Ibid., 34.

[22]Ibid., 35.

[23]Ibid.

[24]Clement of Alexandria *Recognitions* 5.28.

[25]Clement of Alexandria *The Miscellanies* 4.24; 5.14.

[26]Origen talks about this purifying fire in, among other places, *De Principis* 2.10 and *Against Celsus* 4.13; 6.25-26.

[27]Today the idea that God will finally save all people (universalism) seems to have found new appeal—even among some evangelicals. As in Origen's day, the appeal of this position lies largely in the fact that it seems to be far more consistent with the loving character of God as revealed in Jesus Christ than is traditionalism's everlasting torment. The answer to both of those errors is found in accepting the biblical teaching that God's final punishment of the lost will be infallibly *just*, but that it ends in "eternal destruction" and the "second death" (2 Thess 1:6, 9; Rev 21:8).

[28]Arnobius *Adversus Gente* 2.19.

[29]Ibid., 2.62.

[30]Harry Buis, *The Doctrine of Eternal Punishment* (Philadelphia: Presbyterian & Reformed, 1957), p. 61.

[31]Edward Bouverie Pusey, *What Is of Faith as to Everlasting Punishment? In Reply to Dr. Farrar's Challenge in His "Eternal Hope," 1879* (Oxford: James Parker, 1880), p. 172-73.

[32]Augustine "Preface to the Treatise on the Trinity," quoted in James Montgomery Boice, *Does Inerrancy Matter?* (Oakland, Calif.: International Council on Biblical Inerrancy, 1979), p. 22.

[33]The quotations that follow are taken from *The Fathers of the Church: A New Translation*, trans. Gerald G. Walsh and Daniel J. Honan (New York: Fathers of the Church, 1954), pp. 339-413. Page citations likewise refer to this English translation. I discussed Augustine's treatment of hell contained in book 21 of *The City of God* in the first edition of *The Fire That Consumes*, pp. 439-48.

[34]*Fathers of the Church*, pp. 342-43 (emphasis added).

[35]Ibid., p. 343 (emphasis added).

[36]Ibid., pp. 369-70.

[37]Milton McC. Gatch, *Death: Meaning and Mortality in Christian Thought and Contemporary Cul-*

ture (New York: Seabury Press, 1969), p. 94.

[38]Ibid., pp. 97-99.

[39]Edward William Fudge, *The Fire That Consumes: The Biblical Case for Conditional Immortality*, rev. ed. (Carlisle, U.K.: Paternoster, 1994), pp. 35-40.

[40]Emmanuel Petavel, *The Problem of Immortality*, trans. Frederick Ash Freer (London: Elliot Stock, 1892), p. 255.

[41]For a collection of such quotations from Luther, see Norman T. Burns, *Christian Mortalism from Tyndale to Milton* (Cambridge, Mass.: Harvard University Press, 1972), pp. 28-32; and LeRoy Edwin Froom, *The Conditionalist Faith of Our Fathers* (Washington, D.C.: Review & Herald, 1965), 2:74-77.

[42]Quoted in Burns, *Christian Mortalism*, p. 101.

[43]This work is located in John Calvin, *Tracts and Treatises in Defense of the Reformed Faith*, trans. Henry Beveridge (Grand Rapids, Mich.: Eerdmans, 1958), vol. 3. I examined Calvin's *Psychopannychia* in some detail in the first edition of *The Fire That Consumes* (pp. 449-66), which is now out of print.

[44]Calvin, *Tracts and Treatises*, 3:414, 416.

[45]Ibid., 3:490.

[46]There is nothing inherent in the distinctives of Reformed doctrine that requires the traditionalist view of final punishment. However, the Reformed creeds have preserved that tradition and have seemingly presented an insurmountable obstacle in the minds of many good people. This is the case in spite of the fact that the traditional doctrine of hell as everlasting conscious torment seems particularly incongruous with the Reformed teaching that God created some individuals for the specific purpose of sending them to hell.

[47]Burns, *Christian Mortalism*, pp. 32-33.

[48]John H. Gerstner, *Repent or Perish (With a Special Reference to the Conservative Attack on Hell)* (Ligonier, Penn.: Soli Deo Gloria, 1990), p. 32.

[49]Fudge, *Fire That Consumes*, rev. ed., pp. 112-15.

[50]Ibid., p. 93.

[51]F. F. Bruce, who contributed a foreword to *The Fire That Consumes* in which he said he was committed to neither the traditionalist view nor the conditionalist view on hell, nevertheless expected a conscious intermediate state, at least for believers. Bruce writes: "Those who are 'in Christ' and risen with Him in this life will not be separated from Him when they leave this mortal body; and all that is requisite for communicating with their new environment and enjoying the Lord's presence will be supplied: it has been prepared for them already" (F. F. Bruce, *Answers to Questions* [Grand Rapids, Mich.: Zondervan, 1974], p. 101). Notably, Bruce did not base this expectation on the supposed immortality of the soul or spirit but on the believer's union with Christ.

[52]The two most influential conditionalist authors of the nineteenth century, Congregationalist minister Edward White and Anglican minister Henry Constable, held differing views on this subject. See Edward White, *Life in Christ: A Study of the Scripture Doctrine on the Nature of Man, the Object of the Divine Incarnation, and the Conditions of Human Immortality*, 3rd ed. (London: Elliot Stock, 1878); and Henry Constable, *Duration and Nature of Future Punishment*, 6th ed. (London: Edward Hobbs, 1886).

[53]Peterson, *Hell on Trial*, p. 222 n. 9.

[54]Peterson's traditionalist predecessor J. Oliver Buswell seems to have suggested as much. After quoting the Westminster Confession to the effect that Scripture is all-sufficient and that "nothing at any time is to be added" to it, Buswell continues, "Nevertheless it is to be expected that the Holy Spirit will continue to guide the church into a deeper and fuller understanding of

the Scriptures, and that future events will throw light upon questions hitherto unresolved."
The Council of Chalcedon was one example of this, Buswell continues, stating that "the doctrine of the one Person and of the divine and human natures of Christ was not made systematically explicit" until that Council (see J. Oliver Buswell, *A Systematic Theology of the Christian
Religion in One Volume* [Grand Rapids, Mich.: Zondervan, 1969], pp. 383-84). Exactly how
much are we supposed to read into that "Nevertheless"?

[55]It has become almost a stock in trade of contemporary traditionalists to borrow a phrase from
former U.S. president George Bush and accuse conditionalists of simply opting for a "kinder
and gentler" viewpoint. The truth is that most of us point out that biblical exegesis, not senti-
mentalism, must determine what we believe. I almost began *The Fire That Consumes*, for example, with the warning: "if we reject the traditionalist doctrine we must do so not on moral,
philosophical, intuitive, judicial or emotional grounds" because the "only question that matters here is the teaching of Scripture" (Fudge, *Fire That Consumes*, p. 3). This traditionalist
accusation is nothing but a blatant and unfair appeal to prejudice.